MOMENTS IN TIME

*Tuiavii's Way: A South Sea Chief's
Comments on Western Society*
Legacy Editions, Toronto
and Sanseido, Tokyo

A Dangerous Remedy
Legacy Editions, Toronto

How To Invest In Gold
McClelland & Stewart, Toronto
and Follett Publishing, Chicago

Gold, Silver & Strategic Metals
McClelland & Stewart, Toronto
and McGraw Hill, New York

MOMENTS IN TIME

The Experience of My Life

VOLUME 3

Family
Gratitude

PETER C. CAVELTI

ISBN 978-1-7780316-1-8
Library and Archives of Canada

Cavelti, Peter C. (Peter Christian), 1948-
Moments In Time: The Experience Of My Life / Peter C. Cavelti
Volume 3

Cover Design: Richard Moore Associates, New York, Hanoi
and Saigon

Content Design: Laura Brady, Toronto

Manufactured in the United States of America

Family

*N*ow that our grandchildren are in their teens, I frequently look back at how we raised Melissa and Krista. There are things I'm proud of and others that I regret. What it comes down to is this: while I loved both girls deeply and always did what I thought was best for them, some of my judgments could be qualified as too lenient, others as tough love, while yet others appear harsh, perhaps unnecessarily so.

Let me start with Melissa, whose progress through private school, then university was breathtakingly linear and unaccompanied by the kind of defiance that typically characterizes adolescence. If Melissa needed to define herself she did that by excelling at her classical music. She was a serious and reserved girl, sometimes bordering on the awkward, tending to internalize the chaos of growing up, but Caroline and I never doubted that she was capable of deep love and loyalty.

When Melissa graduated from Northwestern University, summa cum laude and with two degrees, we expressed our delight. When she told us how some of her peers were getting BMWs as recognition for their success, I reminded Melissa that I'd just paid a quarter million dollars for her university education, explaining that was equivalent to more than $500,000 in pre-tax earnings. Caroline and I talked about how we could honour Melissa's accomplishments while staying true to our values. We decided to buy her a backpack, an airline ticket to Zurich and a railway pass so that she could explore Europe to her heart's content. We also gave her a gift of $2,500, with the proviso that she had to stay abroad for at least six weeks. We were concerned that Melissa, loving comfort, might otherwise stay in a luxury hotel for a week and return home.

After her trip, Melissa asked me whether she could come to work at Cavelti Capital. I handed her a yellow pages phone book, recommending that she call banks and financial advisors and arrange interviews. When she asked me whether I could call some of my highly connected friends who were in the business, I explained why I preferred not to do that. Not only would she be among the most qualified applicants any given firm would be interviewing, but if I employed her or arranged for a job for her and she did well, she'd never know whether she'd made her own success or whether it was all due to my connections.

I'm incredibly proud of those decisions. Melissa, now in her late forties, uses them as examples of good parenting when talking to her own daughters, Alexandra and Abigail. She explains how, first staying with my family in Switzerland, then travelling eastward, she became truly independent. She loved Salzburg and Vienna, then got onto a train to Prague, always hot on the trail of her favourite classical composers. At the border to Czechoslovakia, in the middle of the night, she got thrown off the train because she didn't have the proper visa.

I remember Melissa calling me from Vienna the following day, crying. She was livid about the injustice and inconvenience the Czechs had subjected her to. When I asked how badly she wanted to see the city in which Smetana, Dvoràk and Mozart had once lived, a resilient and determined Melissa took only seconds to respond. She'd travel all the way back to Berne, tell the Czech consular employees how they'd inconvenienced her and get the right credentials. No one was going to keep her from seeing and experiencing Prague.

When Melissa's trip was over and she settled back in at my mother's house in Herisau, I flew over to surprise her. Together, we explored some of my favourite places. We hiked in and around Herisau; I showed her Chur, where I'd spent so much time with my Grossmami and Grosspapi; and I took her to Sagogn, the place where all Caveltis come from, the gravestones in the tiny cemetery almost invariably making reference to the life and death of one my distant relatives, both husbands and wives often sharing the same birth name.

I'd recently adopted Melissa, which meant that she now was a Cavelti *and a Swiss citizen too, which added significance to the occasion. We crossed the Alps to the Ticino and briefly entered Italy, Melissa laughing when the border guards declined to see her new passport: she was a blonde and looked distinctly Swiss, they joked, and that was sufficient. And finally we headed North again, taking a brief excursion to the lake lands near Gruyeres and Murten, where Melissa badly beat me in a round of mini-golf.*

Getting back home was more traumatic for her, yet I've overheard Melissa talking about how my refusal to employ her, or help her find a job, empowered her. Somehow, she landed a job as a research analyst at Dominion Securities, the Royal Bank's brokerage subsidiary. She worked long hours at an offensively low salary but, before too long, was promoted. And that's when her compensation went from sub-par to exceptional, at least for someone her age. As any successful career, Melissa's was made up of consistently great performance and a few lucky breaks. Eventually she joined my firm, but not before having been a Managing Director at Bank of Montreal Nesbitt Burns, where she supervised a highly successful portfolio management and research team.

Yet, while most of the decisions I made were good ones, I can now see that I made mistakes, too. Based on my own experience of leaving home, an act which I feel contributed positively to my own evolution, I thought the girls should have the same experience. When we returned from Switzerland, Melissa thought she was entitled to some downtime, during which she could look for a job. Caroline and I disagreed; we shared the view that she needed to find employment and a place of her own right away. This led to considerable tension. For the first time, Melissa was seriously upset with us.

What I completely missed was that I'd had a stable and loving upbringing, while Melissa's childhood had been a nightmare of tension and instability. No wonder she wanted to cling to the memories of her teen years at Haddington—how could I have missed it? That we also kept reminding her that we'd soon sell the house made the situation only worse.

When Melissa secured her job and Krista unexpectedly quit university, the two sisters moved in together. I remember visiting them and being deeply disturbed by what I saw. Their place was grimy and their landlord was nasty, but it was all they could afford. They were truly independent now and we had contributed to that, but I felt we could have achieved the same result in a more sensitive way.

IF KRISTA RESENTED having to be on her own, she didn't show it. For her, it had always been about living an independent life. While Melissa loved to nest at home, Krista wanted to sneak out as often as possible. Her elder sister observed boundaries, but for Krista rules were there to be renegotiated. If we set a midnight curfew for a night out, she'd immediately contest it, arguing that her friends could stay out until two. Caroline had figured out how to handle this: while resolutely declaring that two o'clock was unthinkable, she asked Krista what she thought was reasonable. The second proposal was usually quite acceptable, and because it had come from her, Krista would honour it.

Given our preference to be in bed reading by 10:30, how did we know when Krista actually returned home? I came up with a system that did the job for quite some time. Here is how it worked: I set an alarm clock for five minutes after her curfew and placed it outside our bedroom door. If she failed to be back in time to turn it off, Krista was in trouble.

One of the remnants of my army training is that few things escape me, even when I'm asleep. Weekend after weekend, I'd hear Krista come up the stairs, turn off the alarm clock, then return to her room. She had a boyfriend then, an impressive and responsible fellow named Dan who was two years older than her. We credited him for Krista's impeccable behaviour.

Then, one Friday night, the pattern changed. Half-asleep, I heard Krista return as she always did, congratulated myself on my resourcefulness, turned over and fell back into a state of deep relaxation. Later, not sure what the time was, I heard a click, which I dismissed as an outdoor noise, since our window was open. It wasn't until the next morning, when I left to take Charlie the retriever for a walk, that I heard the same sound again. It was opening and re-closing our kitchen door, located exactly below our bedroom, that had produced it. I shared my impression with Caroline, who was in disbelief. I decided to follow up at the next opportunity.

The sequence of events repeated itself the night after: Krista, at her most considerate, tiptoeing up the staircase; Krista picking up the clock and putting it back down; Krista returning downstairs. For twenty minutes or so, nothing happened. And then, the click of the closing kitchen door. I waited for two minutes, got up and left the bedroom quietly, made my way to the downstairs hall closet, slipped my raincoat over my pajamas and put my running shoes on. Next, I left the house through the main door, stepping into the clear, moonlit September night.

I hugged the cedar hedges that surrounded our property, peaking down Haddington Avenue. And there, parked fifty meters away, was Dan's Nissan Stanza wagon. Two people were inside.

I walked around the block so I could approach the vehicle from behind, snuck up its side and entered through the back door. When she realized what was happening, Krista lost it. She accused me of being underhanded and embarrassing her, then left the car and ran back home.

Then I spoke to a speechless Dan, telling him that I was too upset to talk. I suggested we'd do that at 7am the next day at the McDonalds not far from us. When we had coffee together he proved that he could be the man we'd come to appreciate, apologizing and guaranteeing me that his relationship with our Krista was the most important thing to him. He'd never again disappoint us.

THERE WERE THREE *things that distinguished Krista. In most things she did, she was at least two years ahead of her peers. When she made a mistake, she made it at least twice, sometimes three times. And once she absorbed one of life's lessons, she moved on, never admitting to the shortcomings of her approach, but never slipping back.*

After dropping out of her first year of university, she worked as a waitress and steadfastly saved for a car. In time, she bought what was probably the least practical vehicle she could find. I tried to help her buy something that would last, but she insisted it had to be a Nissan ZX sports car. The one she found and could afford with her $2,500 budget was a run-down heap of rust. She spent days sanding down the fenders and touching them up with the help of a cheap can of spray paint. The vehicle looked better, but soon after broke down.

By now, she'd taken a bartending course. The tips she banked were impressive, often amounting to $200 or more a night. That allowed Krista to buy another Nissan ZX, which, like the first one, ended up with the mechanics far too often, before it was totalled by a drunk driver while parked on the street. In the end, she bought a Toyota 4-Runner, not much to look at, but practical and mechanically reliable.

Caroline and I knew that Krista would succeed at anything she took on, but we also understood that her evolution would be littered with false starts. While she studied at Concordia, she became a scuba instructor, which allowed her to spend paid holidays at various Club Med resorts. After graduating, she became a digital designer, then a head-hunter with an employment agency. Eventually, her image popped up at bus shelters and on the top of a couple of buildings. She was one of Toronto's most successful realtors.

Melissa and Krista taught me many things, but the most intriguing lesson was that two sisters can grow up with the same parents and the same conditioning, yet tackle the challenges life throws at them in unthinkably different ways. I shouldn't have been surprised. After all, in terms of behaviour and personal traits, I'm not remotely similar to any of my siblings. What I do have in common with them are shared memories, but even there we frequently differ.

I BELIEVE THAT *our frequent absences from Toronto and their living together brought the girls closer. I also fear that part of their growing friendship grew out of resentment; they weren't happy that we cut them loose and spent significant time in Colorado and, increasingly, on journeys to exotic places. They seemed more detached, often making it known that they thought of us a selfish.*

Caroline and I, in turn, found it difficult to relate to that. We thought we'd done an extraordinary job. Getting the girls through university and seeing them succeed in the workplace were accomplishments that, a few years ago, had seemed impossible. How could they not be grateful?

Everything is humming along at Cavelti Capital, allowing us to settle into a new routine. Whether in Toronto, at the cottage or in Colorado, I devote five to six hours a weekday to my financial work, half in the early morning and half in the afternoon. The middle part of each day and the evening are spent on other pursuits.

We've taken on new creative challenges. Caroline produces encaustic paintings, takes ceramics and jewelry-making courses and learns Spanish. She's even visited San Miguel de Allende, where she's lived with a family and attended language classes. I'm working on the Tuiavii project, write short stories and build a serious tribal mask collection. For fun, I create my own masks to compliment the classic indigenous designs, mostly out of cut-in-half plastic bottles adorned with electronics parts, spent coffee cartridges, newspaper clippings and a few dozen other things.

We're physically more active, too. I've been on my skis more than a hundred days this winter, and at the cottage, spend a lot of time cutting down dead trees and splitting wood. When with us, the girls ask their mother, "What on earth is Peter doing out there?" And Caroline answers, "He's cleaning up the forest." My own story is that interspersing my mental gymnastics with mindless physical work makes for a perfectly balanced day.

TRANSLATING THE SOUTH Sea Chief manuscript turns out to be only half the battle. I think I've succeeded in revealing Tuiavii's message in simple, incisive language appealing to a contemporary audience. The responses from the experts have been more than encouraging.

Yet, most of them have suggestions on how I should proceed from here on. "You must accompany the chief's speeches with a cultural and historical perspective," a British professor tells me, giving me the names of possible sources. Another academic suggests that I should write a foreword about the linguistic challenges I've been facing, after I tell him how impressed I am with Tuiavii's use of similes to describe things that don't exist in his culture. Calling money the "round metal" and the "heavy paper" has particularly got to me—how perfectly these terms evoke the burden money can impose on us!

I'm learning that there are a dozen or so authorities on early 20th century South Sea culture worldwide. Some lecture at universities, some are museum curators, others are experts on art and literature. Each has a new idea for me and gracefully reveals the name of someone who can help me along. I'm deeply grateful for their insights. I can see that my objective to familiarize a new generation of readers with Tuiavii's thoughts requires more than just the body of his speeches: it wants context.

In the end, I decide to bookend the chief's eleven speeches with a lengthy prologue and epilogue, covering most aspects of South Sea life circa 1900 in one, and devoting the other to the many controversies about both Chief Tuiavii and his translator, Erich Scheurmann, which are still much alive nearly a hundred years later. It'll take me another year to get everything together and link each part into a cohesive and captivating narrative. So be it. It's what I want to do.

A few years ago, I was first invited to talk to a group of Toronto Rotarians. I was stunned when, at the onset of the meeting, their leader articulated their belief system, part of which is that whatever interaction takes place, it must be fair and beneficial to both sides. It's what I'd come to believe all by myself and what I'd practiced during my business life. Hearing it as the mission statement of a worldwide movement of professionals impressed me.

I never joined the Rotarians, mostly because the Canadian chapters of the Rotary Club wanted me to raise my water glass and pay allegiance to the Queen, while the Americans paid homage to their flag. Still, I never turned down an invitation by the Rotarians and made myself available whenever invited.

Why was I so surprised to learn that a group as influential as the Rotary Club espoused the same value system I'd adopted? Because it's something that hasn't been taught at business schools for a long, long time, at least not as a guiding principle. A business proposition must benefit both sides.

A COUPLE OF weeks ago, the new managers of Personal Finance, one of America's largest investment magazines, called to announce that I, along with other contributing editors, would no longer be paid the $5,000 I'd been receiving for every published article. Their rationale: they had lots of brokers and investment professionals who'd happily make contributions without charging. When I pointed out that anyone writing without being compensated would probably use their platform to promote their products, they said that was fine with them. Their code of ethics, which until now had prohibited promotional content, was being revised. They hoped I could continue in my past role under their new set of rules. I turned them down.

And now I'm sitting in our board room, facing a man in his mid-thirties. I'm with Kevin MacLean and Heinz Thoma and our guest represents First Union, the sixth largest U.S. bank. He reminds us that the bank's Evergreen Investments subsidiary has just acquired Sheffield Management Company, which operates the Blanchard group of mutual funds whose assets we manage. He also states that he is not an employee of the bank, but of McKinsey & Company, the management consultants. Then he states that he wanted to meet because we are being paid far too much money and that he's here to change that. What's remarkable is that the young man doesn't look at any of us while he says these things. His eyes are firmly trained on the screen of his laptop computer. Neither Kevin, Heinz nor I have ever been in a meeting where someone read from a screen.

I interrupt him, pointing out that it takes two parties to change anything. I also challenge him to explain what he means by "far too much money". He briefly raises his eyes to look at mine, then lowers them again, as if to look for guidance on his machine. Next, to my surprise, he shuts the lid of his laptop, stares at each one of us for a long moment, as if he's just become aware that we're in the room. I wonder whether this is a tactic he picked up at McKinsey.

Then he delivers his message, explaining that we're currently billing the Blanchard funds well over a million dollars a year. First Union is willing to pay us up to $100,000. That, he elaborates, is what their cost would be if the bank brought the management in-house. When I counter that our staff and administrative expenses directly related to the fund are at least half a million dollars, he decides to lecture me. "Look, the one thing I've learned at McKinsey is that there is no difference between a milk store and a money management firm. If you're not competitive, the business goes elsewhere." I notice Kevin shaking his head, mumbling.

I invite our visitor to look at it from our perspective. "A million dollars is roughly one tenth of one percent of the assets we manage. The funds group, soon to be owned the bank you represent, charges fifteen times that much to the client. Yet we do all the research and actual investing. And remember, our performance history has been tops."

His response stuns me: "My client realizes that once the fund is managed in-house, performance will suffer." I ask him where he thinks that'll get them, predicting that they'll soon have a fund without investors.

"And that's where you're wrong," he counters. "Yes, investors will call to complain and the sales staff will express their sympathy. And then they'll recommend a switch to one of the group's best performing funds, and everyone will be happy."

It's the most callous statement I've heard in my nearly three decades in the financial business, but I have to acknowledge that our visitor may be right.

1998 MARKED THE end of Cavelti Capital Management Ltd. We could have continued, and profitably so, but with a sharply lower revenue base I would have had to trim the staff and go back to year-round, twelve-hour working days in Toronto. Now that I'd found a nice balance in my life, a return to the regimen that dictated my Guardian years was unacceptable.

I announced a wind-down period of nearly a year and helped my staff find suitable positions. Next, I sold the managed account program, offering the clients a transfer to Adrian Day Asset Management in Annapolis or to our Swiss affiliate, Camafin Trust. I'd admired Adrian for years and I'd known and trusted Roger Badet since I first arrived in Canada. The three of us shared highly compatible investment philosophies, which gave me comfort that our managed account clients, many of whom had been with me for more than fifteen years, were well taken care of.

Yet, to my surprise, about thirty of my longest-standing clients balked at being transferred to another firm. It was a reaction I hadn't expected and it threw me into a state of inner chaos. I'd worked hard to find continuity for our managed program, but that was obviously not enough.

One of the clients, Fritz Bollinger, the Swiss-Canadian owner of a large transportation business, insisted on a face-to-face meeting, even though he had to drive all the way from Kingston. When we met, he bluntly suggested that I had to find a way to honour his loyalty—walking away from our long-standing relationship was simply not an option. When I explained my dilemma he politely repeated his demand: I had to find a way to be true to myself and handle a bunch of client portfolios and he was confident I could do so. I agreed to think it over.

With the decision to close down Cavelti Capital made and agreements with Adrian Day and Roger Badet negotiated, what was I to do? After days of reflection and numerous talks with Caroline I called the dissenting clients, one by one, and presented my proposal. I'd continue to manage their assets, but only on two conditions. First, I'd focus on only two things: research and performance. Each quarter end, I'd present them with a commentary, in response to which they'd have the option to call me or meet with me. They'd have to agree not to call or e-mail me in between. Second, the infrastructure my company had provided would no longer exist. We'd transfer each client account to a major bank or brokerage firm, where we'd negotiate a discounted trading platform. All administrative work would be performed there. I also explained my personal circumstances, emphasizing the need for balance in my life and expressing my belief that I'd be able to do as good or better a job in less time.

About half of the clients seemed upset by my proposal, mostly taking offense with the idea that they couldn't call me whenever they wanted to. More than one client added, "What kind of business model is that, anyway?" To which I responded that the business model had been my proposal for them to transfer to Adrian Day or Camafin Trust; what we were now discussing was my lifestyle model.

The response from the other half warmed my heart. Without exception, they promised to honour my requests, appreciating that reducing communication and delegating administrative work would free me to focus on performance. A few went as far as to compliment me on taking my personal life as seriously as my profession.

My Swiss-Canadian friend put it best. "You see, you've managed to find a way to help both yourself and the people who've been loyal to you. To me, that means you won't burn out like all those others. I guess my money will be with you for many more years." Given that Fritz was 75, that gave me confidence. And yes, when he passed away at age 90, I was still managing his assets.

THE WIND-UP OF Cavelti Capital and its U.S. affiliate was time-consuming, but liberating. We'd had a remarkable decade-long run. Kevin MacLean moved on to manage the Royal Bank's precious metals fund, Heinz Thoma moved to Annapolis to run Adrian Day's investment management business, and Paul Whelan, who'd been our primary client contact, was quickly recruited by the Bank of Montreal.

I sensed no resentment from any of the people I'd worked with; sometimes I even wondered whether some of them weren't feeling a bit sorry for me. Pity also seemed to be the prevailing sentiment of my friends and competitors in the business community. "You can't be serious, just walking away from everything. You've built such a following…all for nothing?"

One of the financial columnists, the Financial Post's Patrick Bloomfield, called me to report that people were wondering what I'd take on next. He laughed when I told him that I simply wanted more time for my writing and, yes, more fun as well. Besides, I'd still be managing the assets of my fifteen or so favourite clients. "Come on, Peter," he responded. "You've got something up your sleeve, you've done this before. But, fair enough, the only thing I ask is that you let me know first."

*A*m I a great businessman? As I told Alison, a young lady sent to me by Professor Etele, whose Ryerson class I'd occasionally been invited to address, it all depends on definitions. I've been good at building up businesses of a serious scale in record time, but that's only part of the challenge. The other part, at least according to MBA textbooks, is to stay the course.

I gave her the example of Pierre Lassonde, with whom I worked for several years, co-managing two precious metals funds. One day, nearly four decades ago, Pierre announced that he and Seymour Schulich were starting a new gold exploration company, Franco Nevada. Today, their enterprise had a market capitalisation of $36 billion and 36 employees. I doubted there was another company that had accomplished anything similar.

"But my professor said I should connect with you, because you succeeded at everything you ever did," Alison interjected, looking a bit confused.

"Well I have, in a way." I clarified. "But I didn't see things through to the end. Sometimes because I stopped having fun and sometimes because there were other interests that beckoned. Giving my life to a commercial enterprise simply wasn't me." Then I moved on to elaborate on the things that business courses tend to skip: the human and social capital an enterprise can build. "You know, I knew the names of my employees' spouses, knew if they had children and where they lived," I explained. "And I made it possible for Torontonians to do their banking before ten in the morning and after three in the hope that those things may be more important measures of success than what return a company achieves on its capital."

When Alison left, she seemed shaken up. I wondered whether I'd given her anything that would benefit her academically. I also suspected that Professor Etele was unlikely to ask me to see other students.

IF I'M NOT *a great business man, am I at least a good investor? Kevin MacLean shed some light on that subject during our farewell lunch. He told me he'd analyzed our track record at Cavelti Capital and he thought I'd get a kick out of the results. "Out of ten investment bets in the Blanchard Precious Metals Fund, how many do you think were winners?" he started. I suggested that we'd have to define what a winner was. "Okay, then. How many were sold at a profit?"*

I gave it some thought. We'd consistently been in the top decile of the performance spectrum, so presumably the majority of our bets had paid off. Kevin told me to try again, then let on that only five out of ten positions we'd initiated during our eleven-year run had been winners. This despite the fact that we'd spent days researching each new bet and that we had easy and virtually unlimited access to each corporation's management. I was in disbelief, yet Kevin, true to form, unveiled a spreadsheet that confirmed his findings.

When I took a look at it, I understood. What had really kept us on top was our unorthodox approach. Most of our competitors reduced risk by holding fifty or more positions. We limited our portfolio to twenty, but used rigid risk controls. If any of our bets lost 15% of their value we sold them, while we let the winners run. In short, it wasn't our experience or brilliant investment analysis that had led to our success, it was a set of rules.

In my personal life, I frequently violated such guidelines, usually because I let emotion interfere. Twice, I missed out on small bets that could have made me many millions of dollars. When Pierre Lassonde and Seymour Schulich started Franco Nevada, they allotted me 10,000 founder shares at $1 each. But the start-up period for the company was rocky. Its exploration program depended on higher gold prices and gold was in decline. I watched this for a while, then sold my shares for a hefty 50% profit, congratulating myself on my success.

When I learned that Pierre and Seymour abandoned their

exploration-based business model I viewed that as an admission of defeat. When they spent $2 million to acquire a royalty on Nevada's Goldstrike property, I wondered what they were doing. Having closely worked with and always admired the two founders, who were also by far the largest Franco Nevada shareholders, I should have known better. Two years later Barrick Gold bought Goldstrike and found fifty million ounces of gold, which so far has earned Franco Nevada more than a billion dollars. Had I kept my shares, they'd be worth close to four million dollars.

Unlike Lassonde and Schulich, who were serious investors, Murray Pezim was a classical stock promoter. His record as an investor was speckled with spectacular successes, painful failures and even fraud charges. But Pezim controlled a huge slice of junior mining stock offerings, the most speculative part of the market. Every now and then he called or showed up at our offices, typically with a great story. None of the gold funds we managed invested in speculative grade juniors, but I personally bought stock in Pezim controlled promotions and invariably, lost the money I'd put in, usually $10,000 or less.

And then, in the late 1980s, at a Blanchard organized investment conference in Bermuda, not long after deciding never to invest with Pezim again, I ran into a tall, exceptionally well-dressed man called John Reynolds, who introduced himself as a Vancouver-based federal parliamentarian. He handed me his card, told me he'd listened to my speech and invited me for lunch.

When he showed up with Pezim I was intrigued. But this time, Murray said little and Reynolds did the talking. He described how he'd become involved in what was surely going to be one of Canada's biggest gold discoveries and that I should consider an investment too. I listened politely, declined and returned to my room, convinced that my judgment on gold related matters was far superior to that of a politician.

Instead, I should have wondered why a member of parliament would

*involve himself in a gold mining venture. Had I done so, a small invest-
ment would have yielded insane returns. This time Pezim hit the jack-
pot—the Hemlo property in Northern Ontario was to become one of the
continent's most prolific gold resources, yielding well over twenty million
ounces of the yellow metal.*

*Are these missed opportunities mere flukes that any investment pro-
fessional would experience during a career spanning more than half a
century? I think there's more to it.*

*As a generality, I've always done better for my clients than for myself.
Part of that may be related to the fact that I don't have the time to review
my own affairs with the regularity with which I look at client portfolios. When I analyzed my performance during the Guardian Trust
and Cavelti Capital years, I was appalled. While our clients routinely
earned double digit annual returns, mine averaged less than three percent. Fortunately, the amount of money I made on my Guardian shares
and my compensation from Cavelti Capital still left me well rewarded.*

WHEN I LOOK *back at my career as a businessman and investment professional, I'm stunned that I did so well. It seems the people I competed
against and worked with at my level were all possessed by an ambition
to win and a capacity to fight that I completely lacked. For some of my
peers, such determination paid off. People like Ned Goodman, Seymour
Schulich and Pierre Lassonde were in the class of the comfortably wealthy
when I first worked with them. Now they're in the pantheon of the bil-
lionaires, something that has never been a goal for me. On the contrary,
I've often asked myself why, as a society, we value money so much and
why so many people define success in monetary terms.*

*So, how do I view money? Curiously, not much has changed since I
was in my mid-thirties, when I first realized that I'd managed to build
a comfortable cash reserve. If I succeeded in keeping some of it, chances*

were that I'd never have to compromise my values. By now, life had taught me that, every now and then, I'd find myself in disagreeable professional or personal circumstances. The next time that happened, I'd simply quit, walk away and allow myself sufficient time to reconsider how I wanted to live my life. My savings would allow me to do that.

When I quit Guardian Trust, and again, when I decided to sell Cavelti Capital, that is exactly how it turned out: money gave me the ability to withdraw into a space where I could regain my energy and self-analyze. It was my Great Reset button.

Obviously, money has many other advantages. One of the most rewarding experiences is to explore what it can do for others. It was not until I reached my fifties that I started to realize that helping those who had none of the opportunities or luck I had, could vastly add to my happiness.

That it should be me who has the resources to do so still fills me with wonderment and gratitude.

A couple of years ago, Melissa got her own place in the city, a comfortable upstairs apartment on Belsize Drive, not far from our tiny apartment and probably about the same size. She'd earned her Chartered Financial Analyst designation on top of working long hours at the bank, which we knew left her little time for other things. But there was another reason why we weren't seeing much of her: she was in a steady relationship with John Stout, her new boyfriend.

In time, we got to know and love John. He came to the cottage a couple of times, and later spent a week with us in the Bahamas, where we visited Krista, who worked there as a scuba instructor. Watching the sun slowly sink toward the sea, each evening painting water and sky a different hue of red, orange or purple, a cigar in one hand and a drink in the other, John and I had some meaningful conversations. I came to appreciate his sincerity, but also his unpretentiousness and his sense of humour. By the end of the holiday, Caroline and I agreed that he was perfect for our daughter.

Now, at the legendary Little Nell hotel in Aspen, we're celebrating Melissa and John's engagement, starting off with a bottle of champagne. We've chosen Bollinger to acknowledge John's addiction to James Bond movies. He knows each one of them and can sing the respective theme song—a bit off key, but with enormous enthusiasm.

Before they leave, Melissa and John let it slip that they've started looking for a house. Caroline and I are also planning to move. Our rental apartment has been too uncomfortable and my new business circumstances mandate a space large enough to store my files, meet with the clients I have left and seat two or three employees. We've bought two adjoining lofts in a building zoned for both residential and commercial use. When in Toronto, I'll have an enviably short commute to work. I'll be walking from unit 707 to unit 706.

HERE IS SOMETHING else to celebrate. Sam Hiyate, a relatively new arrival in my life, but one with whom I've spent a lot of time during the past weeks, is stepping up to the podium to introduce me. Round-faced and chubby Sam is infectiously exuberant and counter-culture, traits that have always appealed to me. He's also one of the most honest people I've ever worked with, making no bones about the fact that he's as penniless as his enterprise, a small publishing company called Gutter Press.

Sam knows everyone; he's already booked me a reading at Indigo's Toronto flagship book store and got me favourable reviews in several papers and magazines. How well he is connected becomes evident as I look around me: there are well over a hundred people that have come to my book launch party. Technically it's not even a launch. Tuiavii's Way was first published two years ago, with a small print run and little publicity. Now, Sam feels, it's the time to put it on the map. A celebration then.

There are other writers here tonight, a few publishers, agents and journalists even, and of course a bunch of my friends—all packed into the large and very stylish industrial space that is Rob Davidson's studio. I've known Rob since my days in the annex; once he turned to professional photography, I hired him to shoot piles of precious metals for Guardian Trust's and the Royal Canadian Mint's marketing materials. When I told him about my book he was happy to offer his space.

Another friend from the past, Hart Melvin, is here offering a selection of spectacular gelati and sorbets. Our paths have crossed a few times since I met him in Greece in the mid-1970s. Hart has moved from running a small shop selling Tibetan rugs and artifacts to owning the Toronto franchise of a well-known luggage maker to building Gelato Fresco, a company that now supplies top-end hotels and restaurants with his creations. At one point I brought an exhibit of gold, complete with security guards, to help him draw customers to his Eaton Centre store opening. Now Hart is here reciprocating in his inimitably generous way, leaving the assembled crowd, used to celebrating book launches in dark, smoke-filled basement spaces, speechless.

The Tuiavii project has taken me on a long and deeply satisfying journey. I've had a thorough education in South Sea culture and, unexpectedly, stumbled into a huge controversy. While Erich Scheurman, who brought the young chief's speeches to Germany nearly a hundred years ago, was widely admired, the literary establishment belittled or even vilified him. I learned that other South Sea writers, including Robert Louis Stevenson, had received similar treatment. It seems that any portrayal of a workable alternative to colonialism was unacceptable to Europe's establishment.

Still, there was one accusation that I couldn't ignore: a prominent German bibliographer asserted that Scheurmann had made up not just Tuiavii's speeches, but that the chief may never have existed. I talked about this to the South Sea experts on my list; none of them had an opinion on the subject, but they were all aware of the allegation. So, I read and reread the speeches, in Scheurmann's German version and my English translation, then discussed the controversy in great detail in my epilogue.

In the end, whether Tuiavii's words or even Tuiavii himself were made up mattered little. If the message they contained came from a young Samoan chief, they deserved to rank among the great texts of wisdom. If Scheurmann had invented them, he'd given us a stark reminder of where Western society had gone wrong and an invaluable blueprint for a more wholesome alternative.

It's late on a Friday afternoon. The taxi ride South is smooth and fast; all the traffic is coming from downtown. There have been a few annoying snags in winding up Cavelti Capital and the stock market is going through a nasty sell-off. I predicted it, but that doesn't make me feel better; the clients I have left have only small positions, but even those are shrinking. What's worse, this whole week I didn't find a spare minute to do the things I enjoy most. No wonder I feel sorry for myself.

The man I'm introduced to greets me, then guides me to his office, a tiny hole-in-the-wall crammed with piles of paper. He introduces himself as Fred Sanchez, points to a chair and asks how my week has been. I tell him it was awful, then reciprocate the favour, asking him how he is faring. He shrugs his shoulders, throws up his hands, then kind of points at the space behind me. I turn around and see a whiteboard filled with red and blue scribbles. Most of the writing is illegible, but the column headers give me a clue: Chechnya, Haiti, Ivory Coast, Somalia and a handful of other challenged places—civil war theatres, hotbeds of disease, places where malnutrition and famine reign.

Fred, who is MSF's man in charge of bringing logistical support to these venues, elaborates. MSF is *Médecins Sans Frontières*, or Doctors Without Borders, an organization I've been supporting in a small way for the past twenty years. I'm meeting with Fred because Rebecca Davis, who works with the donor relations team, invited me to come by. Was I curious to learn what MSF did with my annual grants, she asked? Yes, I was.

And here I sit, listening to Fred's account of the week he experienced: a nurse who got raped in Papua-New Guinea, a missing doctor in Nigeria, presumed kidnapped, and raids on MSF assets in the Congo. As I digest this, I start feeling disoriented, even inadequate. Have I been so insulated from the real world that I've lost all context? How could I have thought of the inconsequential setbacks at my office as something that made for a bad week?

Scenes from a lifetime ago pop up: the tent city not far from Calcutta hosting more than half a million refugees from the Bangladesh Genocide, supported by a mere 300 staff. The images are unerasable, but had I allowed my overtaxed brain to push them aside, so that financial formulae and administrative minutiae could take centre stage? I listen to Fred as he takes me through the challenges his people in the field face each day, then ask some questions, but my mind is too busy to pay much attention to the answers. What I see is children passively laying on the ground, bellies swollen and eyes out of focus; a woman hysterically sobbing, collapsed next to her dead toddler; mothers desperately holding their still alive babies to their breast, their infants too exhausted to suck.

I spend nearly two hours with Fred, realizing he's staying late to tell me about his ongoing struggle to stay on top of a dozen large-scale human emergencies. In doing so, he also manages to put the few thousand dollars I give to MSF each year into context. What's been a small amount of money to me seems to have made much more of a difference than I thought possible.

As I leave, I feel curiously reinvigorated, determined to give away much more of my money. The way things will turn out, I won't meet Fred again, but my journey with MSF has only just begun.

I'M DETERMINED TO write a novel. Once I have a first draft, Sam has promised to take a look at it and, if he thinks it's worthy, help me with the promotion. As I've found out, Caroline is an excellent editor, too. As I struggle through the pages, tracing Christian Unger's terrifying journey to protect his family from the psychotic wrath of his lover's ex-husband, she helps me with issues of character development and pacing. Sometimes I lose my way altogether and she helps me regain objectivity. Caroline has even come up with the right title, *A Dangerous Remedy*.

I write, go for a walk or do something physical when I need distance from my emerging opus, then hand Caroline a few new pages. She then sits, usually in the courtyard of our Colorado garden, wearing her wide-brimmed straw hat, or in the shade of the cottage porch, considering my work. When she summons me for her comments, I always find them thoughtful and balanced. She makes me see things through a reader's eyes. This is remarkable given the story, which contains segments of Caroline's history, including glimpses into the pathology of abuse she and the girls suffered.

Why would I write a book about her former husband? Actually, that's not what it is. What the novel does explore is what would have happened if Don had allowed his rage to take him a few steps further. What if he'd engaged the help of criminals to deal with Caroline and me? What moral boundaries would I have had to cross? It was a question I asked myself when Don did make threats, did casually turn on our gas barbeque when dropping off Melissa and Krista, and eventually, did steal a quarter million dollars from the girls' educational trust. As it happened, things never went further, but the experience of being on the wrong side of someone so profoundly vindictive had left me consistently unsettled and in fear. It's that state of mind that I want to explore in my novel.

KRISTA HAS A steady boyfriend too, but seems to prefer coming up North alone. She even has ideas on how we could improve the cottage. She wants to make the tiny open attic space into a bedroom for herself, a project I've volunteered to do with her, envisioning that the experience would leave us with cherished shared memories. Now, having climbed up the newly built oaken ladder, we are busy installing the walls, Krista handing me the boards and I fixing them to the joists, both of us dodging the beams of the slanted roof. I'm enjoying myself immensely and, occasionally looking up at Krista's face, I can see that it's the same for her. We've been at it since morning and soon it'll be time for a shower and a sumptuous dinner. It's Thanksgiving Day; a few feet below us, Caroline is cooking.

With the walls finished, only one thing is yet to be done: the small door, which I built the previous day, needs to be mounted. Caroline doubts whether we can get it all done today; she keeps reminding us that the turkey is almost done. I ask Krista to help me hold up the door and, with my other hand, grab the post that will support it. It's half an inch too wide. "One more cut, Caroline, and will be ready to shower and help you," I holler. Then I climb down, walk out onto the porch, kneel down next to my table saw and turn it on. "Almost done," I say to myself, as I guide the piece of wood toward the whining blade.

On the boat, an ice cold dishtowel holding my hand together as we motor through the dark toward Parry Sound, I wonder what exactly happened. Later, in the emergency room of the hospital, a man whose son has shot himself in the leg, asks me the same question. I tell him I nearly sliced off a finger. "Table saw kicking back, eh?" he says knowingly, then holds up a hand with two missing fingers.

I feel badly for the surgeon. As she cuts off bits of skin and gore, then stitches up my hand, I can see that her back or neck is trou-bling her. When I ask she tells me she's been at it for eight hours. "Thanksgiving," she shrugs. "It's the same every year."

I'm sufficiently medicated not to feel any pain as we return at eleven at night, Caroline holding up the powerful light and I at the helm. When we re-enter the cottage I even feel hungry. I can't operate the corkscrew, though. Krista has to do that.

SOME CHRISTMAS BREAKS are more memorable than others. This year we got together for three family celebrations: one at Mike and Nellie's place, another at Melissa and John's new house, and a third at our newly built loft. Then we flew to Colorado, where Stephanie and her friend Jim came to visit us, so we could together usher in the new millennium. Yesterday, we spent most of the day painting prayer flags and suspending them from the beams of our pergola. Now, on the first morning of the year 2000, we watch our messages of hope snap in the crisp morning breeze, the sky behind them perfect in its cloudless intensity. It's hard to look at it without squinting.

I stop reading, put Mami's letter aside and close my eyes. What comes up first is the memory of Gaby and Kurt showing me their new house in Brunnadern. My sister had won a major battle, hav-ing gained a new kidney and pancreas, but we all knew she was losing the war. Decades of insulin consumption had caused her capillaries to degenerate. She'd lost a toe, then another. Walking had become a problem, especially during the dark winter months. She'd given up her job.

But now, in their new house, they'd have more light, and

modifications were made to accommodate her frailties. Outside, additional lights were being installed; inside, there would be hand-rails along the staircases and some of the walls. Even better, Flavia and her family lived next door. There would always be help if she needed it, even when Kurt was at work.

Nothing ever happened while Gaby was home alone, and when all went inconceivably wrong it wasn't with her, but Kurt. I still find it difficult to adjust to the reality of my sister as a widow, deprived of income, her ability to go to work or other places impaired by her eyesight and her mangled feet.

I spent three weeks with her not long after she lost Kurt, trying to find a way to help, but I left despondent, my mission unaccomplished. It turned out that Gaby didn't want help. She was so full of anger at having become dependent that her one and only goal was to become free again. It took us a while to understand what she had in mind. For now, all we could do was back off.

My sister once told me that what defined whether or not our lives were lived successfully, was how we tolerated or stood up against adversity. She had done a lot of both with distinction: tolerating the gradual deterioration of her body since she was a child, and resisting when she felt she needed to take a stand.

Within a few weeks, Gaby managed to subdue her anger and focus on healing. She remembered her typing skills and practiced on Kurt's typewriter until she was near perfect. Mami proof-read, reported on progress and even found an engineering firm whose principals still dictated on tape the old fashioned way. They started mailing Gaby tapes and she typed the recorded protocols and letters onto their stationery. Adjusted for the amount of time she took with each assignment, her pay was absurdly low, but that didn't matter. For the first time in months, she felt a measure of satisfaction.

One day her contact at the engineering firm called her and asked if she had ever worked on a computer. A conversion was planned in a few months' time. Gaby was devastated. She understood that she'd be obsolete if she didn't adapt. Someone at the Institute for the Blind told her that if she bought a computer, they would help with the purchase cost and send a tutor as part of a rehabilitation program. The desktop she got came with a huge monitor, which featured contrast enhancements for the visually impaired. Within a month, Gaby was reasonably proficient on her new computer.

But while my partially blind sister managed the switch from typewriter to state-of-the-art technology, her friends at the engineering firm fell behind, then chose not to proceed. Disappointed, Gaby decided to look for a new employer and asked around. One of the people who learned about her quest was Dr. Kuhn, her physician of nearly 35 years, who was intimately familiar with her personal circumstances. To Gaby's amazement, he offered her a position at the hospital, where he headed the surgery department, provided that she'd physically go to work there. He explained the reason for his condition: my sister didn't just need a job, she also needed a new start in her social life.

For a day or so, Gaby felt sorry for herself. Accepting the offer involved walking to the station and getting into and out of a train, which was a skill she didn't have. Once in Herisau, she'd have to hike up a hill to the hospital and in winter it would be dark and icy. And all this for only four hours of work each day—two before lunch and two after—because that was as long as she could work without encountering devastating eyestrain.

But then she took the plunge. Dr. Kuhn, whose technical transcripts she now types, demanded perfection. As Gaby related it to me in one of our frequent phone conversations, every sentence had at least two or three special terms in it, usually in Latin. She was ecstatic: apart from being independent and needed, she was becoming an expert in medical terminology.

THINKING OF HOW Gaby's soaring spirit was once again eclipsing challenges that would have driven most others to thorough despair, I'm picking up my mother's letter once more. Three pages of type-written words. A smile comes to my face as I recall my sister's account of how she'd gifted Kurt's almost new typewriter to Mami.

Yet, as I read on, deep sadness overcomes me again. Apparently, when trying to board the train to Herisau, Gaby had missed the step and fallen. Luckily, the conductor had seen it, or she would have ended up under the departing carriage. I look at the sky outside my office, the clouds racing across the horizon turning into a shapeless smear as my eyes fill with tears. I try to envision the scene, attempt to feel the terror that must have engulfed Gaby as she slipped, then lay there helplessly, in the semi-dark space between the hard train platform and the rails below, the massive wheels coming for her within moments.

Eventually, I return to my mother's lines and soon feel a bit better. Apparently, Gaby has decided to sell the house and move to a condominium in Herisau. She understands that keeping her job at the hospital is paramount; it's what motivates and defines her.

Perhaps Mami needs to redefine herself too. Not long ago, she volunteered for Amnesty International and the museum; she's since quit both engagements. Maybe my mother and sister can help each other. I stay with that thought for a moment, realizing that Mami is close to eighty. Looking after Gaby may characterize her remaining years.

*T*uiavii's words have changed me in profound ways. I elaborated on my transition when invited by the CBC's book reviewer Shelagh Rogers, and in even greater detail when John's dad, the CTV network's distinguished anchor, Larry Stout, graciously invited me to the studio to do an in-depth interview.

I was turning fifty when the book was first published and felt as awed by the simplicity of the young chief's insights as I had been twenty-five years earlier, when I first considered them. I still feel the same way as I'm interviewed for an Amazon promotion; I'm in my early seventies now. In the meantime, Tuiavii's Way has become a designated study material at some top U.S. universities and mandated reading for English language students at Japanese high schools. This is what I always hoped for: that young people will draw inspiration from the chief's wisdom.

WHEN CONSIDERING MY own journey, what amazes me most is how the demands of professional life crowded out my youthful idealism—at least for the better part of two decades. Here I was in my early twenties, convinced of the merits of socialism, and a few years later, embracing the doctrine of free markets. Much had to do with what capitalism did for me: I was one of the fortunate few to be given virtually free reign by figures like Nicholas Deak and Howard Kelly. The only barriers to commercial success were my creativity and a commitment to accept responsibility and long working hours. In return, the system rewarded me with endless promotions and handsome compensation. No wonder I adored unbridled capitalism!

I remember contrasting Ronald Reagan's bold promises to reduce the role and size of America's government with Canada's clumsy attempts to *go in the opposite direction, all at enormous cost to the taxpayer. Sometime in the early 1990s, as we spent more and more time in the United States, I seriously contemplated a change in residence. Many others went a step further: thousands of doctors, engineers and business people left Canada.*

Then came the Tuiavii project which, bit by bit, changed my perspective. I turned softer, started to see the world in which we lived differently. As I studied the economic and socio-political landscape, I started to understand that both capitalism and socialism, the way they were applied, were doomed. As workable doctrines they both had strong merits, but as practical organisms they were at the mercy of perverted political structures.

The enemy was the growing centralization of power, in every field of endeavour. In Canada, the U.S., Europe and Japan—whether the ideology favoured socialism or capitalism, the power dynamic seemed to be identical. Economic expansions and recessions alike served to increase the might of the ruling establishment. The social contract between employers and employees that had ruled through the early years of my career was dead; competition was being stifled by ever further consolidation, which served a single purpose: to expand the power of the monopolists. Already, the politicians and the media were their loyal servants. Down the road, they'd become handmaidens of an inescapable tyranny.

I might have come to all these conclusions without Tuiavii's help, but scrutinizing the merits of his message in enormous detail and over a long period of time made me look at the sustainability of our policies more closely. The U.S., for which I'd developed such admiration, used the collapse of Soviet Communism as a pretense to build an empire, spending ever more money on the military and less on its social programs. The European Union, sold to its voting public as a means to gain economies of scale, quickly transformed itself into a colossal and inefficient bureaucracy.

INDOCTRINATED BY THE *German missionaries who'd come to his native Samoa, Tuiavii had wanted nothing more than to visit and experience European culture. When first exposed to it he was awestruck by its glamorous inventions; after a while, he started to understand its dark side. Selfishness, greed and hypocrisy ruled. That's when he decided to return home and do the only thing he could: to warn his fellow islanders.*

My journey was similar. I was as overwhelmed by the positive attitude of my American friends as by their country's wealth. Yet, as I listened, I realized that a lot of their patriotic and self-congratulatory talk was parroted propaganda. America's systems, no matter how widely copied elsewhere in the developed world, were not only unsustainable, but designed to benefit not its people but a narrow oligarchy.

What was I to do? I decided to change the focus of my research, broadening it to include a lot more geo-political and social policy content. To accommodate that I started Perspectives, a monthly review that was available to not just my clients, but the public at large. Instead of paying a subscription fee Perspectives subscribers had to donate $100 to Doctors Without Borders each year.

Much of my focus in Perspectives was on analyzing the roots of our problems. I soon convinced myself that centralization was the enemy of societal well-being and a comprehensive effort to devolve power to smaller scales the only solution. Some of my observations were quoted, but found not much of an echo. Still, many of the themes regularly discussed in Perspectives twenty years ago—the inevitable explosion in U.S. wealth inequality, the intensification of American military adventures into a 'forever-war', and the militarization of the country's police forces which would eventually have to be deployed against rebelling citizens—have all become reality.

WORKING ON THE *Tuiavii project also redefined my social orientation—not because of the chief's message, but because of the people I worked and started to hang out with: publishers, agents and other authors. With my gold books, my encounters were largely confined to negotiating a royalty arrangement with a senior operative at a major publishing firm and the odd joint appearance with another investment writer. The group Sam Hiyate routinely brought together was far more colourful and interesting. In a way, it was like a return to the bohemian crowd I'd been part of when living in the annex. Vibrant discussions, excessive drinking and the odd karaoke night were all part of the fun. I realized how sheltered I'd been during my twenty-plus years as an executive. Someone had told me that Sam Hiyate's Gutter Press brand referred to Oscar Wilde's aphorism, "We are all in the gutter, but some of us are looking at the stars." This resonated—there was a lot of that when congregating with Sam and his friends.*

One stargazer who was to become a close friend was Larry Gaudet who, at the time we met, was working on a tome of his own, 'The Peacekeeper's Teahouse'. The novel's central character was a burned-out U.N. peace-negotiator who'd returned home to Canada from the ravages of war and hoped to find solitude in the teahouse he built himself. There, he realized that while he'd escaped one horror, his own backyard had become a battlefield of deception, drama, and betrayal.

Unlike Larry's peacekeeper, I never felt discouraged or even disillusioned. But I did start to relate to the economic and political environment in which I was destined to live as a theatre of the absurd, its coaches, stage designers and actors blindly executing the director's program. Over time my relationship with the symbols of statehood underwent a profound change. I no longer viewed flags and anthems as benign icons of shared values, but as propaganda tools used in the spreading of lies and hypocrisy, and as instruments of duality and domination.

While I kept most of my darker views out of the pages of my published communications, I didn't hesitate to bring them up when asked.

This led to some interesting conversations with our American friends. At dinner parties or when I gave a speech, with surprising frequency someone would ask how I, as a Canadian with a foothold in Europe, viewed the United States. My responses were unguarded at first, naïve even, with predictable results. As I roundly condemned the culture of military interventions, labelling them as a brutally callous business model, there was always someone who reacted with hostility. More than once I was asked to get out of America, if I couldn't stand the place.

As the years went by, I learned to modify my comments, drawing a distinction between individual Americans and the government. I liked, even admired the people, but I loathed the power structure. For a brief moment that earned me kudos from at least half the listeners—if the administration was Republican, the Democrats would cheer me on, and vice versa. But once I got around to explaining that I thought both parties were utterly corrupt and that most members of Congress were no more than paid servants of various industry lobbies, I was quickly relegated to my status as the ugly stranger.

Finally, I think I've got it right. When being asked, I now counter by voicing discomfort. "Gee, I'm not sure you are ready for my assessment. You may not like it." There's always someone who dismisses my hesitation to engage. "No, we do want to hear what you have to say," or, "Come on now, no need to be polite in our company." That gives me the opportunity to make my audience laugh. "Okay," I'll say, "we all love America because of its one indisputable advantage: a much superior climate than what Canada or large parts of Europe can boast of."

Then, careful to draw a distinction between the country's people and its government, I give voice to my opinions. And when closing, I'm careful to add that there are other nations that are as dysfunctional as theirs—the U.S. just matters more because its actions are so consequential. Going at it this way works better, and those who are open to my message get it just the same as if I let my oratory passions run wild.

It's been fifteen years since I first met Melissa, ten years since I started thinking of her as my daughter and offered to adopt her. Today, at Toronto's Hunt Club, she's getting married. The day is spectacular; the flower-covered portal under which Melissa and John say their vows seems to float atop Lake Ontario. It's hard to imagine that we're anywhere close to an urban centre.

Melissa has everyone's admiration. A couple of days ago, she put out her back; it's evident that she's in severe pain. We doubt whether she can last through the evening and wonder how she'll endure the ten hour flight that will take her to her honeymoon in Europe tomorrow.

Later, while family and guests nibble on freshly-shucked oysters and sip champagne, I give my speech. In its midst, I notice that I'm losing people's attention, but I can't see why. Everyone's eyes seem focused on a spot just below the platform I stand on. I'll later learn that one of the ladies fainted; her skirt was lifted in the process and, apparently, she wasn't wearing underpants.

The wedding celebration is perfect. None of the speeches are too long, the dinner service is well-paced, and everyone seems to enjoy the entertainment. Even the salsa dancing segment that Caroline arranged and Melissa vigorously opposed is met with enthusiasm. The hired professionals first demonstrate, then instruct those courageous enough to join in.

Around ten, one of the guests enters the room and suggests we come outside. Out of the black lake of an hour ago the moon has risen, bathing the vast waters before us and our small group in a gentle, then progressively exuberant glaze.

On the way home to our new condominium, I taunt Lea, who's

flown over from Switzerland for the occasion, suggesting that she may be next to be married. "I noticed that you've been paying attention to every detail," I tease. Lea dismisses the idea, betting that Krista, who brought her friend Nick along and is talking about moving together with him, will be first.

Only seven flights a week are destined for Bhutan and the only carrier allowed to land here is the country's own DrukAir. Most of the flight from Bangkok has been unremarkable, but now, as our small plane descends toward a deep valley, I realize that landing here must be a challenge. The trek ahead of us will be similar to what we did in Mustang—several weeks in largely unexplored territory— but the scenery is distinctly different. While the ascent through the Kali Gandaki gorge into Upper Mustang led us through largely treeless desert, Bhutan is heavily forested. After a couple of days in Thimphu, the capital, we'll be driving to Bumthang in the country's middle, then walk East along a route dotted with small settlements toward Tashigang, before turning South into an area that's not yet been mapped for trekkers, into India's Assam state.

We've read several articles on Bhutan, often with a sentimental overlay based on one of the kingdom's propaganda pieces. "Instead of Gross National Product, an economic measurement," one article in the New York Times proclaimed, "Bhutan uses Gross National Happiness as its philosophy." That kind of hype makes me deeply suspicious, despite Richard and Noriko Moore's reassurances. Our friends have spent considerable time in Bhutan, Richard having been retained as the country's marketing communications advisor.

As we arrive, we're impressed. While Thimphu, a town of less than 50,000 people, is remarkably uninspiring from an architectural viewpoint, it has a highly compelling social profile. Wherever we walk within the small capital, no effort is spared to make us feel at home and expose us to Bhutan's customs and culture. Food and accommodation are very simple, but we never have the impression that anyone holds anything back or that there is a commercial motive. Nothing seems to involve a deliberate effort. I'm asking myself if I've ever visited a capital where no one asked for a handout, or even a piece of candy, or where everyone seemed so content.

Perhaps, such modesty is possible because the vast majority of the country's population engages in farming and is completely self-sufficient. In other words, no commercial effort is necessary to survive. Our guide, a robustly built, tall, pockmarked thirty-year old explains during a bland dinner at our modest hotel that people freely drift in and out of their isolated hamlets, visiting a nearby settlement, or occasionally a major town. It's understood that wherever they go they'll be looked after, without consideration of recompense. I'm still in doubt about the practicality of such an arrangement, but remind myself that I've witnessed similar conventions elsewhere: when I crossed Africa 30 years ago and, more recently, when Caroline and I reached other truly remote parts of the Himalayas.

I remember Richard Moore's comments too: that the gracious simplicity of the Bhutanese is enabled by the country's policy of opening up to outside influences at a deliberately slow pace. Tourism, for example, is at once welcomed and discouraged. There's a stringent limit on visas issued each year and, to keep the small supply of permits in line with demand, a stiff daily fee is imposed.

The effort to protect Bhutan's cultural identity is evident everywhere. I ask our guide, Wangchuck, about his dress, virtually identical to what every other male wears. We learn that the knee-length, robe-like cloth that envelops their bodies and is secured by a belt is known as a Gho. The women wear an apron-like dress called a Kira. Conventional garb is compulsory. While patterns and the extent of embroidery allow for a degree individuality, the basic design is mandated to be the same for all.

As we leave Thimphu we quickly realize how uniformly stunning Bhutan's scenery is. We drive the first hundred miles or so, then start walking, getting the first glimpses of the pristine Himalayan peaks to the North, many of them yet unclimbed. To our South are lush valleys, which teem with subtropical vegetation. In the mornings, Bhutan's woods are shrouded in mist, which gives them the type of mysterious air one associates with a Himalayan kingdom.

NEARLY A MONTH later, as our adventure nears its end, we're still not used to the abundance and size of shrubs, bushes and trees. Most frequent are the rhododendrons and wild poinsettias, covering hues of red from rose to crimson and garnet, which are often the size of trees. Even more impressive are Bhutan's vast virgin forests—cypresses, cedars, oaks and pines, covering hills so steep it's hard to comprehend how the soil can support the weight of the often hundred-foot-high trunks.

There have been unforgettable physical challenges, along the way. As we had on our Mustang expedition, we faced our share of high passes, including the 13,800 foot high Rodung La. But the hardest part came near the end, as we descended some 8,000 vertical feet of steep forest terrain that was covered with dense undergrowth. We soon realized that walking it was impossible without a crew of half a dozen machete-wielding helpers. We were also lost; the map Wangchuck had been given by the authorities had been reasonably accurate as long as there were paths linking human settlement, but now that we were in largely uncharted territory it was useless. We discussed our options and realized that our only chance was to find, then follow, the creek that appeared to be near us.

We separated into six groups of two people each, instead of going downhill spreading out along the slope, promising that whoever heard running water would alert the others. Finding the gurgling creek was easy; following it downhill proved treacherous and frustrating. In order to find a passage through the impenetrable vegetation on both sides of the rushing water, we had to follow the creek's rocky bed, jumping from boulder to wet and often frozen boulder. More than once, we feared that dusk would fall before we reached a flat piece of land where we could put up our tents. Some of us fell during the perilous descent; Caroline took a more serious spill, cracking her tailbone.

WE'VE ALSO LEARNED a lot about Bhutan's cultural complexities and contradictions. The rarely visited monuments and monasteries we've seen in the past few days as we traversed Bhutan's easternmost part, strike me as stirring spiritual manifestations of Buddhism, quite different from the fortress-like symbols designed to defend feudal regimes that dominated the major towns closer to the capital. We reach the hillside town of Trashigang, which marks the end of our trek, in time for its Tschechu, an annual festival, where monks enact classical morality plays in which good triumphs over evil. As foreigners, we are allowed into the monastery's courtyard, where we press ourselves against the tall, intricately carved and painted walls, allowing the colourfully dressed masked dancers to enact their drama, taking their cues from a cacophony of gongs, drums and Tibetan horns. Yet, despite the proximity to all this, centre stage is two floors up, where a half-dozen apprentice monks, boys in their early teens wearing their orange robes, stand at a window-like opening, their faces radiating purest joy.

Trashigang, much the same as the hamlets we've come through on the way here, have made Thimphu, with its many identical looking buildings and its indistinguishably dressed people, look contrived. The villagers who've come together here also wear their mandated Ghos and Kiras, but in these surroundings their outfits appear genuine and culturally integrated.

Curiously, after our dinner, we end up talking about this with Wangchuck, who tells us how he and many other young people in Thimphu prefer casual Western clothing and how, at night, they often venture out in jeans and T-shirts. He seems comfortable enough with us to tell us more. One night, he confesses, he was on his way to meet up with friends outside the capital when the police caught him. The only reason he escaped a stiff jail term was because his father, a government official, intervened.

We're offered additional insights into Bhutan's tenuous socio-economic structure during our drive toward the Indian border. As we leave Trashigang, the road is a potholed dirt track, barely able to accommodate crossing vehicles. A couple of hours later it broadens into a generous, beautifully paved two-lane highway. Now, at regular intervals, we notice sizeable logging equipment along its side. The hotel in Deothang, where we spend our last night, could be anywhere in Western Europe or America. Except for the staff, no one here wears the traditional garb, not even the Bhutanese guests.

Back in the bus the next day, sitting next to Wangchuck, Caroline and I ask about what we've seen. His answer surprises us. Wangchuck explains that the king is married to two sisters, whose father not only owns the hotel we just stayed at, but also the logging monopoly that clear-cuts some of Bhutan's oldest forests, then trucks the wood to India.

As we cross the Indian border and leave Bhutan behind, our feelings are complex. We've learned to love the generosity and grace of the Bhutanese people, but have also seen evidence of hypocrisy and corruption.

In between treks and climbs, at the campfire or at the dinner table of a guest house, we've had the odd opportunity to ask both ordinary Bhutanese, as well as a few civil servants and members of the country's small elite about their hopes for the future. Without fail, members of the peasant class praised their monarch, while those elevated a few notches by education expressed admiration for their monarch but expected trouble ahead. They feared that technology and gradually rising education levels would before long subvert government narratives.

As I consider all this I realize that, perversely, the king's determination to resist modernization, has helped me gain perspective. It's made it possible to once more step back in time, into a world far simpler, less hurried and more caring, made possible by the coincidence of the country's remoteness and the self-sufficiency of its farming communities. That and spending a month trekking, each day sampling an offering of the unexpected, not knowing where we'd next pitch our tent, is more than adventure. It's untainted, immeasurable privilege.

Melissa and John have left not long ago, both have become solid skiers. Now Krista and Nick are with us. A few months ago, they moved in together; now they want to get married.

Caroline and I are concerned, partly because we've noticed that Krista is in too much of a hurry to follow Melissa's path. We both feel that she hasn't known Nick nearly long enough, and we know that our Krista tends to make weighty decisions that she soon after regrets.

"Live with him for a couple of years first, and see how that goes," I've suggested. "Why get married and buy a house before you really know what it's like to be with Nick?" I've even put my thoughts on paper, thinking I may get through to her. To her credit, she read my letter and said she appreciated the thought I put into it. Nevertheless, she'd get married, and soon.

Now that the two are in Colorado, I'm trying to get to know Nick better. Chatting with him riding the chairlift to the top and watching him ski and interact with other skiers on the way down helps. Nick seems eager to show me how good a skier he is, and wants to take on some of the expert runs, including the Hanging Valley Wall, an iconic near-vertical chute. I feel that his technical skills are strong enough, but emphasize that there is no room for error. Krista, listening to our conversation, is completely opposed to the idea. She announces that she'll hold me accountable if anything goes wrong, to which I respond with a compromise solution. I suggest we tackle some of the other wilderness runs, where the consequences of a mistake would be less dramatic. But Nick is determined.

Half an hour later, having hiked uphill and skied to the top of a narrow and near vertical chute flanked by barren rocks, we stop. I give Nick a preview of what is to follow, warning him not to veer to the sides, but head straight down to where the chimney-like channel opens into a bowl. "That stuff to the sides looks like nice, forgivable powder, Nick. But in reality it's just last night's quarter-inch snowfall…underneath it is a layer of ice and, below that, sheer granite." I explain that if he turns on that, his edges will slip and he'll fall and careen down the whole hundred meters or so. I point to a table-sized rectangular boulder sticking some four feet out of the snowpack, far below us, suggesting that is where he'd end up.

Nick looks less confident now, so I remind him that he's a good skier and can absolutely do this—as long as he follows my instructions. When I ask if he wants me to go first, Nick looks at me doubtfully and pushes off. Instead of diving right into the abyss, he opts for the seemingly more cautious alternative and initiates his first turn off to the side. As his skis slip from under him, he falls and moves downward, head first. His bindings release almost immediately, then, as his body flips and bounces, he loses his poles. He tries to resist his fall and change direction, but his trajectory is assured. I watch helplessly as he surrenders and rapidly slides down the fall line. My emotions flounder between anger, fear and the realization that I'll have to explain this to Krista.

Nick is gaining speed, heading straight for the rock I'd pointed out. Just before he gets there he hits a small rise in the terrain, which gets him airborne and helps his head and torso avoid the obstacle, but as far as I can make out his legs come crashing down on it hard. Then, just below the boulder, Nick's body comes to a rest.

Moments later, kneeling by his side, I have a chance to assess the damage. The one positive is that my future son-in-law is alive. One of his hands is cut up; apparently, the glove came off along with his pole. Far worse, his Kevlar ski pants are ripped open and the bits of exposed leg are a bloody mess. Nick looks completely drained and can hardly talk. I ponder how we'll get to the bottom, which is when I realize I forgot to bring down his skis and poles, which are somewhere near the top of the chute, probably deeply buried in snow.

No matter what happens next, Krista, who's waiting for us at the mountain restaurant below, will be livid.

Getting Melissa and Krista through their teen years demanded time and dedication. When they reached adulthood, I assumed my life would now enter a quieter phase. My engagement in the world of business was nicely slowing and I suddenly had more time for travel, exercise and creative pursuits. Even better, I had Caroline. The two of us spent an enormous amount of time together, hiking, skiing or swimming, reading the same books, seeing the same people. For a while, we even meditated together, albeit each in our unique way—Caroline taking the time necessary to reach and dwell in a space of absolute quiet, me devoting exactly 30 minutes per day to the task, so I could follow the ebb and flow of my mind and then record my experience in spreadsheet form.

Even the things we did when we were apart were eerily similar. I'd turn to my writing or get involved with a new art project, while Caroline learned to make pottery and craft jewelry. So comfortable were we with our new life, we never gave much thought to its inevitable next chapter.

Occasionally, while visiting Switzerland and sitting in Flavia and Urs' idyllic garden we watched their three kids—Christian, Roman and Nina—take delight in a new game they'd invented and, moments later, fight about how it should be played. Sometimes the children sorted things out by themselves and sometimes their parents had to intervene. Occasionally Flavia and Urs argued about who was at fault and how the crisis should be managed. These were scenes that Caroline and I were too familiar with. As grandparents, we imagined, we'd be in far better position: we'd be spectators of a delightful performance when the little ones behaved and we could get up and leave when things turned ugly.

What we could not have guessed was how soon both Melissa and Krista would be married and have children. We were delighted with such an outcome, but it took us a while to adjust to a completely different life than the one we were just getting used to.

It's in the fifth episode of the 26-part series 'The World at War' that Sir Lawrence Olivier narrates Operation Barbarossa, the ill-fated 1941 invasion of the Soviet Union. The cinematography is pitiless, the pace cruelly slow. Relentless winter storms batter the German foot soldiers who at first progress, then utterly defeated return across hundreds of kilometers of snow covered flat territory, unable to see more than a few feet ahead of themselves. Many perish.

As I watched the series at our new Colorado house, I felt a sense of curiosity. Much of what I saw seemed eerily familiar. And then the Barbarossa ordeal—I knew I'd been there, as a German soldier. I tried to listen to Olivier's words, but what I heard was the unyielding howl of the wind and what I felt was the weight of my boots, the feet inside already lifeless. I cried then, not knowing what else to do.

The next day, certain that my experience would be less disturbing or that there may be some explanation for my reaction, I watched it again. I'd been there, there was no doubt, this time wondering how we'd gone from marching through conquered small towns, cheered on by residents not too many weeks ago, to the shame of retreat, even the starving farmers we passed pitying us. Again I cried, feeling the agonizing hole in my stomach, my frozen limbs. I wasn't sure whether I'd returned home— wherever that was—and died there, or whether I'd perished in that godless, shapeless stretch of uncaring white.

Deeply disturbed, but intrigued, I spent the following days listening to German folksongs and military tunes that were popular during the Hitler years. Remarkably, I knew the words before I heard them. The melodies, too, seemed etched into my soul—readily recallable, the refrains echoing through the towns we'd once marched through, the clack-ing of hobnailed boots ensuring perfect rhythm. Had I loved the tunes for their melodious characteristics or had I been attracted by their capacity to make me feel part of something compelling and mighty? I couldn't tell.

TO A LARGE *extent, my detour into the realm of the past was propelled by my new habit to meditate, which made me realize how little time I spent in the present. There I was most mornings after taking my shower, clad in my oversized white bathrobe, settling into a contemplative pos-ture. That was the easy part; retreating into a truly quiet space proved far more challenging. My eyes closed, I concentrated on my breathing, intending to stop the flow of thoughts.*

It always worked for a minute or two, but then, resting in the soothing pattern of my inhalations and exhalations, I noticed that I was thinking again. It was as if I beheld a peacefully, silently flowing river and sud-denly spotted a vessel that must have stealthily advanced from outside the periphery of my vision to its centre, without me seeing it. Some of the thought vessels drifting by delighted and reassured, brightly painted and sporting colourful flags snapping in the breeze; others, seemingly not car-ried along by the current, but ruling the waters around them, demanded vigilance or instilled fear. Some pointed to a near or distant past, some to the future. Others focused me on what I thought of as now, but actually had little to do with the present moment. It was the Tuiavii chapter I'd been working on last night or the urgent phone call I planned to make after breakfast that my thoughts dwelled on.

I considered the matter in the context of my everyday activities. When I worked on analyzing a company's balance sheet, where were my thoughts? Typically, on how much better or worse that balance sheet had looked a year ago, if I wasn't speculating about the company's future prospects. I wondered how much attention I gave the physical and emotional sensations of cuddling Cleo, the cat Krista had found and raised and who was now our constant companion. Not much, I realized. When Cleo rested in my lap, my mind was mostly on what I could do to get her to purr, or that I had better place my full-to-the-rim tea mug on a solid surface in case Cleo decided to jump. And when I walked up our spectacular road, did I do the incomparable mountain scenery justice, or contemplate the sour-sweet scent of a million choke cherry blossoms, or watch the plethora of birds, some resting in the bushes that lined the street, some majestically riding the currents far above me? No, I usually thought about what tasks awaited me at my desk or in the garden, or chose the exact place where I'd place a speed limit sign if I were in charge of the Snowmass Village police.

Of course there are things that arrest thought and let us savour the moment. Letting a lump of pistachio ice cream slowly melt on my tongue, being stung by a bee and feeling my finger swell up, losing control of my car on an ice patch—all make for a few seconds of absolute presence and lucidity. Sometimes, when I watch the sun slowly melt into the horizon the sensation lasts as long as a minute or two, but rarely without me catching myself comparing the experience to a previous one.

What I had related to throughout my life as the present seemed actually non-existent; my mind was always to either side of the moment. Perhaps the real now was only attainable when thought was altogether absent—a state I became determined to summon, and in time, master.

When that proved difficult I felt annoyed. The interference of my restless mind and, more so, my inability to put a stop to it, frustrated me. Talking about it with Caroline helped, as did the suggestions from our friend Theophane, the Trappist monk. He told us we should view the thought parade with tolerance, even amusement. The mind was an important ally that deserved to be honoured—just be aware of its tendency to dominate and crowd out silence.

In time, our inquiry led us to the better known thinkers and writers on spiritual matters: Ramana Maharshi, Omar Khayam, Krishnamurti, Thich Nhat Hanh, Jon Kabat-Zinn, David Bohm and Eckhart Tolle. We both read their works, then discussed our findings. They echoed Theophane's input: be aware of the seemingly relentless flow of thoughts, while asking what it is that holds that awareness. Gradually, we learned to see that concepts like time and reality, the way we had been conditioned to see them, were no more than a given way to manage our experience of consciousness, and perhaps an illusion. The need to keep my spreadsheet on spiritual progress up-to-date soon evaporated.

OVER TIME, CAROLINE *pursued her spiritual practice with far more devotion than I did. Eventually, she was asked to teach; guiding others has since become her main purpose.*

The journey I followed has been less focused, but the insights I've gained are still deeply rewarding. My explorations of consciousness have profoundly changed the way I perceive and look at things. I'm still struggling with being in the real present, and probably always will be, but I've come to realize that musing about the future is a ridiculously unworthy pursuit.

What's curious is that Kevin MacLean and I had concluded just that when we closed down Cavelti Capital. Our forecasting ability had been unexceptional, even though we had access to as much or more information than our competitors. What kept us at the very top of the performance spectrum was only one thing: our recognition that we needed a formula to safeguard against the erroneous projections that accompanied us wherever we ventured.

Plans, it seems, are useful as long as they allow for different possibilities. As the scenery changes, they can be adjusted, but never must we allow our emotions to become married to a given outcome.

AS I LABELLED *the future as unworthy of much further thought and resigned myself to the perpetual difficulty of dwelling in the real present, I paid more attention to the past. Once Melissa and Krista brought us grandchildren we became a four-generation family. I started considering the vastly different ways each of us experience life and how we recall what is behind us. Mike and Nellie's upbringing in rural Ukraine during Stalin's time, and their struggle through the Great Depression once they were in Canada, distinctly coloured the way they saw the world. When Mike saw anything made of concrete he related to it as beautiful, mainly because to him it represented prosperity. If we took him to the cottage, he saw the trees surrounding us as things that obstructed progress and should ideally come down. The deprivations of his upbringing as one of the many children of a tenant farmer warped his perception of many things.*

I wonder what distortions I've allowed into my story. Is my rise from the depths of failure as miraculous as I make it out to be? Are my adventures as a backpacker as romantic and my successes in the world of finance as noteworthy as I think of them?

And what about my journey into the past life of a German soldier, one moment being cheered on by townsfolk while chanting a nationalistic tune and feeling invincible, and not long after limping homeward along a stretch of icy tundra, drained and fatigued, my uniform in tatters, bits of frozen blue skin showing through. Did I make it home or had I collapsed and perished along with tens of thousands of others, a heap of bones partly covered by a snowdrift, there for the wolves and crows to feast on? Are my ingrained suspicion of government and my intense dislike of flags and anthems the product of not just this life's experiences, but previous ones as well?

Four intense years have passed. Shedding professional responsibilities and spending more time reflecting have helped, but I'm once again having a hard time coping. Weddings, the arrival of babies, visiting friends and family, trips, adventures and health scares and, yes, even death, have filled our days, quite apart from my writing projects and renewed pressures on the business front. The bad thing is that the balance I recreated is once again wobbling; the good thing is that I see quite clearly what activities I cherish and which ones need to be cut. Family and writing are first, professional engagements can be tossed overboard.

NOT ONLY DID Krista and Nick get married on a beach in Mexico, to which a sizeable contingent of friends and family members travelled, but we now have three healthy grandchildren who've helped us see the world in ways we never could have imagined.

Watching Alexandra standing on top of our cottage bed, holding on to the window sill and looking out at the forest, her eyes unimaginably large and expressive, saying the word "tree" to herself over and over, weighing each expression of the one syllable as if she were surprised that she could create sound, makes for one of my favourite things. At two and a half, Alexandra is starting to like my computer too. She crawls toward me when I sit in front of it, compelling me to lift her into my lap and show her pictures of her Mom and Dad, her Nana Caroline, or animals she's familiar with.

Krista's son Cameron, only a few months old, is inquisitive and tactile. He doesn't politely point at things like his cousin, but has to touch and turn, open and close them. When he's asked to be still, he fidgets; when strapped into his high chair, he tries to wiggle free.

Abigail, Alexandra's younger sister who's only just been born, is a pudgy and content baby who is happiest when carried by her daddy, whose thumb she enthusiastically sucks.

OUR RECENT MOVEMENTS have largely been determined by outside events. Even though we concluded that we're most content in the Colorado mountains, family events have frequently summoned us to Toronto and Switzerland. Caroline's dad celebrated his 90th and our mothers both turned 80. The birth of Alexandra, Abigail and Cameron have lured us back home, too — in Cameron's case, Caroline was even there to cut his umbilical cord.

In turn, we've been visited more often than we're used to. Flavia's family spent nearly a month at the cottage and in the city with us, and, within a few months of their birth, our grandchildren visited us in Snowmass Village, their parents proudly showing off the passports they secured for their babies. Our summers at the cottage now typically involve canoeing adventures with baby Alexandra, Melissa making us promise that we won't have our usual rum and coke before taking their daughter onto the water.

We still find time for travel, but our excursions are shorter now and our destinations less daring: road trips from Colorado to nearby Utah, Arizona and New Mexico; dashes within Switzerland to medieval Alpine hamlets or to Zurich and Geneva; the odd flight to London or, most recently, to Malaga, from where we toured Andalusia's major cities and the spectacular Moorish White Towns.

A few days ago, Aspen Public Radio, talk-show host Richard Sherman quizzed me about my critical views on America and the corporate world. He seemed to agree with much of what I said, frequently urging listeners to subscribe to my newsletter.

Then, a couple of minutes before our half hour ended, he asked me why I put so much effort into writing Perspectives. Without hesitation, I said that it was a way to help charity. "No, let's go deeper than that, Peter—why do you put so much effort into writing it?" he asked. I reiterated that charity came to my mind first. Sherman persisted, suggesting there was another reason, which left me bewildered. Now I found myself getting defensive, emphasizing that I didn't get a penny out of my efforts while Doctors Without Borders benefitted handsomely. The host shook his head, drily stating that he thought there was a deeper reason, one that wasn't based on monetary equations. "I think the real reason is that you love writing the damn thing, Peter, and it comes across." And with that he terminated the interview, but not without recommending Perspectives one more time.

On my twenty-minute drive home I fumed. I felt I'd been publicly embarrassed and vowed never to return to Richard Sherman's show. Yet a bit later, after talking to Caroline about it, I reversed course. My wife thought that Sherman had done me an enormous favour and that his conclusion may have been dead on. "Everyone can see that the charity angle is a wonderful thing, but is it really the underlying reason why you write Perspectives?" Caroline suggested I ask myself, which I did during a long walk.

When I returned I could see that Sherman was not only an exceptional interviewer, he had seen right through me—a capacity I apparently lacked.

Why is Perspectives so important to me? Most likely, because it helps me sort out an array of recent economic, social and political developments that challenge the values I've come to embrace and leave me deeply disturbed. Writing about them forces me to think them through and search for context, something that appears to be missing in most articles carried in the press.

I've come to look at my own past commentaries as flawed, as well. No matter how confidently I broadcast them in my newsletter articles, when I look at them now, only a few stand out as profound or even original. Far too many of my theses appear to be based on little more than commonly accepted "facts" and conclusions adjusted to my personal biases.

My approach to Perspectives, I believe, is completely different: it's an exploration, rather than a mission to establish certainty or forecast specific outcomes. Also, I try to focus on the truly large themes of our age—the emergence of a unipolar imperialistic world order dominated by the United States, advanced by lies and hypocrisy and facilitated by the growing corruption of legislators and a collaborative media complex; the gradual takeover of the economy by ever larger monopolistic entities operated on sociopathic principles and the breakdown of the social contract; the rapidly escalating disparity of wealth and the erosion of social networks; and, worst of all, the speed and enthusiasm with which these America-initiated changes are copied in Europe, Japan, Canada and down under.

Will I ever fully comprehend the causes or consequences of these weighty dynamics? Not likely at all, but I feel it's an investigative journey I need to stay with and share. Once I feel I'm nearing its end, I can move on to something different.

I'M AGGRESSIVELY CUTTING back on things that don't fit into my new world, which seems to center on family, writing and business—in that order. The hardest decisions are those related to my professional engagements. I realize that I need to look after our personal assets, which have become significant enough to take two or three hours out of each day. Luckily, my clients are content with the idea that I manage their accounts identically to mine, so continuing to attend to the affairs of the people I looked after at Guardian Trust and later Cavelti Capital seems to be logical and wholesome.

But there are other things I can let go. Among them are my directorships. The one that's taking up an enormous amount of time is Dundee Precious Metals, the company I co-founded with Beutel Goodman and N.M. Rothschild twenty years ago, which has since morphed from a precious metals fund into an active mining company. The assets we bought, some at the exploration and development stage and others already in production, are far afield and require significant attention, not only to the logistical realities of mining and smelting, but also to cultural realities. As a member of the board's Audit Committee and the head of its Corporate Governance Committee, I have to deal with a host of new government regulations that appear logical in the Canadian context, but are particularly hard to implement in Bulgaria, where our two major mining operations are centered. Attempts by regional and local government figures to secure bribes are a challenge, as is the theft of expensive equipment, sometimes perpetrated by the very security staff we hired to protect it. Luckily, we have some highly experienced mining executives on our board: our Chairman, Bill Wilson, is the former CEO of Cominco, while Peter Steen held the top office at Homestake Mining.

Still, while working with such veterans of the mining industry is both educational and comforting, the workload is far too significant to fit into my life. For a while now, I've been complaining and feeling sorry for myself. Now, I decide, it's time to resign from my remaining board obligations. Writing my resignation letters is easy, communicating the decision to the people I've worked with for a couple of decades more difficult. Even at the goodbye party Ned Goodman throws in my honour, I can see the bewilderment in my colleagues' eyes. Why is he walking away from something he worked for so many years to build?

My waking hours are filled with the richness of new experiences. So much is happening around us, it's difficult to process it all. Seeing the world through Alexandra, Cameron and Abigail's eyes is a gift I could never have imagined. The experience of my day is changing; my priorities are continuously shifting. I want nothing more than to witness the way my grandchildren experience each moment, to share their journey through childhood, to protect them as they grow.

When I looked after Gaby, Flavia and Reto for a few hours at a time, I did it through the eyes of an older brother, following my parents instructions. The emphasis wasn't on observing while the little ones explored their world, but on keeping them within the confines of good behaviour, as defined by the elders. Melissa and John, Krista and Nick act much as my parents did then. They're preoccupied and nervous, juggling the many new duties on top of the responsibilities that were there before. I observe our grandchildren when they're with their parents: content when they find themselves in a space of harmony and calm; agitated and needy when the tranquility of a few moments ago is replaced by tension.

It's easy for Caroline and me to give Abigail, Cameron or Alexandra a few hours or even a day of our undivided attention. After all, we can plan ahead and take chunks of time out of our schedule, an advantage the parents don't have. The rewards are extraordinary. When we're together, our grandchildren instill a peacefulness in us that we're not used to, which in turn allows us to bathe the little ones in a sphere of acceptance and love that keeps them content. I realize it's a relationship that is completely different from that between parent and child. Perhaps it explains why my bond with my Grossmami and Grosspapi was such a profound and resilient one. It wasn't that I loved my parents less or felt less loved by them. The difference was that I felt that my grandparents offered me a level of acceptance of who I was and what I did that my parents never could. Parents, after all, feel responsible for the outcome of their upbringing. Grandparents don't carry that burden.

From a space where my professional duties dominated my thoughts, I've migrated to a space where family seems to take center stage. My grandparents and my father, long dead now, routinely make appearances during my sleeping hours. Mami and my siblings are there, too. Occasionally even an aunt or uncle or my cousins join in. Sometimes my encounters are one on one, at other times we're all reunited.

During the day, too, I spend more time on family matters. Since Papi died, I've dutifully visited my mother once each year; after Kurt died I decided to do it twice. I've made it a habit to frequently phone, as well. And all along, I've kept up a vigorous correspondence with my mother, each of us reporting from our home front. Mami writes about Reto being offered a very senior programming job at the bank, one of my cousins getting divorced, or my childhood friend Martin becoming dean of the university. In turn, I update her about Melissa's and Krista's latest accomplishments, report on what their husbands are like, or a holiday Caroline and I have just returned from.

Most recently, with Gaby living close by and needing Mami's continuous support, the tone of our written and verbal communications has shifted. We've transcended our mother-son relationship; we've become friends. At times, her comments stun me. My strong, proud, aloof mother admitting to her growing anxieties—fears over Gaby's deteriorating health; worries that she herself might fall ill and not be there for her ailing daughter. Now that she knows me to be a good and caring listener who doesn't respond to her comments with judgments, she's also talking about Papi. She makes reference to his attempts to get close to her, then touches on his infidelities, only to conclude that she had perhaps failed him. "And how do you feel about Papi now?" I ask. "What comes up when you think of him?" She answers that she'd marry him all over again. I tell her that's all that matters.

MELISSA AND KRISTA are on my mind a lot.

Melissa's ascent in the financial world has been straight and uncompromising. She's only in her very early thirties, yet she's already in a senior position at Nesbitt Burns, Bank of Montreal's brokerage division. I keep thinking of her late teen years, when she confessed to being in love with the then 50-year old Patrick Stewart, Star Trek's Captain Picard. Caroline and I teased her about it, but we also wondered what the starship commander's appeal was. My conclusion was that it was the captain's goal to "boldly go where no man has gone before" that resonated with our Melissa. Back then, she probably hoped to be taken by the hand by someone and led toward some imaginary ideal, but as it happened she's done it all alone, and in record time.

Yet, while I'm incredibly proud of Melissa's professional success, I'm now finding myself fussing over her role as a mother. What's on my mind is the widely instituted 'maternity leave, then back to work' protocol. Will spending the largest part of the day with a nanny or in day-care be a good solution for babies Alexandra and Abigail? Or was the system my mother's and Caroline's generation observed—stepping back from their work life and spending the child-rearing years at home—any better? When I think about it this way, I can see that Melissa's approach may be preferrable, but is still far from perfect.

Luckily we're all living close to each other, making it easy to help each other out. We're in our Eglinton Avenue loft, Melissa and John live in their new house in nearby Leaside, and Krista and Nick have bought a place in between. We're all within a 5-minute car ride or a 20-minute walk from each other—provided that Caroline and I are not in Colorado, at the cottage or travelling somewhere.

Krista has turned into a strong and independent woman, as well. She's 30 now and I shouldn't worry about her any longer, but I do. She's followed a far more unconventional path than her sister, but I feel she's finally found her calling—in real estate. Less than a year ago, she showed me a neighbourhood property that was for sale. She felt it could be renovated and sold at a substantial, quick profit. Krista's business plan was compelling; she'd even taken a builder there and obtained a preliminary estimate. We decided to go into business together. I'd put up the required capital and Krista would do all the work. Six months later our little enterprise had realized a hefty profit. Now, while on maternity leave, Krista is taking her real estate exam, while renovating another, larger house. We've formed a company; we're calling it 4Now Investment Corporation.

I know that working with me means a lot to Krista. Melissa and I have always had a lot in common: our love for classical music, our interest in the economy and financial markets. Melissa was the one who wanted to visit Switzerland, who studied German, who wanted to be adopted. Krista, when offered the same things, politely declined, probably because she wanted to be different than her sister. Now we've finally found something we can do together: rebuilding and flipping properties, something I'd never have thought up on my own.

Yet, despite her successes, I can tell Krista isn't happy. The reason is Nick. As little Cameron contemplates his first steps, I see signs and overhear comments that make me realize their marriage is falling apart. What Krista has admired in Nick so much—his need to project a lifestyle beyond what he can afford and his ability to tell her and others what they want to hear—no longer impresses her. She sees the man who swept her off her feet as self-centered and irresponsible.

By now, Caroline and I know that the girls aren't happy with our lifestyle; they've frequently commented on our being away far too often. We talk about it, not sure whether we should be flattered that Melissa and Krista want us to play a bigger part in their lives, or whether we should view their criticism as an unwarranted interference in the routines we've fashioned for ourselves. Maybe we are too self-absorbed.

There are other reminders that our many absences from Canada are becoming logistically unmanageable. Not long ago, while we were hiking in the Colorado Rockies, a mother bear broke into the cottage, bringing two cubs along. The damage, as reported by the contractor who was supposed to close up the place, was extensive. Trying to get in, the adult simply buried her claws under the frame of the kitchen window and pulled the whole thing out of the wall. Once inside, she saw the gallon of brown stain I'd left. Unable to remove the lid, she grabbed the metal can by its sides and pushed, forcing the lid to fly through the air and the stain to explode onto the kitchen counter, herself and the cubs. The result of that small episode: nice, brown paw prints on our furniture and the heritage quilts that cover our beds. When we finally got back to inspect, we were faced with the scope of the damage: most of our wooden walls were badly scratched up and the fridge was torn apart. Maybe we have too many places.

Another issue: Caroline's parents have become more dependent on help. They'd never admit to such a thing or even ask for our assistance, but we can see that some tasks are now out of reach for them. Not long ago, we were there to help them move from their house to a more manageable condominium—a monumental task that involved the organization of a garage sale comprising mostly worthless, but to Mike and Nellie cherished, pieces of furniture, tools and trinkets accumulated over a period of 40 years. But not long after, when Mike fell ill with pneumonia, we were once again out of the country and Melissa had to engage.

I'd also like to spend more time with Gaby. She spends most of her time alone, no longer able to work, our mother being her only consistent contact. I think she appreciates Mami's efforts, but frequently tires of it.

Last fall, on my trip to Switzerland, I was stunned by my sister's condition. Her energy level was still astoundingly high, but her eyesight had dramatically deteriorated. She showed me her new cassette player, courtesy of the Institute for the Blind, as if she were the luckiest person on earth. She opened the catalogue of books she could order and we earmarked a dozen or so novels I thought she might enjoy. A few times, we went for short walks, Gaby probing her way forward with her white cane. We spent longer times at our favourite restaurants, the same places that had been there decades ago, when Papi took out the family for Sunday lunch. Once there, we ordered Prosecco, now Gaby's favourite drink, and red wine for me, then studied the food selections which appeared unchanged from our childhood.

I saw Gaby again in May. She was upbeat and full of ideas of how we could spend our time together. More than once, we picked up Mami, then visited Flavia and her family at their home, next to where Gaby and Kurt had lived not that long ago. The weather was spectacular, allowing us to sit outside, Urs grilling fish and chicken and the kids helping with the table and in the kitchen. Christian, at 18 the eldest, told me he'd like to come to North America one day. Roman and Nina, his younger siblings, were less talkative. One day I took Gaby to a furniture store in St. Gallen to buy her a comfortable office chair. She told me I was the best brother she could ever have wished for, which focused me on how much more I might be able to do.

Mami had told me that Gaby had recently collapsed and, when recovering consciousness, had told her that she wouldn't mind slipping away if that happened again. I was tempted to talk to her about it, but decided it would be better to stick to pleasant things. Feeling a bit awkward, perhaps even guilty, I then decided to surprise Gaby with another visit on her birthday, only five months away.

A COUPLE OF days ago, in our weekly phone conversation, we touched on last year's ill-fated invasion of Iraq. Always fervently on the side of justice, Gaby lamented the death of so many children, questioning whether Americans understood how evil their government was. Perhaps they didn't appreciate that Iraq had nothing to do with the events of 9/11.

As we got talking about the World Trade attack I told her how I'd learned about what was unfolding that fateful September morning, how it would always stay with me, much like the Kennedy assassination or the moon landing. It was early morning in Colorado, just before seven, I explained, when the phone rang. Krista's voice was on edge. I could tell something unsettling, maybe even terrible, had happened. Her first words were, "I'm not sure I'm dreaming this or whether it's all made up, but you have to turn on the TV and see for yourself." Seconds later I saw a part of New York I'm very familiar with. One of the downtown skyscrapers was in flames and a plane was headed for the second one. I called Caroline over to my office and we watched, disbelieving and utterly bewildered.

Gaby told me she'd only heard about it when watching the evening news. I tried to imagine what it would be like to live a life as isolated as hers. Mami and her television set were now her only consistent sources of information.

We talked about our 82 year-old mother for bit, Gaby expressing gratitude for Mami's help, taking her to doctor's appointments and checking on her daily to make sure she was fine. And then I sprang the surprise on her: "I'll be there for your birthday, Gaby. The trip is booked. I'll see you in just a few days' time!" My sister expressed disbelief, told me she was going to cry, but then thought better of it and came up with ideas of how we could celebrate. I was as excited as she was.

Then, a couple of days before my departure, the call from my mother. It was afternoon in Switzerland, morning my time. My sister had died.

Mami explained how she tried to phone Gaby as she did most mornings. When there was no answer, she walked over to check. Even before she opened the door, she heard Sasha's agitated meows. Inside, the cat led her to the bedroom, where Gaby lay dead in her bed. She'd had a heart attack while sleeping.

GLIMPSES OF MY sister have entertained and tortured me along the seemingly endless, sleepless flight across the ocean and, now, on the short drive to Herisau. There is no chronology to what I see. Some memories are compressed and fleeting, others play out over several minutes. The image of Gaby's hand rolling up the side of her sweater and undershirt comes up more than once, the syringe full of insulin gently pushing into flesh that looks like a collage of puncture marks and bruises. I see the two of us dancing to the latest Beach Boys song: "Wouldn't It Be Nice If We Were Older…" And that, in turn, evokes the image of Gaby and me listening to the Radio Luxemburg hit parade—more dancing, this time while carrying our much younger siblings, Flavia and Reto, both still wearing diapers.

The movie of Kurt and Gaby holding hands at one of the darker tables in Herisau's only bar plays next, and then I see the two of them posing outside the church for their wedding picture, both exuding shyness and innocence as they look at the photographer, but then their eyes settle on each other and purest tenderness shines through. My sister cooks perch from Lake Constance for Caroline and me, her speciality. And an instant later an ashen-faced truck driver makes his appearance, climbing down from his cab, convinced the girl that's disappeared between the front wheels of his vehicle is dead. Then Gaby emerges, scratched up a bit and crying, but unscathed.

My sister the teenager appears next, telling our mother not to be such a lamb and once in a while stand up to Papi. Both our parents look stunned and I find myself smiling. And there I am, having returned from South Africa and my backpacking adventure around the world, Gaby proudly telling me that she's landed a job as an executive assistant to the general manager of the bank. I watch the two of us as infants, playing in the small bedroom we shared.

Gaby caresses her white fluffy lamb doll with the droopy ears and I'm holding Maxli the dwarf, a red smile sewn onto his face and a pointed hat that covers his ears atop his knitted face. I look around to take in the room, but realize I have forgotten what it looked like.

Then screams: my five-year old sister in a hospital bed, hallucinating, convinced a crocodile is in her bed, gnawing at her feet. Mami and Papi are there, too, distressed, barely coping. Aunt Gaby plays with Flavia's children in their shared backyard next. Then Gaby the widow, laughing about something I said, as if her ailments and her loss were imaginary, and a moment later Gaby questioning the fairness of it all.

Once in Herisau, I hold my utterly exhausted mother for a few precious seconds, then share the next few hours with her. She tells me how Gaby lay in her bed when she found her, how she washed bits of drool off her lips and chin, how she dressed Gaby in a white sleeping gown and sat with her, resting in the peace she exuded. My childhood friend Urs, the doctor, arrived soon after, assuring Mami that Gaby hadn't suffered and commenting that she looked like an angel.

I'm not sure whether I've ever seen my mother cry, but I can tell she's fighting back tears now, as she reveals how Gaby lost consciousness on several recent occasions, how she lay there all by herself, until Mami found her or she woke up. The last time this happened, Gaby described how she looked at the commotion from above, and how pleasant that felt. "She said she wouldn't have minded floating forever. I never told you, because I didn't want to worry you."

Then Mami returns to the events of yesterday. How the undertakers came to take Gaby to the crematorium far too soon, and how she wishes I could have seen my sister one last time instead of arriving in time for the funeral. She says she took a photograph;

I'll be able to see it once the film is developed. We hold onto each other's hands and I cry.

Now I'm in Gaby's bed, the one she died in two nights ago. I wanted it that way. Sasha the cat is here too. Flavia will pick her up and take her to a family with children who look forward to having a pet.

But that will be tomorrow or the day after. For now, Sasha is feverishly pacing around the bed, endlessly crying. I know she'll lament my sister's loss all night long and I wonder whether I'll ever sleep again.

FOR WEEKS AND months to come, Gaby stayed with me, one moment distinct and the next blurry, but constant in her presence. First came funereal business, rituals that kept my mind occupied, preventing deep reflection. I kept seeing the wooden box holding my sister's ashes placed on the sober earth, around it flowers already wilting under a sprinkling of early snow. Mami was part of that mind-loop too, putting her hand on the gravestone saying "Kurt", noting how deeply his name was chiselled into the granite spotted with bits of greyish green moss and rust-coloured lichen, and how the letters extended right to the edges. Then she pointed to the place below where Gaby's name would be.

The rest of my Switzerland trip took me to the meetings I had planned to attend, long drives to Geneva, then Zurich, the rental car devouring the white lines ahead and Gaby floating somewhere above, oblivious to the business of life, sharing the sky with whisps of cloud. Soon after I returned to Toronto, where life's tedious demands pressed in, attempting to erase the images I held. Yet, by Christmas time, I dwelled in Gaby's presence once more, scribbling bits of what came up onto whatever scrap of paper was at hand,

and, eventually, organizing them into an elegy, a love poem from brother to sister.

I told Caroline I'd write it all down in my best calligraphy, then take it back to Switzerland in spring. I'd ask Flavia to take me on the walk along the river, where she had told me Gaby and Kurt had loved to walk. I'd let Flavia guide me to an appropriate spot, where we'd summon Gaby and dwell in her presence for a while. And when the time was right, I'd read my words out loud, before setting them on fire.

We'd planned a launch party for my morality thriller and even announced the event; it was to have taken place the week after Gaby's death. But even without it, Sam Hiyate's been busy promoting A Dangerous Remedy, securing decent reviews with the major papers and getting me onto a couple of interviews. The tag line from the Globe & Mail, "A creditable debut from an author whose moral message shouldn't be ignored," was enough to keep me motivated. I'm already working on a new novel, The Sweet Spot—a work I'll finish in record time, then keep under wraps for many years.

THE GRANDCHILDREN OCCUPY an ever larger part of our life. Caroline and I realize we've been together for two full decades; Alexandra, Cameron and Abigail provide us with a deeply satisfying way to celebrate that. The eldest, at three and a half, now insists on joining her Nana in her yoga exercises and already has a Colorado skiing holiday behind her—initially practicing the "pizza wedge", snugly held between my legs, which caused me serious backpain, and soon after on her own, pole-less, squealing with delight, convinced she could soon best her parents. At the cottage, she wants to create art: we collect bird feathers and clam shells and paint them.

Abigail's and Cameron's ways to express themselves are more unsophisticated. Abby likes to be held and hugged and read to. Cameron prefers having baths in the kitchen sink, being taken for hikes in the backpack or playing with my collection of Dinky Toys I brought over from Switzerland. Trucks of any description are his favourites.

Our parents are on our minds more often. Caroline's mom keeps fainting and her dad has developed a respiratory condition. Yet in between such episodes, they effortlessly cope, walking several miles a day, restlessly exploring their neighbourhood. My mother is in robust health, dealing with the sale of Gaby's condominium and the settlement of her estate, but I can tell how heavily the loss of her daughter and companion weighs. We talk once, sometimes twice a week, usually for an hour or longer. No topic is off limits; we're becoming good friends.

IN MAY, AS we set out from Flavia's house, my sister is edgy, not quite sure what to expect but sensing this is a momentous occasion. But once we reach the nearby Necker river, its waters boosted by the spring melt of the nearby mountains, my sister starts talking. We cross a narrow wooden bridge, its planks not far above the turbulent waters, and reach a meadow teeming with buttercups, asters and mallows. Bees and June bugs are everywhere. "This is where I bring my children's classes to play once the weather turns warm," Flavia explains. "And over there is where I take them swimming, but only after summer break—the water will be lower and more accessible then." She points at a spot a bit ahead, wider and less rocky than the other parts of the river.

Before long, we arrive at a narrow grassy area littered with a few boulders, large and flat enough to comfortably sit on. It's as far as Gaby usually walked, Flavia says; sometimes she sat down here before turning around.

The reading turns out to be harder than I'd thought. The passages commenting on the difficulty of Gaby's life and how she inspired come easily, but when I get closer to her death my voice starts to falter. Competing with the noise of rushing water is one challenge, but now I have to struggle with the rising intensity of my emotions.

It had been the priest's words that focused me on why Gaby came to my life and changed me forever. At the service in the small cemetery chapel, he'd asked Flavia's youngest, Nina, to light six candles, then asked a question of each flame and challenged us to meditate upon it.

I'D INCORPORATED THEM into my poem:

The first light asked: What was it I enjoyed about you, Gaby?
Your openness, your honesty.

And what united me with you, the second flame was asking?
My heart grew light; I knew that yours would too.
The same upbringing—mother, father—for a start,
But there was more, much more.
We loved to laugh and liked to hug together
and shared a vision for the world.

Another flame: Where did we fail to share? And did we irk
    each other?
I felt your anger when you lost your limbs and sight,

but didn't share it with you.
I could have come along onto your final journey, yet withdrew.
Nice meals and small talk marked our last few get-togethers.

The priest's voice asked about regrets:
What debts are left unpaid, what doubts remain?
I should have seen you often, Gaby, not just once or twice a
     year.
And how you would have loved to see more of the world!
I vowed to take you, countless times, and never did.

The priest again: What did I learn from you?
You taught me courage and you taught me hope.
And more: while I was well, you were afflicted,
while I had family you were alone and struggled.
And you accepted that with generosity.

And finally, the last and most important flame:
What was your essence? What memory to cherish most?
Oh Gaby, Gaby—what a life, if we can call it that.
No one should have to suffer like you did,
Yet that you mastered.
And in the midst of misery you could laugh—that is what's
     you.

I drive once more and see the road ahead meet the horizon
and think of you above,
with carefree, weightless clouds as friends.
And you rejoice, freed of your irksome body,
your afflictions gone, your pain dissolved.
And only one thing's left: a memory.

The memory is you, the way you really were, before your
    sickness:
You're in a meadow doing cartwheels.
You stop and look at me, deep in the grass, free of all care,
and I see gaps between your teeth
and hear the tinkle of your laughter.

And one more thing.
No candle asked: What is the meaning?
I think I know.
You were my gift and always will be.
You help me see things clearly.

When I finally strike a match, the spring breeze quickly extin-
guishes it. Flavia points at one of the larger rocks, suggesting it
may give us shelter, and we both crouch behind it. She holds out
the pages I'd written and I try again, this time cradling my hands
around the tiny flame, and then a corner starts burning brightly
and Flavia drops the pages onto the ground, where we watch bits
of inky, medieval looking letters merge into a spreading expanse of
black, until it all turns into a crumbled mess of ashes.

We sit for a while longer, Flavia and I, both feeling better now,
and aware of Gaby's final gift. She's brought the two of us closer
than we've ever been.

Not long ago, my 70th birthday made me wonder how much time I had left. Even if I reached my eighties or nineties, getting there with my reliably robust health intact seemed a stretch. I needed to focus on how I wanted to spend my remaining years and change my life accordingly, and now was the time to make the necessary changes.

I started out by creating a spreadsheet, organizing my routine daily activities into columns: things I felt enthusiastic about, things that I merely enjoyed, things that I might dislike but that were necessary and, finally, things I was determined to stop doing.

Once that was done I felt a lot better, perhaps because the column on the far right contained a conspicuously large number of entries. It listed things like cleaning the boat, dealing with dead trees near the cottage and helping clean up the kitchen. If I got rid of all these activities, life would be unspoiled.

Next, I shared my findings with Caroline, who wisely suggested that I put my spreadsheet away and look at it with fresh eyes in a few days' time. "Then," she added, "ask yourself whether you still feel the same and, if so, what you want to do about it."

Her last comment annoyed me. I know what to do, I thought—that was the whole damned point of my list. Then I started to think. How sure was I that I absolutely didn't want to do the things I'd listed as detestable? Was my spreadsheet a reflection of the truth or was it simply a compilation that had grown out of the frustration of feeling unbalanced and overwhelmed? If I really wanted to know, there was only one way: one by one, I needed to take on each of the undesirable tasks on my list.

The first test was at the cottage, where I took inventory of the trees likely to fall on one of the buildings or the docks. There were two. It would take me half a day to fell them, cut the trunks and branches into fireplace-sized logs, clear up the brush and, finally, carry everything up the hill to where the logs would eventually be split. I knew I loved working with the chainsaw: causing the dead or dying tree to fall just at the right angle required a level of experience I'd built over the past forty years. Cutting the tree up was more chainsaw work; I wasn't enthusiastic about that part, but I didn't mind. What I disliked was lifting and carrying the heavy tree sections; it was boring grunt work that would leave me exhausted.

So here I was, on my first mission: how much did I really loathe the act of hauling 50-pound logs from one place to another? Was my assumption that I hated it true? I thought the best way to ascertain that was to ask myself beforehand, "What comes up as I approach the task?" It turned out to be the easy part; I was convinced there was nothing positive about it. Next, I vowed to observe myself during the actual act of lifting and hauling. How would I experience this key part of the process? I bent down to a crouch, gripped the two sides of the log nearest me, slowly straightened out my knees and lifted the log upwards, trying not to think about my attitude to the process but simply absorbing the sensation of doing it.

My thoughts took me back to a period when I was working on my first novel, a couple of decades ago. Irritated that I could no longer be objective of the quality of my writing after two hours or so, I'd decided on a different approach. I'd write, then split wood, then write again—in two-hour intervals. It was the perfect pace; the woodwork allowed me to reengage with a cleansed mind and see the things I'd written through fresh eyes. How could I have forgotten that? And, more importantly, why did I never see myself as a victim condemned to splitting cord after cord of wood, throughout the summer, back then? Instead, I'd felt satisfaction that the act of doing mindless and tiring outdoor work greatly helped, and congratulated myself on having come up with this insight.

As I mused about this dynamic, I noticed movement under the heap *of leaves close to where I stood. A blue-tailed skink emerged, seemingly dazed for a second or two, as if in need of orienting itself. Then, faster than my eyes could follow, it dashed away and was gone. A few logs later, a racoon slid down the trunk of a nearby oak, impossibly close to where I was working. What about my aversion to carrying wood? I wasn't so sure anymore—right now, I was enjoying myself.*

The final test came when the logs were neatly stacked between two healthy, robust trees. How did I feel now, that the job was done? Terrific, strong, contented! And so it ended up with a surprising number of the tasks I'd marked as undesirable. I approached them half-heartedly, even unenthusiastically, but once I reminded myself to attentively experience the process of performing the work at hand, I felt good. Sometimes I even surprised myself deeply enjoying it. And, almost always, I felt intensely satisfied once the job was done.

There were a handful of chores where that didn't happen. I went back to my spreadsheet and marked them accordingly. I'd find others to tackle them.

July was medical month. First came my regular semi-annual dental event. The hygiene session is always the highlight. I joke with Caroline, briefly a practitioner of the trade herself, beforehand, and we have a good laugh. My prediction: I'll sit back and on command tilt my head and open my mouth wide. Then the hygienist starts poking away at my tartar build up and, while doing so, asks me a question usually one that can't be answered with a simple grunt, the only thing I'm capable of. Despite that, I make a valiant effort, snorting, groaning or grumbling, and sometimes even attempting to nod or shake my head, risking injury to my gums or tongue. Sometimes a second question follows, but more often the hygienist realizes my dilemma and embarks on a droning

monologue. Details of the work hour traffic or an annoying morning encounter at Starbucks follow.

Later in the month came my journey to Sunnybrook Hospital's emergency department. Ten days earlier, at the cottage, I had the bad fortune to stand next to our cooking range, watching Marshall Black, who'd built the place, high up on a ladder, adjusting the vent. When part of the aluminium enclosure came tumbling down, I followed the commands of my brain and tried to catch it. Its corner hit my hand and effortlessly opened it up.

The cut was deep, clearly requiring stitches, but that didn't discourage me from trying to repair the damage myself. As I'd learned in my first aid course in the army, I tightly wrapped a dishtowel around my hand and confidently walked to the bathroom, where I keep what my grandchildren call "Papa's amputation kit." I first doused the wound with antiseptic, then used a couple of emergency do-it-yourself sutures to close the wound, placed sterile gauze over it and bandaged it up. A week later, the incision had nicely closed. The only evidence of my injury was a two inch long, fairly wide reddish-brown crust. That's when I decided to load a heap of wood onto my trailer. I put on my outdoor working gloves and went at it.

The next morning I woke up with a badly swollen hand, which caused Caroline to suggest that we better head for the city. A few hours later, as we drove into Toronto, my wrist was inflamed. By the time I signed in with the triage nurse at the hospital my fingers looked like Swiss sausages and my whole forearm was puffed up. I spent ten hours at Sunnybrook, first being put on an IV drip, then placed under observation, a kind nurse checking in on me every 15 minutes or so. Eventually I had my hand reopened, scooped out and stitched back up by a plastic surgeon. All ended well, but I was told that in another hour or two my organs might have started shutting down.

Normally, when I sign in for a surgical procedure, I carry a file with *me—something I didn't have time to arm myself with on this visit. I do that because I've learned that I'll have to complete a multi-page form asking me lots of questions about my medical history. Part of it commands me to explain what surgeries I've had, offering a tiny space in which to write the answer. I always enjoy watching the practitioners' expression when I hand in my compilation. Invariably, I get a look of disbelief, coupled with the comment, "You've had a lot of procedures," or even, "Is this for real?" To which I say, "Yes, I'm close to seventy—aren't a dozen or more procedures the norm?" The doctor or nurse will think about that and make some non-committal remark, as if something said by a patient had strictly limited validity.*

IMAGINE, FOR A *moment, if the experience of life were to be recorded from the perspective of the physical body alone. Of course, a recount of physical traumas and an ode to the body's fine qualities and its benefits would not make for a gripping tale; it might even be boring. Even though injury and pain draw our attention and focus our awareness like little else in the conscious experience of our life, they are usually sporadic and discontinuous, and therefore of limited importance in an overall context.*

Still, here is a stab at what mine would look like, with surgical procedures in bold type:

Let's start with the agony of being pushed from Mami's womb, followed by the distress of the first inhalation. Then, countless painful sensations, as I get to know my independent body: hitting an extremity or my head against a hard object, hearing a loud noise, tasting what is too hot or bitter for my palate, needing to defecate but being constipated, suffering rashes, or feeling hungry.

Endless new traumas follow as I move through childhood. Learning to walk, the first badly scraped knee, suffering the *flu, enduring an ear-ache, teeth agonizingly pushing through tender, yet untested gums. Next, **tonsils removed**, measles, chicken pox, a **broken forearm** and, a year later, the same **bone fractured** again.*

*Later, adolescence and early adulthood, a **viper bite** below my knee, acne ravaging my face, **wisdom teeth extracted**, cellulitis, a mild case of cholera, followed by acute amoebic infection with attendant sizable weight loss.*

*Soon enough, my body moves on through my thirties and forties It endures **two meniscectomies**, cellulitis (again!), the **tear of an anterior cruciate ligament, the removal of hemorrhoids**, the repair of a **broken small finger, a hernia operation**, a **vasectomy, a cystoscopy, the elimination of a pre-cancerous facial cyst**, as well as severe food allergies with attendant immune system collapse and rapid weight gain (and, due to subsequent correct diagnosis, weight loss and recovery).*

*The fifties bring on a **bletharoplasty, a severed and reattached ring finger**, major neck trauma, lower back problems and yet another **menisectomy**. And, almost forgotten: **a broken toe**. My sixties aren't much better, with **two root canal surgeries**, growing joint problems, loss of nervous capacity resulting in simultaneous **carpal tunnel surgery on both hands**, and a **badly torn rotator cuff**. And yes, for now it ends with my hand injury that led to **sepsis**.*

NOW, LOOKING AT *my list of surgeries, it would be easy to imagine that my body has been, and still is, in a state of continuous disorientation. I don't see it that way at all. On the contrary, I am deeply thankful for what I've been given—the gift of an extremely sophisticated mechanism, through which the universe can observe itself and I can experience myself.*

That alone is an immeasurable blessing, but there is more. My body is a vessel so robust it manages to tolerate, and respond to, unimagined challenges, allowing me to test my human limits again and again, and while doing so, protecting me against adversity. It's kind, too, forgiving frequent abuse and ill-treatment, and miraculously healing itself when sick or injured. What a manifestation of balance and grace my body is, perfect in every way!

And how it manages to register the many offerings coming its way and converts them into undreamed-of pleasures—the sensation of sunshine on my cheeks or a cool summer breeze tousling my hair, the thrill of initiating a turn on my skis and letting the powder below me guide me in a new direction, or the joy of a great back scratch, the tips of Caroline's fingernails ever so softly and slowly descending down the itchy flesh to the sides of my spine.

THERE WERE TIMES *when my life's journey could have abruptly ended, depriving me of the pleasure of compiling my list. I could have been the soldier going over a cliff, after being ordered to keep driving through the night far longer than army regulations allow. The kid coming at me with a knife in a dark corridor in the centre of Tunis could have killed and robbed me, had he not lost his nerve and run. Elsewhere in Africa, and later Asia in South America, I ran into similar predicaments; sometimes they escalated into confrontations, and on other occasions I could see that the would-be perpetrator was merely weighing the odds of a successful attack.*

Years later, when skiing in thick fog in Whistler in my mid-thirties, I flew off a cliff, thinking I was in a completely different spot. Instead of landing on relatively forgivable terrain and ending up with a broken finger and a few facial abrasions, I could easily have crashed onto a pile of rocks.

Maybe the closest call was the visit to my place by several police offi-cers hammering and kicking at my door, demanding that I open up. The day before, I had actually called the cops, telling them that the new tenants next to my stylish Howland Avenue bachelor pad were probably drug dealers, explaining that they'd darkened all their basement and ground level windows and that a steady stream of bikers and drivers of unmarked, windowless vans were picking up and delivering packages all day and night long. Evidently, they sent the swat team to my address instead of raiding the drug den next door.

When I stepped through my front door, wearing nothing more than my white bathrobe, a young officer jumped in front of me, pointing his pistol at my chest, screaming "Freeze" and "Put up your hands," surely the two most overused and asinine of police commands. Two other cops were in a kneeling position further back in the darker part of the entry-way, repeating their colleague's demands.

Immediately understanding what was happening, I was furious. I'd had a long day at the office, been in the middle of a shower, and now these incompetents had come to the wrong house and were threatening me. It didn't help that I had a fairly low opinion of the Toronto Metropolitan Police Force, which seemed far more interested back then in ticketing people drinking beer in public than in solving serious crimes. And that I was used to being a voice of authority during my daytime job, further added to the tension.

I can't remember the exact words I used, but I'm fairly certain I accused the officer of incompetence, clarifying that I was the one who'd called them, while commanding him to stop pointing his damned firearm at me, which miraculously he did. I also demanded to see the person in charge of this bungled raid, who turned out to be a lady officer stepping from behind one of the cruisers sitting at the curb.

As it turned out I got an apology, but I realize the odds of being shot were probably about the same.

I WONDER WHAT will eventually, or perhaps not so eventually, get me. Will it be an accident or illness? Reto's gift of my astrological profile of many years ago addressed the issue, offering some cautionary words about my excretory organs, singling out gallbladder, kidneys, prostate, bladder and urinary tract as likely trouble spots. So far, there have been no major problems on this front. Yes, my day-time peeing frequency can be alarming—my four mugs of Nespresso's richest roast can send me to the bathroom at half-hourly intervals. But my nights are restful, at least since I've started taking a bed-time melatonin.

The astrological narrative addresses the subject of death, as well. It speculates that sudden health scares may place me in mortal danger and that there is a tendency toward accidents that may result in my sudden death.

There are other perspectives on offer. My friend Mel Spira, a highly distinguished surgeon and an ear-on-the-ground in things medical, once told me that if I survived my 72nd birthday, I'd be likely to make it past 90, statistically speaking. Then there was my encounter with the mostly naked, turbaned old soothsayer outside the New Delhi train station more than five decades ago. He predicted I'd be destined to move to a new country, build a family there, and die an old and happy man. But then again, that was in India, where the life expectancy for males was around 50.

What to make of all this? I think it's best to dismiss it all as futile speculation or absurd entertainment. After all, not knowing when life ends is a good thing. Which doesn't mean I can't project a preference: dying all of a sudden is far better than suffering through an odious, lingering demise.

Not long ago, on a spectacular early June weekend, we celebrated Cameron's first birthday. Caroline and I had walked the two blocks to Krista and Nick's modest house; we were surprised by the number of people assembled in the backyard. There were drinks, nibbles and cake for everyone, and many had brought a present. Even so, it was easy to feel the tension. Cameron visibly enjoyed the other children, but acted up when his parents checked up on him. Krista and Nick each huddled with different groups of visitors, plainly avoiding each other.

A couple of months later Krista told us they were filing for divorce. We thought it was the right thing to do. Cameron had turned from a happy baby to a cranky toddler; getting away from the constant squabbles between his mom and dad seemed an imperative. As for Krista, she'd be better off without Nick, too—emotionally and financially. Without offering much detail, she mentioned that Nick tried to control her, giving her instructions on how she should approach her real estate career and how she should invest. The problem: Krista was the one with the real estate exam, the one with a fixed salary, and the one who saved.

Now we're sitting on the couch in her new living room, Krista and I. Caroline is still in Colorado, finishing off a course in pottery, her new passion. I've had a tour of the house, the one we'd been in the midst of renovating when she decided to leave Nick. Instead of reselling the property, I had suggested, Krista should make this her new home. That way, the house she'd shared with Nick could be sold and there would be no dispute over its value.

Everything has turned out perfectly: the interior, tastefully decorated, is just a size too big for a single mother and her son;

outside, the small deck and fenced-in backyard are the perfect training ground for Cameron's walking and climbing aspirations. The location is superb; the bottom of Cleveland Street is quiet and an elementary public school is only a block away. I tell Krista how happy I am for her and she agrees that the house is a dream come true. She moves closer, leans toward me and settles into the crook of my arm. I realize that see she's fighting tears.

Then she tells me how hard things are with Nick, how he keeps interfering with her work schedule. "We have a custody agreement," she says, "but there isn't a week when Nick doesn't change the times he's supposed to pick up and return Cameron back home—always at very short notice." For several months now, Krista has been working for Bosley, an upscale Toronto real estate firm. I can see that Nick's provocations—whether they're deliberate or blunders—would interfere with her job. But I take the conversation elsewhere, telling Krista that Nick's character is obviously incompatible with hers. It's hard not to be frustrated or even angry, I suggest, "but every time this happens, congratulate yourself for leaving him. It'll make you feel a bit less annoyed, and going forward, it's what really matters: that you're back to being you. Strong, uncontrollable Krista, who's only just coming into her own."

I realize I used to say the same thing to Caroline, when she let her former husband's more irritating personality traits get to her. I share that with Krista and she laughs a bit, then tells me that I have no idea of how hard she may have been to live with. I hold her more closely to me and say, "Look, the bottom line is this: Nick tried to control you, and only Mom and I know how uncontrollable you are."

Cuba, January 2006. Our four-generation family is vacationing at the island's legendary Varadero Beach. Stretched out on their deck chairs, Caroline's parents stand out. Bathing suits are clearly not for them. They've dressed down a bit from their wintry Toronto attire, but they're still wearing light sweaters, long pants and socks. As a concession to their surroundings, they've placed their city shoes neatly at the foot of their chairs.

"Why are Baba and Dido wearing socks?" Cameron asks. Melissa and Krista giggle, then discreetly tell him that old people have a hard time keeping warm.

Not far from the hotel pools is the beach, where the grandchildren are building sand castles, then entire sand cities, carving moats around their creations and filling them with water, which quickly drains away. Bucket in hand, they waddle toward the surf to fetch more, the adults keeping a wary eye on them as they dare and dodge the incoming waves.

Krista is hurting; a dark cloud of joylessness envelops her. We try to engage her, pull her out of her funk, asking if she wants to walk the beach or take a spin on one of the small sailboats available to the guests. Then, realizing that we're trying too hard, we let her be. Sometimes she snaps back at us, sometimes she disappears to her room and stays there for a few hours. Cameron, sensing that his mummy is in a bad space, is also on edge. He seems most content when he plays with his cousins.

The evenings are surprisingly precious. We wait for each other outside the dining area, nursing a drink while watching the other resort guests doing the same, some gorgeously dressed and others more casually attired. It's easy to judge how long they've been here: the newcomers are still pasty-skinned, the seasoned vacationers darkly tanned, and the reckless sun addicts repugnantly purple-faced. Every now and then we turn away from the action, taking in the horizon where the lazily descending sun tinges both ocean and sky a reddish gold.

Once we're all assembled, we ask to be led to our table of ten, Mike and Nellie almost immediately deserting the group so that they can check out the meat and seafood offerings beckoning from the lavish buffets. As we settle into our seats, the band is already playing. Some of us recognize the tune from Buena Vista Social Club: Chan Chan. Melissa and I hum along, John rocks back and forth, holding up the drink he brought with him, and we can tell that even Krista is starting to relax. But no one is as fascinated with the musicians as little Cameron. Each night, he insists on having me take him to the edge of the stage, where the elderly guitarist with the battered, strangely fashionable straw hat cheerfully invites him up. It's as if he understands the toddler's anguish and knows that if he lets Cameron touch his instrument, its wood will not only absorb the boy's despair, but grant him calmness and hope.

The other attraction is the night sky. As we walk back toward our rooms, black palm branches swaying above us against the dark night sky, Cameron wants to stay outside a bit longer and search the star-lit firmament for the fledgling sickle he knows the word for: moon. Once he locates it, he keeps repeating its name, persistently pointing it out to me until I pick him up and our faces touch and we both look at it and lovingly label it together. Moon.

Sometimes, along the dark pathways, we encounter one of the elderly resort visitors who walk with the help of a cane. Cameron knowingly says, "Dido", because he thinks anyone limping along like his great-grandfather shares that name.

On the flight home, Cameron is restless. He sits across the aisle from us, insisting to be on Krista's lap. Half an hour into the flight, he demands to come our way. Caroline cradles him for a while, then he climbs across the armrest toward me. Mine is a window seat; for a few minutes I manage to keep him focused on the night sky, challenging him to spot the moon. A row behind us Alexandra peacefully sleeps, while Abigail is snuggled into John's embrace, being read to. Cameron's legs push into my groin; he tries to wiggle out of his seat, wants to go walking down the aisle. I hold him tight, tell him all the squirming, pushing and kicking won't help. I point at the seat belt sign above us, tell him that we aren't allowed to leave our seats. Then I whisper comforting bits of his favourite stories to him, sensing how exhausted, disoriented and distressed he is. Perhaps he's just tired and perhaps he knows that what he's just experienced is coming to an end, that what awaits him is more of the parental bickering and being shuttled around that's made up too many of the past weeks.

When Cameron falls asleep, his head resting against my chest, I focus on my breathing, slow and deep, convinced that the predictable, steady rhythm of my expanding and contracting lungs will comfort him. If only I could calm Krista the same way.

BACK IN TORONTO, a letter from Mami. No 'Dear Peter' this time, nor any other niceties or even introductory words. Blunt, austere, disquieting, it starts out with, "When I die, the following is to be done..." Then follows a set of instructions that leave little room to imagination or judgment. First, Dr. Knaus must be summoned so that he can issue a death certificate. Immediately after, we are to inform the funeral organizers and the Catholic priest. It's equally important to visit the Herisau town office to report her death, Mami writes; this must be done during business hours on the very day of her death. The officials will want to see her documents, which she keeps in a brown binder in the built-in hallway closet.

I stare at the two type-written pages in disbelief. I'd be laughing out loud, were it not for the realization that my mother must have written this in the firm belief that she'll die the way Gaby did: alone, during the night, her body to be found the next day or later, most likely by Flavia. My sister, Mami must be speculating, will then phone me and I, armed with these instructions, will guide her.

I next read about Mami's wishes for a simple funeral and am quite touched by the modesty of her vision. Only family should be invited, she instructs and there can be no speeches other than a brief chronology of her life. Her ashes are to be buried in the communal plot of Herisau's municipal cemetery. It's easy for me to visualize the small piece of lawn where we'll be gathered to say our goodbye, the stately stone wall behind it, and in between the narrow strip of earth where a small opening awaits Mami's urn. Water softly gushes down the greenish-grey granite into which are chiselled the names of other townspeople who opted not to have their own plot. My mind leads me astray: how often does the stone mason come by? Does he update the wall every three months or each time ten new names need to be added?

From the cemetery, I am told, we should proceed to a good restaurant and share a meal. I consider the possibilities, allow myself to dwell in each of the three most logical venues—the same Herisau eateries where Papi would take us for Sunday lunch— then dismiss the first two choices as lacking privacy. It'll be the Landhaus, I decide, then see myself at the head of a long table. I'm wearing a dark suit, white shirt and my only black tie. My brother and sister, nephews and nieces quietly converse with ancient aunts, uncles and cousins we haven't seen for two or three decades. I'm getting up to give my speech, which I'm determined will be more than a mere history of Mami's life. I talk about her childhood in the isolated mountain hamlet, her father the stern station master, the alienation of being brought to Chur, where her simple rural ways clashed with the culture and fashions of an administrative capital. She enters high school, is taught by Catholic nuns for a while and then, innocent and a touch awkward, joins the workforce. It's 1939; Switzerland is mobilizing.

Making reference to a date has got me off track. I hastily calculate, deduct 1939 from my mother's birth year, 1922. Thank God I'm right, she was seventeen and that's when she graduated and was assigned to be trained as a telephone operator.

Then the movie ends on an abrupt note. Just as I lead into the first meeting between my parents, my smile holding the promise of a good story as I look around the table, I realize that half of the relatives sitting there are dead. My eyes skip back to the letter I'm holding.

I start reading again and soon feel better, as the glum funereal content gives way to material issues. Mami turns to the issue of who gets what, a tricky exercise not because Flavia, Reto and I will compete for our mother's cherished armoires, paintings, rugs, clocks and jewellery pieces, but because she has many more treasures than any of us have room for. Someone else in her situation might simply have left the issue unaddressed, but not our mother. She meticulously lists the items that have already been taken away by one of us children and then explains which of her remaining possessions shall belong to whom, adding that we should try to sell whatever we don't want. Or give it away, I think. There must be others, people outside our immediate family, to whom one of Mami's many etchings or paintings, or perhaps one of her many antique books, may have special meaning. I find it curious that there is no mention of that.

The final paragraph names those who have keys to Mami's condominiums and reveals that there are no undeclared bank accounts of safety deposit boxes. Whatever money there will be left should be equally divided between us children. As I come to the end, I realize there is nothing Mami has overlooked, not when it comes to the logistics of dying. Yet, I feel compelled to go back to the beginning of the letter, hastily scanning the lines and paragraphs. Next, I retrieve the envelope from the waste bin, checking if I've missed something. I can't believe there isn't more.

What were Mami's feelings as she contemplated her death? What brought her joy, made her laugh, kept her stable amidst the consistent turmoil that was her life? What did we, her family, mean to her? What would she like to be remembered for?

I'm tempted to call Mami, ask her about the things she left unsaid, then decide not to. Writing her letter may not have been difficult for her, the intensely rational, emotionless thinker, but being asked why she didn't go further would embarrass her.

And now it's summer and Krista is better. She's found a way to reconnect with the miracle that is her child, managed to hold her ground with Nick without letting it affect Cameron. During one of her now regular cottage visits, she confesses that she loves being a mother, adores her new home and is deeply satisfied by her work. In less than two years, she's become a highly successful real estate agent, one of the notable figures in her upscale area.

Not long ago, looking over research reports showing Melissa's name on their cover, then watching Melissa being interviewed on television, I feared what that would do to Krista, who's always struggled with jealousy. Now I see Krista's image on bus shelters and even on a Mt. Pleasant Road rooftop. What a perfect outcome!

KRISTA AND CAMERON are spending a lot of time at the cottage and the timing couldn't be better. We know our daughter, but it's high time we caught up with Cameron, just as we did with Alexandra and Abigail when Melissa and John brought them to Colorado a few weeks ago.

As I do things with each grandchild, I can't help compare their behaviour and characteristics now to what they were only a few months ago. Even at this early stage, the evolution of their personality is clearly discernible. There is Alexandra, showing interest in new things right away, but timid in her first engagement, then enthusiastically embracing the challenge, but not without periodically stepping back to re-evaluate. Abigail is different: she prefers to observe for a long time, looks for reassurance from everyone in her orbit before taking her next step, then never turns back. Cameron, meanwhile, probes, pushes, frequently gets into trouble, sometimes by taking on too much too early, sometimes overstepping his boundaries. Knowing Melissa and Krista, and considering John's and Nick's characteristics, I can see that part of it is genetic, but there is more.

Can it be that the pattern of the relationship we'll have with our grandchildren is being set so early in their lives? I know I won't be decorating snow-witches with Alexandra forever, but will I be skiing with her when she's in her mid-twenties and I'm eighty? Given their love for the stories I read to them now, will Melissa and John's girls want to discuss literature with me when they're adults? Will Abigail, who seems fascinated with paints and paper want to do art projects with me? All three grandkids love the cottage, but Cameron is the one most eager to learn to swim, intent on walking the sand beach with me, stark-naked in our remote bay now that the parents aren't here, delighting in the frogs that leap out of the way. Will he be the one I can share my love of nature and wildlife with?

"DO YOU HAVE any liquids in your carry-on luggage?" the middle-aged check-in lady asks Caroline's mother, who answers in the negative. "Do you mind opening your bag then?" Nellie pulls the zipper and the employee, a knowing look on her face, deftly manoeuvres around the luggage belt and comes to our side of the counter. She doesn't appear surprised at all, as she pulls an aerosol can, a weighty bottle and a straight razor from the purse—weapons that could be used to first blind someone, then cut their throat.

I hastily retrieve Nellie's suitcase from the weighing platform and start moving the forbidden items over. I overhear Caroline apologizing to the agent, who reassures her it's okay. "You have no idea of the things I've seen," the lady elaborates, before softly adding, "You know, elderly passengers…"

Mike, meanwhile, is unsteadily clinging to the counter. He isn't feeling well at all, which isn't related to his general state of health, but to the fact that he ate too much last night. Caroline's brother Bob, who dropped the parents off at the airport provided the context, telling us how Nellie had explained the situation, when he picked them up an hour earlier. "We didn't want to throw anything out and I couldn't eat any more, so dad had the rest." Caroline demanded to know what the rest had consisted of, to which her mother vaguely answered, "bacon and some other things that were left." Apparently, Mike had spent the night puking and was still sick when Bob showed up.

When another Air Canada employee arrives with the wheelchair, Caroline's dad looks confused, even panicked. Not only has he never been in a wheelchair, but we haven't told him that we asked for one. Concerned that we'd never get through U.S. customs with an ashen-faced 94-year old, who was visibly suffering from severe acid reflux and might throw up again at any time, I innocently asked the agent how long the walk to the gate would be, suggesting that it may be too much for Mike.

Despite these challenges, everything is working out wonderfully. The uniformed young man taking charge of Mike tells us to follow him, then blithely bypasses the long line-up in the customs hall and winks at the officer, who waves us through without asking a question. We're dropped off at the gate. "Thank God this is how it's turned out," Caroline nudges me.

Not at all sure that we're in the clear, I repeatedly ask Mike how he feels, to which he keeps answering in an uncharacteristically faint voice, "Not so good." But before long, we board our flight to Denver, buckle ourselves up and Mike's persistent burps gradually recede.

IF THE JOURNEY here was a reminder of Mike's and Nellie's advanced age, our days in Snowmass are providing ample perspective of their robust health. I take in the scene at the kitchen counter, the two of them busy converting the choke cherries they've picked on the lengthy hike up our road into jam. The high altitude, a challenge for many visitors, hasn't been a problem for them; their only complaint is that there isn't that much to do here.

As I watch Mike chopping the fruit, images of him crawling from under his cottage, where he averted a plumbing emergency, and Caroline summoning him off the roof, flick through my mind. He was close to his 90th birthday then. Next, I see Mike at the wheel of his burgundy Oldsmobile, confidently passing an 18-wheeler, cutting in front of the vehicle a second or two before the oncoming vehicle would have struck us. Mike drove for another three years until, just over a year ago, he blanked out and rear-ended a series of cars waiting at a red light. Miraculously, no one was seriously hurt. That was the end of Mike's driving career.

Now we're sitting in Aspen's Isis Theatre, taking in one of

Franco Zeffirelli's movies, Tea With Mussolini. Mike loves the female cast—Cher, Judy Dench, Joan Plowright, Maggie Smith and Lily Tomlin—all fussing over an orphaned Italian boy. But nothing pleases Mike like the discipline the Italian fascists impose on society. As a steam locomotive is seen entering a railway station, he loudly declares, "Look! Mussolini…he made the trains run on time." Uncomfortably many heads in front of us turn to see where the voice comes from, but fortunately, with the theatre two thirds full, it's impossible to tell.

During the car-ride back to near-by Snowmass, Mike talks about the hardships of his upbringing, the adversity he encountered when he came to Canada, the years of long hours at his dry cleaning business. I try to make him feel better, reminding him of how well he's done, giving his children a good education, having acquired a house, two rental properties and a cottage, having paid off the mortgages, and now, after all is sold, sitting on a big pile of cash.

Caroline supports me, but Mike views such comments as a challenge to his experience of life as an onslaught of negatives. All right, I say, so you've done really well overcoming all the challenges fate threw at you—isn't that something worth celebrating? Mike decides not to argue my point, but I can tell it's because he feels he's been out-manoeuvred. He still doesn't think we appreciate what he had to endure.

I reflect on the differences between us. Mike's hardships were imposed on him; when I experienced adversity it was because I sought it out. He was forced to emigrate; I wanted nothing more than to emigrate. He viewed his job as a necessary precondition to life; I saw my employment positions as an opportunity to realize myself.

I suppose the principal difference between us is that Mike never felt he was in control of his destiny. There were times in my life when I thought I was no longer motivated, no longer had fun, could no longer feel good about what I was doing. When that happened I usually moved on, something that Mike would have dismissed as risk-prone and therefore foolish.

Then I feel a jolt, challenging my smug analysis. Mike is a child of war and depression; I am a child of post-war recovery, economic growth and opportunity. How can I make comparisons and judgments without having experienced both?

Throughout my adult life, I've come across extraordinary people. Some were iconic figures I met at conferences, on book tours or on the sets of movie productions Guardian Trust was involved with: the likes of Alan Greenspan, Yehudi Menuhin or Michael Douglas. We chatted, had a cup of coffee or a quick meal together, then went about our business again. I felt like the pretender in the presence of the authentic; they'd spent decades to get where they were now, while I, a mere kid, had been ushered into their ranks by sheer luck. I intended to remember each of these giants forever, but was convinced they'd forget me within a week.

Then there were all kinds of exceptional people I had dealings with in my positions as an investment professional or interacted on various corporate or public boards. They weren't as universally famous, but many left a deep impression on me. I imagine that those who still live remember me as well. Initially, I was the kid who knew far less about financial practices than they did, but didn't think twice about challenging them. Intuitively, I understood what the customers wanted, picked great employees and kept them motivated, while revving up the corporate revenues, traits that must have left them utterly bewildered. Later on, as I rode the wave that carried me through my professional years, they could relate to me no better: I darted in and out of the business in staccato fashion, telling them that I was on to something more interesting, perhaps leaving them wondering why staying on the path we'd briefly shared wasn't exciting enough. I met most in this group repeatedly, over a period of years, but our discussions rarely transcended business topics, probably because our personal interests were too far apart.

My writing projects, outdoor activities and travel adventures exposed me to yet another set of memorable characters. What's interesting is that these encounters, too, rarely led to the kind of deep and ongoing explorations that distinguish friendship from mere acquaintance. Initially this puzzled me. Every now and then I longingly thought back to my days in Toronto's Annex, when gatherings with my bohemian friends, who I saw with great regularity, habitually ended in deep and lengthy explorations of interests we shared. Then I realized that it was my moving around that interfered with such get-togethers. Never being in Toronto, at the cottage or in Colorado for more than a few weeks at a time made the forging of meaningful friendships difficult. Our pursuit of solitary activities didn't help either. Neither Caroline nor I sought out social activities; instead we typically spent our evenings reading or attending to our creative interests. Caroline and I still cherished and nurtured the relationships we had with our four or five closest friends, but there was no time for more.

IT WAS IN my sixties when I initiated friendships of a kind I'd never experienced. We now routinely spent part of the summer and the entire winter in Snowmass Village. I didn't go out of my way to seek more companionship, but life brought me encounters that gradually deepened. Some of the characters I bonded with popped up at the talks I gave once or twice a year at the Aspen business lunches, while others called me after reading a recent issue of Perspectives. There was Charles Dean Ray, who suggested we meet for a private lunch. I could immediately tell that he'd given much thought to my commentaries. Even better, he made me aware of some fresh angles, especially in regard to the radicalization of Islam, a subject he'd researched at great depth.

Charlie and I were fascinated by each other, probably because we were opposites. A highly accomplished scientist with more than 50 patents and over 300 published papers to his name, he had approached entire bodies of science with the sole purpose of understanding every detail they encompassed. My style couldn't have been more different. I *readily threw facts overboard when I thought they were unnecessary or hindered my grasp of a subject; instead I tried to go at it from a different angle. Charlie had the capacity of focusing deeply, of turning myopic when circumstances demanded it, while I approached things from the top down and intuitively. My new friend held doctorates in medicine, engineering and Egyptology, while I was a school dropout who'd learned most of what he knew from practical experience. He was a highly con-nected professional who played by the rules of the professional estab-lishment, while I was a loner who'd avoided social networks. In short, Charlie fit the definition of a scholar, while I suspect most people slotted me as undefinable. No wonder we saw things differently!*

We sat in his condominium in Snowmass one day, a bottle of Kirsch flanked by steaming cups of coffee and a tempting array of chocolates between us. Charlie explained that it evoked his time in Basel, where he worked with Hoffman LaRoche, one of the Swiss pharmaceutical giants. Soon, we were discussing America's interventions in Iraq and Afghanistan, agreeing that they were immoral and ill-conceived, but diverging on where they would lead. He felt the U.S. would rule major parts of the Middle East for decades to come, but worried whether Washington's imperialists had the know-how to govern an inherently corrupt society. My belief was that America would have no problem adjusting to a more crude model of sleaze than the highly refined cor-ruption that existed at home, but that it would fail spectacularly on the military front.

As I tried to explain the principles of asymmetrical warfare, Charlie abruptly rose, telling me he'd need to get something from his office. Moments later he returned, struggling with a massive bundle of papers. "This", he announced, "is what I've been working on for the past few years. Close to two thousand pages and there will be more. And you'll be the first person to read them, Peter."

I looked at the ridiculously tall stack of paper on the table between us and asked what it was. "It will be the guide to everything," Charlie confidently declared. "It'll explain how things evolved and what lies ahead on every front. Astronomy, agriculture, architecture, law, medicine, and yes—the economy and politics, which is where I could use help. I wonder if you'd be my editor." I evaded Charlie's request, knowing that I'd never find the time to do his book justice and that I wasn't particularly interested in reading a history of everything. Instead, I found myself commenting on the merit of his idea.

I told him I admired his drive, his desire to dissect everything in a reductionist Newtonian kind of way, reverse-engineering the proverbial frog, limb by limb, organ by organ, to see how it worked and truly understand it, largely because I'd never had the required discipline. Then I suggested that his approach could never work when it came to geopolitics, social behaviour or the economy, areas where emotion and crowd psychology could derail or overthrow established state policy in a short period of time.

Charlie said that was why he needed me, that these were areas outside of his expertise, while I tried to explain that it just couldn't be done. We both talked and neither of us listened, yet we enjoyed each other's company. And then, as we were halfway through the bottle of Kirsch, the conversation drifted to the adventure of our lives and I started to recognize another Charlie—a man who'd travelled the world and allowed it to change him. A man who collected stories and could communicate with anyone. I visualized him in a track suit, talking to the seniors on a park bench or the Mexican berry picker riding the bus. I recognized he was someone anyone could relate to. It didn't matter whether we agreed. We liked each other and we'd keep spending time together.

It was still a few years before Caroline and I visited Charlie in Santa Barbara. We stayed at his unpretentious yet magnificently proportioned house, had meals together, took walks in his lush California garden and ventured to the ocean front. Sometimes we talked about his book, which was still, and would always be, a work in progress. Charlie showed us his avocado trees, pointed to the plump mangoes and papayas, proudly elaborated on the water system that connected his terraced ponds and irrigated the soil. Even here, Charlie commanded scientific authority. He'd made it his business to know all about the lilies on his ponds. He gave us a brief history of the avocado.

Not long after, Charlie suffered a massive stroke. Driving his car, he was on his way to an appointment. His daughter Marlene happened to look out of her office window and saw the traffic jam below, then realized the problem car was her father's. She called an ambulance, then rushed to the elevator.

Charlie couldn't talk, couldn't write. No one knew how much he could comprehend. The therapist working with him felt he may remember Tic-Tac-Toe. It turned out that he could signal the next logical move on the game board held up to him.

Eventually Charlie succumbed, but the distressing thoughts of his slow death stayed with me long beyond that. Here I'd known one of the world's most distinguished scientists, as erudite in articulating academic concepts as in weaving life stories everyone could relate to. Next thing, he couldn't make himself understood.

ANOTHER NOTABLE MAN who became a good friend to both Caroline and I was Curt Strand. Like Charlie, he'd come to my talks, but we only got to know him well after his wife Fleur, a renowned geneticist, died of cancer. While Charlie had been twenty years our senior, Curt was even older. He was well into his nineties when we commenced our friendship and he was to last several more years. During that time, we had regular get-togethers at our respective homes or at Curt's favoured eateries, which inevitably escalated into vibrant discussions. Caroline used to joke that my purpose in Curt's life was to periodically raise his blood pressure.

We were opposites in personality and differed dramatically in how we saw the world. Curt's mannerism was gentle; his long life as a skilled establishment operator had taught him to keep his thoughts to himself—until my candidness left him no choice but to reveal himself. We debated many issues, from colonialism (Curt thinking it had bestowed great gifts upon the less developed world), to running a business (Curt concluding that the only thing that mattered was to displace competitors), to politics (Curt believing that America's growing disfunction was a very temporary problem). Sometimes, friends or acquaintances of Curt urged me to pay more restraint; after all, he was a nonagenarian and we had to treat him gently. Yet, every time I heeded their advice, it was Curt who prevailed and moved me back into vigorous debate.

Knowing his background, his views came as no surprise. He was a former intelligence officer, the President and Chairman of Hilton International, and a director of numerous large corporations. His closest friends had been Robert McNamara, John F. Kennedy's Secretary of Defense during the Vietnam War and General Dynamics CEO Lester Crown. He had met numerous heads of state and was a Fellow of the Aspen Institute.

What I found remarkable about Curt is that, throughout his nineties, he gradually changed his views of the institutions and policies he'd spent a lifetime believing in. When I read to him from Tuiavii's Way, he confessed to never having thought of colonization from the viewpoint of someone 'uncivilized'. In time, he could even agree that very attribution of the term 'civilized' to what Britain or France or Spain brought to perfectly functional societies, was unjustifiable. Gradually, his assessment of the country he loved so much changed as well. He watched Ken Burns' Vietnam series and promptly adjusted his previous conviction that America was the upholder of morality. At one particularly memorable dinner he told me that he agreed with my assessment, but that he had long ago vowed never to speak badly of his country—I took that to be a reference to the oath he must have sworn when he joined the intelligence services.

Even more remarkable, Curt's transition from ideologue to truth-seeker was entirely unrelated to his gradual physical decay. Until the very end, he dazzled with his mental acuity. During the last several months of his life, Caroline and I spent Saturday evenings with him. It was the height of the Covid-lockdown. For us Canadians, the pandemic meant that we couldn't return home—we were stuck in paradise, hiking the valley's magnificent mountain trails and tending to our spectacular garden. For Curt, the restrictions were much harder to tolerate. The Snowmass Club's gym, where he'd become an iconic figure, visiting daily to spend half an hour on a recumbent exercise bike, was now off limits. And his favourite restaurants, where he enjoyed holding court, were closed. So, as the weekend approached, we'd find ourselves signing in with Curt to coordinate a martini-and-nibbles summit.

As an aside, to Curt martinis were an elementary component of refined life. He'd introduced me to the only cultured way to drink a cocktail when we first met; as it happened, I'd never had a martini. Over time, I learned that in most elevated dining establishments in Snowmass Village and even Aspen, ordering a "Curt Strand" meant that I'd get a locally made potato-only vodka martini, straight up, with a twist of lemon, well chilled, but without any of the ice showing.

We usually arrived around six for our summit. Curt wouldn't have us at a less civilized, earlier hour. Quite often, Barbara Lynn Bloemsma, who'd looked after our friend ever since his wife died, or one of the elves Barbara had summoned to his side, joined us. And before long, we were deep into discussing the state of the world and, more specifically, America's many woes. Yet, no matter how contentious the topic of our discourse, Curt never lost his composure. The hand cradling his glass remained steady, the insights he presented were as sharp as they would have been many years earlier, and his faith in mankind's ability to resolve *the grave problems at hand remained untainted. His 100th birthday was just a few months away.*

The last of our martini sessions took place less than two weeks before his passing. Despite his curtailed social life and the fact that his legs no longer carried him, Curt was still optimistic. He projected that things would soon return to normal and he'd once more get together with all his friends.

We saw Curt one last time. He'd withdrawn to a place of humility and grace. Socio-political reflections and martinis were no longer relevant; he was accepting what lay ahead. His surrender was profoundly inspiring.

THE SESSIONS WITH *Curt Strand led me to suggest a similar routine to my friends Larry Gaudet and Steve Cornish, whom I knew from his days at Doctors Without Borders. Soon after, Richard Moore joined us, as well. The four of us weren't able to meet face-to-face; we lived in different parts of the continent and the Covid pandemic had made physical meetings difficult. So we resorted to internet-technology, holding our Sunday evening events, the weekly Whiskey Summits, virtually.*

Before long even that became difficult. Larry now lived in rural Nova Scotia, while I went back and forth between the cottage, Toronto and Colorado. Richard commuted between Hanoi and New York, while Steve, now living in Geneva, continuously dashed off to Africa's and Asia's more notorious trouble spots. Yet, week by week, we adjusted. Often, two of our group joined in with their morning tea or coffee, while the other two sipped at a glass of well-aged spirits.

The Whiskey Summits have taught me a lot, both about technology and friendship. A puritan about human interaction, I often alienate kids and grandkids with my insistence on face-to-face encounters. If that isn't possible, I can live with a phone conversation—at least it allows me to adjust what is being said for the inflections in the other person's voice. On the other hand, texting, for anything other than a convenience-driven brief blast (like the plumber signalling that he's on his way), will never work for me.

Given my prejudices against tech-inspired communication modes, I was stunned to learn of the merits of Zoom and other virtual meeting platforms. Here we were able to see each other, read facial expressions and body language. Larry could swivel the computer around and show the rest of us how well the construction of his new barn was coming along, while Richard could show off the Vietnamese breakfast he was served in his hotel room while in quarantine. I loved seeing the group's reaction when I made a debatable geopolitical judgment, Steve giving me a dubious look as I was explaining why it was fine to criticize China for its human rights record, but not without holding the United States and its allies to the same standard.

Our summits were a gift not only in terms of the vibrancy of our discussions, they also gave me an insight into how friendship works. Our commitment to spending a full hour a week together led to a comfortable exchange of what was new with each of us and what social or political developments were worthy of examination. That in itself was rewarding, even if some of it could be dismissed as enjoyable banter. What I found far more remarkable was how our group rose to the occasion when one of us sought input or help.

When Steve admitted to some confusion about how to profile himself with Doctors Without Borders' Geneva-based recruiters, who were interviewing applicants for the post of Director General of Operations, we all came up with what proved to be effective insights. Not long after, Larry articulated ideas for his next book and the group quickly focused him on what would and would not find an echo with readers. Richard, still running his Vietnamese firm, was planning a weekend presentation on ideation and asked for input; Larry, a veteran of communications, *provided valuable help. I routinely use our group to test the conclusions I've come to in my work of analyzing geopolitical, social or economic trends. One of my fellow summiteers always has something profound to add to or detract from my assessment.*

Best of all, we haven't only been there for each other with advice we can each draw on in the areas of our particular expertise. Intuitively, we've also made ourselves vulnerable to each other, sometimes admitting to our feelings of confusion or even bewilderment, sometimes sharing a journey into a deeply personal choice we're contemplating. If it weren't named after what we first drank during our virtual get-togethers, we could label it after its most precious attribute: the Trust Summit.

Being able to dial up my friends' faces, hear their voice and read their expressions while they talk, has renewed and even revolutionized my communications. After the first three months of highly successful Whiskey Summits, I suggested the practice to my other close friends and family. Gradually, my regular phone calls with Stephanie and Jim in Maine, or with my siblings or my nephews in Switzerland, were replaced by video calls. Gone were the days when we wandered the rooms of our house attending to household tasks while talking to each other. We now sat down and stayed, giving each other the gift of attention—and getting so much more out of our discourse.

DID I EVER *think that the latest gift from technology could resonate with me and enhance the experience of my life? I'll answer that with an anecdote.*

I think it was in the mid-1990's when I first showed Hong Kong, where I'd regularly visited on business, to Caroline. We enjoyed ourselves immensely, frequently ferrying between Kowloon and the central part of Hong Kong Island, where we stayed. What always brought excitement was our last walk of the day; we followed the bustling main arteries, then darted off into dimly lit, narrow side streets and alleys. Most were strangely deserted, some leading steeply uphill. If we followed them we might eventually reach Victoria Peak.

One night, trying to find our way back to the hotel, we got lost in Lan Kwai Fong, the cradle of Hong Kong's night life. The streets were no wider here, but everything was brightly lit, bustling with people, many stopping to look inside the bars and restaurants, from which appetite inducing smells emanated—roasted fowl or pork, spices we tried to identify but couldn't quite place. Others paced restlessly forward, as if guided by some remote puppet master—we couldn't tell whether they were lost, looking for an escape, or whether they were on track to a specific destination.

And if you looked for them, there were the ladies of the night, standing in sheltered doorways or a space between buildings, always in light just strong enough to allow their would-be customers to assess their attributes, but sufficiently mellow to grant discretion, should a negotiation ensue.

The night was still young when we passed through. Many of the prostitutes were waiting for business, and remarkably many were talking into something we rarely got to see in North America: a cell phone. "Who do you think they're talking to?" asked Caroline. I answered that I had no idea—maybe other hookers, maybe potential clients, maybe their mothers.

As we maneuvered through the crowds, we looked for other people who might be talking on cell phones, but couldn't see any. The fact that all prostitutes seemed to have these very expensive devices was puzzling us. We concluded that they must have been given to them by their pimps, who needed to reach them if their service was requested. We both seemed satisfied with that possibility.

Later, as we entered the hotel lobby, Caroline wondered whether we'd soon see more cell phones in the U.S. and Canada. "Never," I confidently declared. "It's not a technology that's going to make it. What kind of person would want to be reachable at all times?" Then I added, "Except a hooker, of course."

I bought my first cell phone in 2017, more than twenty years later, a few years after my pre-teen grandchildren got theirs. I joked that there were now only fourteen people without a cell phone left—worldwide. If I'd waited a bit longer, I would have become famous.

Has it changed my life? Not a bit, but then I'm not letting it. The weekly Apple summary of my device usage routinely tells me that I've been connected for less than 20 minutes.

Like breath on a mirror, haze has lately obscured the Colorado sky. A West coast fire is sending its pall across the Rockies, the postmaster told me. But today all is perfect. The air is crisp and translucent. I look out on miles of aspens, the patches touched by autumn's first frost changed to yellow and copper, others still a summery green. Above them sits a layer of sturdy conifers, and higher still the horizon of snow clashes with the radiance of a cloudless sky.

Earlier, I did my morning work, had a light lunch and played some tennis. My partner and I talked about the faultlessness of the day. The luminescence of the high-altitude light, the drama of the topography surrounding us, the piercing crispness of the air and the absence of tourists at this best time of the year. Who could ask for more?

Now I'm back at my desk, my eldest nephew sitting at his computer a few feet away from me and Caroline in her office downstairs. Half a year ago, after a barbecue in Flavia's garden, Christian shily asked me whether he could spend some time living with us, taking a break between high school and university. Knowing that Lea, the daughter of my school friends, had done that and loved it, gave him confidence. We agreed on terms: for the duration of a year, Christian was to be by my side, wherever I went, and help with whatever needed to be done. In return, Caroline and I would teach him what we knew: how to analyze a company, deal with banks, grow vegetables and prepare a pasta dish, use a chain saw and stack wood, write a decent essay and prepare an impressive resume. Yesterday we hiked up to Cathedral Lake, a nine kilometer pump cresting at 3,600 meters; now we sit side by side, Christian entering data into a spreadsheet, me contemplating a portfolio adjustment.

THE PHONE RINGS twice before I pick it up. I hear only noise, at first, the sound of machinery intruding on my senses or an ocean of static caving in on me. But already I know that something is not right.

And then a tear-choked voice, barely audible at first, then softly wailing. It takes me three or four seconds to realize it's Melissa. My mind leaps four steps ahead. Something is wrong with Caroline's 95 year-old dad, it says, and then moves to the next square. He's had a good, healthy life; we have to be thankful for that.

But then Melissa says Krista's name. Her heart has stopped; they're trying to resuscitate her. The message can't be authentic, the voice too far back in Melissa's throat to be real. But then it breaks. She'll die.

I hear myself answer. We can't think that way, mustn't allow ourselves to go to that place. And all along my mind races on, tries to fill in blanks. I learn that Krista's heart hasn't beaten for at least ten minutes. The brittle mountain scape outside looks unreal, bizarre even. Inside me darkness descends; I feel black ink running down my chest cavity. My heart is drowning.

Curiously, it's not Krista I cry for yet. I haven't allowed myself to think she's dead or even dying. It's Melissa that's on my mind; Melissa who has to carry the burden once again. When my wife's father collapsed, I was at the cottage and Caroline at an art camp in Haliburton. Melissa was summoned. The same with half a dozen other family emergencies. I don't feel guilty about this, just enormous sadness that it is always Melissa who has to be there.

I recall her words, distorted by sobs. "She's had some kind of liposuction and now she's dying." I hear myself ask where she's calling from. "Driving to North York General, with John. That's where they've taken her." Then fifteen, twenty seconds of silence, punctuated by Melissa's convulsions and traffic noise. "You know, she's put me down as next of kin and she didn't even tell me what she was doing."

My mind turns to Krista and the talks we had about her operation, the e-mails we exchanged. Caroline and I trying to dissuade her and Krista saying she wanted all the loose skin around her middle tucked in. "Ever since I had Cameron…the Caesarean has left me with all this flab, you know." I can hear her voice now, explaining, and inside my head is the reaction I had then. She's vulnerable, looking for a man again. She wants to be beautiful; how can I argue with that? It was a tummy tuck she had planned then and we managed to talk her out of it. Instead, she explained just a week ago, she was going to have a liposuction.

"It's not nearly as risky." Krista's words echo through the dome of my head. I remember hanging up and wondering if I could still talk her out of it, checking out websites for an hour or so, looking for risks related to liposuction and not coming up with much. I was sitting in my office in Colorado then, much as I'm now. But now all is different.

I share what's going on with my nephew Christian, whose face is turning pasty. I keep repeating it can't be true, just can't be. I must be dreaming this. And then I go to tell my wife. Not more than five minutes ago, Caroline went downstairs to her office, to make sure there would be flowers at Krista's house when she got home.

CAROLINE TREMBLES AS I hold her, looks at me with eyes that seem to have broken. We stand for half a minute, supporting each other. Then she takes charge, makes decisions that stun me. "Get me a flight; I have to be there with Krista." I thankfully react, dial, talk to our travel agent. I learn that a plane is leaving in fifty minutes and book a seat.

Things turn frantic now. John is on the phone: they're fighting traffic trying to get to North York. They should be there soon. A few minutes later, Melissa again. They're at the hospital. Nick is there too. He volunteered to take Krista home from the clinic and instead ended up in the ambulance taking her to the hospital. Later I learn how he was sitting in the front, crying and praying, with the paramedics desperately trying to resuscitate Krista. How strange: he'd broken up with our daughter to go his own way, and yet he was the one destined to accompany her on her most fateful journey.

AT NORTH YORK General, a team of six is trying to get Krista's heart to beat again, while giving her massive blood transfusions. I listen to Melissa's frightened voice, the background no longer traffic noise, but shouting and the beeps of machines. Then I hear someone else talk, a male. The tone is soft, composed. It must be a doctor talking to Melissa. I can't make out what's being said, but I sense the pain spreading through Melissa, the vise gripping and squeezing her heart.

When Melissa continues, her voice is different, further back in her throat and more tortured than before. "They want me to make a decision," she sobs. "How can I make that decision?" I try to stay calm, tell her that no, she doesn't need to make that decision, that it isn't fair to ask her. Something has happened to my voice cords, too. "They can't make me kill my sister. I'd rather have her brain dead than make that decision."

I want to die. If we have to make that decision, we will make it together, I say—all of us. Or I will make it. Just not you, Melissa. And then I notice no one's on the phone.

Seconds pass, no beeps and shouts now, just the whooshing sound of a voiceless phone connection. Then John comes on. I tell him the same thing, repeat that Melissa shouldn't, mustn't, make that decision, and then I hear John saying it's not needed right now. Apparently, the surgeon has gone back through the doors.

I picture those doors, wings to purgatory, and I imagine what Melissa must be seeing when they swing open and shut. John tells me they've got Krista back and they're giving her blood. Massive amounts of blood. They want to see if her heart can manage on its own.

Caroline is next to me; we need to get her to the airport. I ask John to call us. As we drive, we evoke images of Krista and pray. And wonder what we should be praying for.

The drive to the Aspen airport is short. The other passengers for the afternoon flight have all checked in; Caroline gets processed in a matter of five minutes. We hug and seek each other's eyes, tear-stained mirrors of knowing.

SNAKING MY WAY back up to Snowmass Village, I try to visualize the scene at North York General, let random images of horror flood my mind, then decide to block them. I brush emotion aside, instead trying to evoke rational thoughts. There must be meaning in this. What can it be?

The bus in front of me distracts me. It's moving too slowly and I contemplate passing it, even though I can't see ahead. I need to get back home to catch up with what is happening at North York General. My mind is in overdrive now. First it presents me with the scenery of a crash—me slamming into an oncoming vehicle—then it tells me that such a thing is impossible. The probability of Krista and I staring death in the face at the same time is minuscule.

Next, I feel the tension leave, as if it were ordered away by an overtaxed neural system. A more peaceful state enters. For a few moments, I try to define it: is it calm or an absence of caring? I wonder why I would feel composed during such acute crisis and already there's a voice telling me that I have no right to feel this way, not now. A dozen images of Krista—my Kristabelle, as I always call her—start flooding my brain. Some bring a smile to my face and when that happens, the wrinkles that form to the sides of my eyes turn into passages for my tears.

Yet, unexpectedly, the images of Krista settle me down even more, and it's the descending tranquility that once again makes me aware of the incomparable beauty of the land before me: gold, white and cornflower blue. A portrait of joy, not death. It seems inappropriate that tragedy should occur on such a day. Not only inappropriate, but unjust. Sleet coming from stormy, gun-metal grey skies would be fitting, but not the beauty of a perfect fall day. I ask myself why the sky can't fall in, a rockslide bury my car and take me instead of my Krista.

My heart is heavy when I get back to the house. My nephew Christian looks up at me and I can tell that no one has phoned. His expression says he wonders if I know more. But I don't and so I keep weighing what may be best. Melissa's tear-choked words get played over and over in my mind: "They want me to make a decision."

And then the call, but not from John or Melissa as I have come to expect. It's Caroline, from inside the plane. She tells me that as she boarded, looked for her seat, her cell phone rang. She tells me Krista is dead.

Her voice, distant as though it were filtered through protective layers of armor, says, "I can't believe it—what a waste." And then I hear someone tell her she can't make calls while on the plane.

I close my eyes, try to absorb what is now a reality, then let my windows to the world open again and the first thing I notice is that the mountains are still as snow-capped as this morning and the ridge is still embraced by the gold of aspens as it was when Krista was still alive.

I hear myself moan, "Oh Krista, my Kristabelle," and then my nephew is at my side holding me.

BY THE TIME I lie in bed, it's two in the morning. Even though the house is well heated and I've been wearing my heavy sweater, I've been shivering all afternoon and evening. A great void has spread through my body, its unmistakable pain numbing my nervous system. But my mind has continued to function independently of my physical deterioration. Sporadically, I've tried to focus on Krista, what she meant to me and what's happened, only to find my attempts drowned out by a chorus of logistical demands. Move the potted plants into the house; I won't be here for the first frost or maybe even snow. Explain to Christian how to adjust the thermostats. Make sure there's enough cat food, the type Cleo likes—Cleo, the cat that used to be Melissa's, then Krista's, and has lately been living with us.

Even now, in bed, the impulses keep coming, like fat snowflakes from a busy sky. I take note of each and file it away, before another settles on top and demands my attention. What's amazing is that I don't feel the least overwhelmed, not yet. I almost welcome the onslaught, but then pull back, disgusted with myself. Krista has died and here I am fussing over cat food and thermostats. I think I can comprehend what's happening. The mind noise says, 'Leave notes on who to call if there's an emergency,' and then it gets interrupted by a note of sanity. What emergency could there possibly be, after what happened today? There will never again be emergencies, not compared to this. I'm shivering almost uncontrollably.

I get up, resolving to take a steam bath, then change my mind. I'll go to the kitchen and make a hot water bottle. As I stand at the stove, more logistical details come at me. I remember the plane tickets I booked for Krista and Cameron. I hear Krista tell me that she lent money to a friend. I wonder what will happen to Cameron's day care routine now. I have to write all this down or chaos will ensue.

When I return to the bedroom I realize that I've forgotten the hot water bottle and am instead carrying a pen and a pad of paper. I stare at the lines I scribbled while I was waiting for the water to boil.

THE NIGHT IS long and mostly sleepless. "Krista is no longer," is the thought that keeps arising. In between, fragments of things that have been experienced and said since I got that first phone call from Melissa.

John's words, before he tried to go to sleep, are woven into the tapestry of today's tragedy as well. How many units of blood were given to Krista, how long the clinic waited before calling an ambulance, and that Melissa was very angry. For a while, I dwell on what John told me the surgeon at North York General said—that one thing we could be sure of was that Krista did not suffer. I try to weigh the significance of that statement, then conclude that it has no meaning, not without context, and that I don't have.

"Krista is no longer." I keep trying to convince myself, but can't accept the truth of that thought. Even if she's left her human form behind, even if her spent bodily shell is somewhere in the coroner's building, as I've learned from John, she's still here. I can feel her presence as I lay awake. I open myself to it, feel Krista's spirit envelop and comfort me, visualize myself taking her into my soothing embrace, and it helps me cope. And later, when around four o'clock I fall asleep, Krista is in my dreams.

An hour and a half later I stand under the shower, feeling the sting of the almost unbearably hot water particles. Occasionally, I move the top of my head under the spray and feel the water running down my face wash away my tears.

I feel different this morning; yesterday's barrage of logistical challenges has subsided. I'm still completely disoriented, as I look out at the changing dawn sky, one moment sobbing with grief, and the next asking myself whether it's all a bad dream. Then Christian comes down to make his tea and I know.

I spend the morning cancelling appointments and calling people whose help is needed while I'm away. And as I do so, I observe myself indulging in a strange ritual. I tell the people I phone that I must leave because my daughter has died. Some of the calls are to friends, of course, and their reactions consist of disbelief, expressions of love and offers of help. But when I talk to others, who don't know me well or at all, I sense they feel bewilderment and curiosity—they are wondering why I'm telling them.

Later, when I check in at Aspen's tiny airport, it's the same. The check-in agent, whom I remember from previous flights, comments on the high airfare I'm paying. I end up telling her about Krista, and immediately wonder why. "It must have been your wife I helped yesterday," she says, her eyes brimming with sympathy. She reaches across the counter, touches my hand and tells me how sorry she is.

THANK GOD THE flight is half-empty. I'm alone in my seat row, images of Krista racing by and a narrative of who she was and the enormity of what we've lost taking shape. I see Krista at the dinner table, having finished high school with distinction, declaring that she won't go to university yet, not before she'll complete the optional Grade 13 year in a non-private school. We've had this conversation before and Caroline and I have steadfastly refused her wish. But now, an extraordinary offering of honesty makes us reconsider. "Can't you see this has nothing to do with education?" a teary-eyed Krista screams at us. "Christ, all I want is to have a life for one year." A smile crosses my lips. It's what I liked best about Krista, her capacity to resist, to make a decision for herself and stay the course.

After that morning, Krista always had a life of her own making. She rappelled off cliffs and bungee-jumped across gorges, explored the swirl of the party-circuit and experimented with solitude, checked out marine life on barrier reefs and took turns on her snowboard. Krista was complex and hard to get close to. She'd be my little girl wanting to be cuddly one evening, and then I'd feel her need to be aloof and alone for weeks and sometimes months after. One time I told her she reminded me of Paul Simon's song, "I am a rock, I am an Island."

Who was Krista? As I attempt to merge my thoughts about her into some seamless collage, I find myself more confused than ever. I conclude that it was impossible to understand Krista, yet I also feel that I managed to cross the moat to her heart, especially these past two or three years, and that realization opens the gates to an onslaught of memories.

I see Krista sitting in her hotel suite, the wedding only three hours away, making herself beautiful for Nick, all softness and grace now. A black-and-white image of Krista shortly before giving birth follows, her extended belly carrying the boy we all love so much miraculously exposed. Then Caroline, in surgical scrubs, cutting Cameron's umbilical cord. I wasn't there for Cameron's birth, but I well know and cherish the picture. How I loved Caroline for finding a way to get the hospital to allow her to be with Krista while she gave birth, and how I admired Krista for embracing the idea.

Krista in tears. Her marriage has failed. Krista, at our last dinner together, telling me that Nick was going to get remarried. Angela, his wife to be, she explains, is a caring person—good to Cameron and right for Nick.

Krista is seeking comfort with her family again. I see images of her and Cameron with Melissa, John and the girls, and with Caroline and me at the cottage. I'm sitting on the dock, looking at the water below me, where the late summer breeze has created a carpet of miniature whitecaps. I'm staring out at the black of the night sky, jet engines droning somewhere in the far distance, but what I hear is Krista's and Cameron's joyful laughter and what I see are a million diamond-like sparkles, and in between float Krista and, held up by his mom and a yellow swim-vest, little Cameron, so fragile and so full of life. They look at each other adoringly.

IT'S CLOSE TO midnight when the limo driver drops me off at John and Melissa's house. As I watch the vehicle pull away, the door opens and John stands there, his face a mask of pain, his voice so soft I can hardly understand him. We talk outside his front door for a minute; I understand, the girls are asleep. Melissa, I'm told, has gone to bed too, and Caroline, who's spent most of the day here, is resting downstairs in the guest bedroom. She must be exhausted; she's probably nodded off by now.

But a moment later Caroline emerges. I hold her, feel her numbness, her shoulders and back hard as marble. When she raises her eyes to mine, they're alive with hurt, burn with pleading—pleading for something that's become impossible, I immediately realize. Caroline wants a different outcome, wants her Krista to be alive.

I've always been able to help Caroline get what she wanted. How can I help her now?

The next day I finally get to see Melissa. Her is body is more pliant than Caroline's, but as I hug and hold her there is no response. Her eyes are dead too, expressionless. I suggest we go upstairs, just the two of us, and that's where we sit on her bedroom floor, just looking at each other at first, then connecting, bit by bit, then holding each other. I tell her how sorry I am that it was she who had to endure such horrors, that Caroline and I weren't here to carry the load. I manage to get her to talk a bit, which makes me cry. Tears form in Melissa eyes, too, but she can't let go yet, is still too angry to do that—angry with Krista, angry with Caroline and me, angry with the world and its injustices.

When we return to the living room, Alexandra and Abigail are there. They manage a smile when I hug them and we chat a bit, but as they answer my questions they look at John for reassurance. They're disoriented and don't know how to handle the reality of what they've been told has happened. We adults have heard of death, have long known that the loss of a parent, siblings, friend or even a child was always a possibility. No one has prepared the girls, aged five and three, for such an outcome.

I LOVE CAMERON'S raspy boy-voice. Whenever I lift the receiver and hear the words, "Hi Papa," I'm transported into a state of bliss.

Now I hear Cameron's voice and feel the vibration on his chest. I'm sitting on a ledge outside Shoppers Drug Mart and Cameron is resting on my lap. My hands are clasped around him. He's asking, "When can I visit my Mummy in the angel house?" and I tell him that we can't visit angels, and that's why we're all so sad.

"I'm not sad," Cameron says. "I just want to visit my Mummy."

And then, as an afterthought, he adds, "Or maybe Mummy can come from the angel house and visit me."

"But Mummy is watching over you all the time, Cameron. She's here right now, just as your Daddy told you."

"Is she up in the sky, Papa?"

"Yes, she is."

"Right up there?" He points to the bit of crisp blue between the high-rises and I feel tears well up. I'm glad I'm wearing my sunglasses.

Two days ago, Nick told me he'd consult with a psychologist and then talk to Cameron about what happened. I remember being suspicious, wanting to be part of that conversation. What if the psychologist subscribed to some off-the-wall theory, recommended some trendy new approach? It was difficult for me to trust Nick when I felt so compelled to protect my grandson. Now I'm reflecting on how well Cameron is handling his Mummy's death.

"Papa, if we can't see Mummy and the people in the angel house, how come Mummy can see us?" I ponder different answers that might work, and settle on one that's not an answer at all, realizing that my three-year old grandson's questions are the same that have challenged humans for millennia. But before I can reply, Cameron goes on. "Maybe, we can't see the angels because they're blind, Papa."

"Because they are invisible," I hear myself say. This clarification is lost on Cameron, but it helps me. It's a safety line that gets me back into the realm of logic.

Cameron stirs on my lap: "Listen, Papa. It's a fire siren." He asks me to lift him up so that he can see. Cars slow and pull over toward the sidewalk and then, in all its magnificence, a ladder truck approaches, its lights flashing and the bursts of its horn drowning out even the ear-splitting wail of its siren. And for a few moments, Cameron is in heaven alongside his Mummy.

When the noise has died down, we sit back down and I ask Cameron if he's ever seen a fire engine this large before. He dodges the question. "What I really want to see is an ambulance, Papa." He pronounces it ammulanse. "Tell me, Papa. Was my Mummy in an ammulanse when she went to hospital?"

More tears flood my eyes and this time the sunglasses won't cover them.

Less than two months have passed. And yet, so much has happened. Caroline and I are in Ojo Caliente, a spa in New Mexico. This isn't a spa where the moneyed crowd gets massaged and manicured after a bit of horseback riding. No visitors lounge in cushioned chairs, cell phone in one hand and martini in the other. In fact, no food or drinks are served in the resting areas, and inside the plain restaurant diet-conscious visitors will find the menu surprisingly robust. There is no cell phone signal and the modest rooms don't have telephone service. There is a public phone in the lobby, but when we try it to let Melissa know where we are, it doesn't work.

This is a spa in the old style. The bath attendants aren't muscle toned early-thirties kids picked for their looks, but stocky native women from the nearby pueblos. The brochure makes the claim that Ojo Caliente medicinal springs are North America's oldest. The local Tewa Indians took baths here hundreds of years ago.

It's easy to visualize that. Think away the few simple adobe structures where the guests stay, and what's left are rock pools containing arsenic, lithium, sodium, iron and soda. Ojo Caliente is the only place in the world where springs offering this array of minerals exist.

ACCORDING TO BUDDHIST belief, tomorrow will be the day when Krista's soul will be reincarnated. Not long ago, when reading the *The Tibetan Book of the Dead*, I learned that the period between death and rebirth takes 49 days.

We're at a crucial point in our journey, Caroline and I. We feel an energy we're not used to—perhaps because my calendar reminds us of the imporant day that lays ahead, but more likely because of our unusual surroundings. The walls of the primordial canyons and mesas that rise around us sober our minds, as the womblike fold that holds the mineral springs soothes.

Before leaving our Snowmass house, when checking my e-mail, I found an inspirational piece that said: "Feeling anger and grief are parts of life that need to be fully felt and experienced, so that we can maintain our mental, emotional and even physical health. The next step, however, is up to us." Curiously, the message wasn't addressed to me, just part of a mass mailing that I would normally have discarded. But it struck me as relevant to where we were on our journey and so I filed it away in one of the drawers of my mind, resolving to bring it up with Caroline when the time was right.

Now, tired from the six-hour drive but thoroughly calmed by a long soak in the mineral pools and an unrushed dinner, we sit outside our room, moonlight bathing us in its gentle light. Caroline is sipping at her glass of water, while I swirl the bit of red wine that's left in my glass. We reflect on how much we've endured and learned.

The agonizing first few days after Krista's death, each of us family members dealing with our pain in a different way, our emotions like colliding missiles—the concerns for Cameron we shared and our fear of seeing him less often or not at all; the shock of seeing our daughter's image on the front page of the paper and the search for details of what exactly had gone wrong; the press coverage implying negligence by the anaesthesiologist and incompetence by the surgeon; the invasive attempts by reporters for the leading media outlets to get us to comment and our struggle to preserve our privacy; the debates on what we, as a family, could do to change the medical regulations, so that what happened to Krista could not happen to others.

Then, as it always does, our talk gradually turns to other, better aspects of our journey. Our first, awkward meeting with Nick and his new partner, Angela, whom we'd never met. The kindness of our friends—Stephanie, now living in Maine, taking the first available flight to Buffalo, and from there driving a rental car to be at our side; Caroline's friend Sartaj offering to help in every way; my friend Larry holding me in his arms before the memorial service, saying, "Peter—fuck, fuck, fuck," the most profound words conveyable under such circumstances, words that left me stunned by their purity.

We remember the service itself, how devoid it was from the hollowness we'd experienced at other funerals—how genuine the expressions of those who'd been touched by Krista during her 32 years, school mates, friends and co-workers, and the many others who didn't know our Krista well but were there to offer words of support. I tell Caroline of how awed I was by her strength, she who still spent her nights shivering and sobbing and, during the daytime, was a faint shadow of her former self. I tried to shelter her, telling her she did not need to speak to the many people who'd assembled, that I would take care of all that, but Caroline insisted on eulogizing Krista in her own words, marshalling a fortitude that left me stunned. I talked about Krista who lived her days fully, who danced the zig-zag through her short life; Caroline paid homage to Krista's softer side, her big heart and, what was more, shared her sad journey of suffering. Several others spoke, but no one's words gripped me like Janet's, the friend Krista had always needed and never found until near the end. Her ode to Krista was pure and courageous, a memory of intensely personal experiences the two of them had shared, some serious and profound and others outrageous—an insight into a friendship between deeply linked souls.

FINALLY, OUR VOICES soft as the blanket of stars illuminating the desert sky above us, we touch on the subject of miracles, reflect on the outcomes we hadn't dared hope for. Angela vowing to be there for our Cameron and Nick assuring us that we'd see as much of Cameron as if Krista were still alive. Our family, managing to gradually come together and rediscover what the agony of loss had temporarily buried: the love for each other. It's like Leonard Cohen expresses in what has become one of our favourite songs, *Anthem*. "There is a crack, a crack in everything. That's how the light gets in." Krista's passing cracked our hearts wide open, and what made its way in was light, the light of acceptance, tenderness and love.

It's close to midnight when Caroline shares a thought. "Once we've been resting with our pain," she explains, "it's up to us to decide what to do. We can grieve forever, or we can move on and return to life." I tell her how, a few days ago, I received an e-mail message saying much the same, and we hug.

There is a change within us. It feels as though our internal clock of grieving has completed its first circle. Yet, I can't help wonder: how trapped are we still in the clutches of our pain, how much healing still lies ahead?

AFTER A NIGHT of deep and uninterrupted sleep, we wake up to the 49th day. It's dark outside. We help ourselves to a small breakfast and a cup of tea, then take a walk up an ochre canyon. Thousands of birds are making themselves heard in the bushes around us, heralding the impending sunrise. Cacti, their red and yellow blossoms lifeless but still colourful, line the paths. Up on top we have a spectacular view; the hamlet below us is incidental, easy to think away. The winding river and the clusters of green along it dominate the otherwise bland valley.

Once we reach the table-like top, we take in the rising sun. There are junipers up here and sage brush, holy plants to natives across this continent. Yesterday we learned about Posi-Ouinge, a Tewa settlement whose history could not be more relevant to our situation. We follow the winding and often hardly noticeable dirt path, then start noticing pottery shards, increasingly large numbers of them, reminders of lives once lived up here.

Posi's history is a metaphor. Once, eons ago, the Tewa were one people. But then they divided themselves into two groups, the Summer People and the Winter People. Each travelled along the banks of the two great rivers of the area, the Rio Grande and the Rio Chama, where they built many villages. But in the end they reunited and that is when they built one last village together: Posi-Ouinge. And here we are, Caroline and I, still in the summer of our lives, reunited at this ancient, sacred site with our Krista, who left us not that long ago for the banks of another river.

Like Posi-Ouinge, of which we find nothing but shards in a place of stunning beauty, what we have of Krista are the memories of the times we briefly shared, the spirit with which she infused us, and what we learned from her during her life and through her death.

The rest of the day is uneventful. We go through the motions of soaking up minerals, of being good to our bodies, but all along our thoughts are with Krista. We think of what she was to us and what we may have been to her, what we'd say to her if she were here.

In the evening, after the cold descends, we celebrate Krista's memory in front of the small fireplace in our bedroom. Caroline places a picture on the low, rough-hewn table and lights a candle. When we turn down the light, the flickering of the logs seems to bring Krista's dark eyes alive. Now we tell her how much she meant to us and how much we learned from having her in our lives. And we wish her well on her journey, tell her to shine on and keep dancing. "Wherever you go next, bring your spirit along, my Krista," Caroline pleads.

WE'VE HAD VIBRANT Krista-dreams, all of us.

Melissa lives through the horrors of the hospital, again and again. Angela reports that she saw Krista inside a subway car and ran toward it, but the doors closed and the train pulled away before she could get in. Yet, Krista spoke to her, telling her to look not only after Cameron, but also Nick. Caroline was visited by Krista too; the message was identical. "It's Nick I'm worried about most," she said.

Krista makes her nightly appearance in my dream world, too, but she hasn't shared any concerns with me. She's just there, walking alongside me down Bayview Avenue, close to where she lived, or sitting outside on John and Melissa's deck with a bunch of us, watching Cameron play with his cousins. Sometimes we eat and she raises her glass to me, without saying anything. At other times I watch her from afar, going up an escalator or disappearing into a building.

But tonight's dream is about Cameron. We're kneeling in the sand, building a tower, the two of us. Behind us are the calm waters of our bay and above us the cottage. The breeze carries bits of conversation from the porch and we can hear the clanking of dishes and cutlery.

"Let's make it really high, so that Mummy can see our tower from up high," I suggest. Cameron's reply is instant. "My Mummy can see everything, even small things. She's dead now; she's in heaven."

I agree and for a time we quietly keep building. The tower's base keeps getting broader and its tapered top reaches almost to my waist. I'm excited, both because we're doing so well and because we do something to keep Krista's memory alive. But Cameron, I notice, is losing interest. He's standing to the side, watching me add sand and smooth the surface. His head is cocked; I can tell he's thinking.

And then, without any warning, his arms dart forward and he smashes the tower off its foundation. I look at him, both surprised and disappointed, and he meets my gaze. "I smash my Mummy's tower, Papa," he states factually. "I smash it."

I absorb what's happened, take a while to respond, and then I reach out for Cameron, hold him tightly for a long time, and keep repeating, "It's all right, Cameron. You smashed it. It's all right."

*O*nce again, I find myself thinking of that night in Ojo Caliente, pondering Caroline's assessment of where we then stood. Once we've rested with our pain, she said, it's up to us what we want to do. Did we keep grieving or did we move on?

While we were united in our intention to return to the business of life, processing what had happened took time. I have no better way to express how I felt than to say that my heart was wounded. I'm not referring to the stinging sense of loss and the emotional upheaval I experienced—those were there too, and they were inescapable. But there was more: I could feel a deep cut right through my heart, could trace its course with my fingers, top to bottom, at a slight angle. For months, the pain stayed with me, throughout the day and when I woke up at night, made only worse by the mind games triggered by doubt and guilt. Could I have talked Krista out of having the operation if I'd only tried harder? I'd succeeded in getting her to listen to my concerns—why hadn't I persisted? Melissa was on my mind just as much. We'd always seen her as strong and rational, able to look after herself; perhaps Caroline and I hadn't been there for her when she needed us.

If I was going through this, I wondered, then what about Caroline? The nights of torment, her fragile body convulsing for hours, continued for weeks. During one particularly troubled episode, while holding her in a tight embrace, I suggested that perhaps she needed counselling. That evoked a reaction that made me realize what toll the loss of a child could take, even on an exceptionally successful relationship. For Caroline, it was no longer the memories that inflicted pain, but the hurt itself. How to accept that there would always be hurt?

We spent half the night talking, me trying to impress on Caroline how much I wanted to be there for her and how frustrated I was, having failed in my efforts. Caroline, in turn, felt that I wasn't there for her, which caused me to accuse her of not letting go of her grief, of being hostage to it, of not letting me in to help. We agreed to see a counsellor, together.

A few days later, we met with a lady psychologist in Aspen, who listened to us for the better part of two hours. It was the only session we ever needed. After hearing both Caroline's and my own perspectives, she told us that our relationship was safe and sound, but not without telling me that a mother's loss of her child was something I would never be able to relate to, and not without reminding Caroline of what she already knew: she could dwell with her grief or embrace life anew.

A couple of days later, at the Aspen farmer's market, a friend spotted us. She walked up to us, opened her arms to Caroline, then held her tightly, saying, "You know, you still have so much living to do."

LITTLE BY LITTLE, we managed to let go of our pain and find comfort in each other, but the ongoing fallout from the tragedy we thought we'd left behind continued to haunt us. There was disagreement about what we should do about the surgeon advertising herself to be a specialist who wasn't anything of the kind; the anaesthesiologist who was mandated to keep an eye on his patients while they were in recovery, but who was unavailable when Krista was found to be suffering from heavy internal bleeding; and a medical system that took far too long to summon an ambulance to take Krista to a hospital that could deal with resuscitation.

Nick was determined to sue, a course our family resisted. All it would bring on, we thought, was even more negative energy and a lot of publicity. We were particularly concerned what ongoing media attention would do to Cameron. A monetary settlement held no attraction for us; we needed to change the system. It's what we felt our Krista would have wanted out of this.

My idea was to put pressure on the College of Physicians and Surgeons to openly address the inadequacies of their regulations. If they didn't investigate and make changes, we'd engage with the media and make them look irresponsible. John took another approach. He had several meetings with the senior people at the Ministry of Health, the body that needed to approve proposed regulatory changes. Caroline's and Melissa's hearts were in the same spot as John's and mine—the sequence of events that led to Krista's completely unnecessary death must never occur again.

In the end, all of us prevailed. Our family's impact statements at the administrative trial helped to strip Dr. Yazdanfar, who botched the operation and didn't have the decency to reach out to any of us, of her license. Dr. Liberman, the anaesthesiologist, shared her fate, after he was found incompetent, dishonest and lacking in judgment. John's meetings with the health ministry also paid off; some of the regulations allowing medical doctors to perform specialty surgery without a specific license, were changed. And Nick eventually won his lawsuit against the two medical professionals; a significant sum of money was placed in a trust for Cameron's benefit. It took four long years for the regulators to indict Yazdanfar and Liberman, and even longer for Nick to secure the financial settlement—each stage of the process stirring our emotions once more.

Yet, while the ongoing hearings and their coverage in the media irritated and exhausted, nothing was more heart-breaking than Cameron's reaction to his mother's death. Comprehending that he came from Krista's tummy and that he'd lost his Mummy because something had gone wrong with her tummy, he convinced himself that he was somehow responsible for her death. It's not something he shared with Nick and Angela, but brought up with me repeatedly. I encouraged him to talk, so that we could examine his account and I could show him where he went wrong. But nothing I said would detract him from his course of self-imposed guilt. In the end, the best I could do was to play with him, let him open one of the many drawers and cabinets that lined our office walls, which contained things that fascinated him—an old pair of binoculars, sketch books and crayons, albums filled with postage stamps. He loved coming to the office with me.

I think Cameron was five when, one summer afternoon, we were working on what came to be known as the Avenue of the Flags. His role was to use my world atlas and identify a country, then call it up on one of our computers. Together, we'd then print out a small image of that country's flag, cut it out and tape it to a wooden skewer. Over the course of a year, we completed a three-foot long collage sporting some fifty flags, many of them exotic and little-known, Cameron reciting their names to everyone's surprise and delight.

I'm not sure what caused Cameron's change of mood that afternoon. It could have been that he looked at the photograph of Krista that sits on my credenza along with other family pictures, or it could have been something else. I was looking through a document when I noticed Cameron attempting to climb one of the rolling office chairs. Concerned that he might fall I asked him what he was doing, and when he turned to look at me, I could see that something was terribly wrong. His expression of contentment had given way to a mask of pain and hostility. I asked him what was wrong, but he wouldn't answer. From the chair, he climbed to the top of a long office table that was parked against the window, and then he reached up to the sliding window above him and told me he'd jump.

An instant later I was grabbing a screaming Cameron, holding him tightly to me, as he kicked and pummelled me with his little fists. I carried him to the guest room where our friends and clients stay when they visit Toronto, and allowed the two of us to collapse onto the bed, Cameron crying now, in between violent sobs still repeating that he wanted to die. We lay there for a long time, holding on to each other, me out of fear that I might lose him too, he for the comfort of being loved.

Later, he wanted to look at the book I'd made for him, 'My Mummy Krista'—a record of the three years Cameron and his mother had together. In time, he'd learn to read the captions. "I have arrived" (picture of baby Cameron with his exuberant Mom and Dad); "Mummy can bake" (showing one of my favourite images of Krista, sporting an apron and showing off one of her culinary productions); "A Bath in the Sink" (depicting Caroline and Krista at our Colorado kitchen sink, washing tiny Cameron, who looks a little bewildered).

Healing took longer for Cameron than any of us. Even once he understood that he had no part in the tragedy that took his mother's life, he still had trouble relating to an existence without her. We spent a lot of time with him, Angela and Nick graciously accommodating us, knowing that it was good for Cameron to be with his cousins, his aunt and uncle, and his grandparents.

For the following few years, on the anniversary of his mother's death, we walked over to Sherwood Park, where we stood above the vibrantly coloured ravine and evoked memories of our Krista. Cameron carried the balloon he'd inscribed with his messages of love and longing, and when the time was right, let go of it. Then, squinting into the dazzling sky for several minutes, we all followed its slow ascent heavenwards, until it was no longer visible, Cameron content that his offering would soon meet up with and delight his Mummy Krista.

For some time now, a bench we commissioned has been sitting on the spot we gathered to watch Cameron's balloon float away. An engraved plaque is attached to its backrest. It reads:

IN MEMORY OF

KRISTA STRYLAND

WHO BROUGHT US TOGETHER IN LOVE.

YOUR LAUGHTER AND SPIRIT LIVES IN OUR HEARTS.

Cameron is in his mid-teens now, but when he visits us in the city we still go to Sherwood Park, resting on the "Mummy bench" for a while, contemplating what could have been.

It's nearly three years ago, but it seems like yesterday that we were at Melissa's and John's house. Mike and Nellie were there, as were Caroline's brother Bob with his wife Nella and their two teenagers, Kayla and Nicholas. Christian, who'd become an integral part of the family, was with us too, experiencing his first Christmas away from home. He was at the half-way mark of his year in North America.

I was sitting on an easy chair next to the richly decorated tree, dressed in a red outfit with fuzzy white-woolen trim, sporting a massive beard. I was Santa. Five-year old Alexandra could tell that something was off, but wasn't sure what it was. The younger two children, still only three, bought into my ruse. Abigail sat on my lap opening a present, intrigued but a bit intimidated; you didn't get that close to Santa Claus that often. And Cameron kept running to the front door, asking where Papa was, determined that we shouldn't start exchanging presents without Papa in attendance.

It was the children who helped us heal. Most of our get-togethers revolved around them, and so it was that Christmas evening. Caroline had told us that only love could get us back together, but each of us had a different understanding of that concept. Now we saw that she was right. All of us found refuge in the children's focus on simple pleasures—how easily they could withdraw from the horrors that lay in the past and the fears of the future! By watching them, we adults could comprehend that, no matter what had happened, we still had each other, which helped us let go of our burden for a few hours, even though we knew that the day after we'd be back to sorting out our emotions and looking for common ground on how to tackle a load of logistical challenges.

Early in the new year Caroline, Christian and I took Cameron to Colorado with us; two weeks later Nick followed. We built snow castles, played with the Dinky Toy cars and trucks I enjoyed when I was Cameron's age, and of course skied. Next, Melissa, John and the girls arrived. More outdoor adventures, more healing.

My old friend Roger Badet and I have a lot to discuss. We've been playing tennis in the morning, working through the middle part of our days together and talking most of the evening away.

Both of us have weathered the worst global recession in decades with distinction, having built large cash positions well before markets crashed. Still, when it happened, the shock of seeing key stock indices fall by over 40% left me completely disoriented. Over dinner, sitting at a table overlooking Lake Zurich, I'm describing to Roger how I felt like a veteran sailor who had survived a horrific storm and now found himself adrift in the middle of a vast ocean. I'd correctly anticipated the storm and done all the right things to avoid being shipwrecked. And now that I was ready to resume my voyage I found my compass gone.

I explain how I struggled, as major banks failed and were bailed out, again and again delaying the overdue market update I was supposed to send to our clients. After weeks of holding back and being frustrated, I finally sat down and forced myself to write, articulating the situation the way I perceived it. I laid out the one fact that mattered: while everyone knew what had happened, neither I nor anyone else could anticipate what lay ahead.

When I finished my commentary I finally understood. Not knowing should not terrify me. On the contrary, the crisis was effectively relieving me of the burden of having to predict outcomes. I'd continue to try my best and that was all I could do. It was an insight that left me feeling completely liberated.

"What does it all mean for our small firm?" I ask Roger. Cavelti & Associates has done far better than almost all of the large financial institutions. There is only one negative: we've lost our largest private client, a former Goldman Sachs partner, who was unwilling to pay us a fee for sitting on the sidelines. He moved his millions to fraudster Bernie Maddoff, whose Ponzi scheme collapsed not long after. Roger thinks that's funny.

Next, we talk about Camafin Trust AG, the Swiss firm we started together. From a performance perspective, we've done equally well, but now we still find ourselves in a precarious situation. Not long before my trip here, the U.S. announced sweeping new regulations to curb banking secrecy. The effect of the changes to a small institution like ours is devastating. Unlike the Swiss banks, we've always demanded that our U.S. account holders be tax compliant, yet the new regulations will implicate us as 'co-conspirators' if a client breaks the rules. Given the new circumstances, Roger and I agree on a simple solution. We'll close our jointly-owned firm down and move all accounts to one of the big banks, where Roger will continue to manage them.

Our plan works for both of us: less administrative and legal headaches for Roger, one less business engagement for me.

HOW DIFFERENT WE are, Reto and I. Few people would ever guess that we are brothers.

Right now, waiting for our meal to arrive, Reto noisily broadcasts his fairly radical political and social views, making some of the guests at near-by tables feel visibly uncomfortable. I'm embarrassed, wishing I could hide under the table.

I used to argue with my brother, giving voice to what I thought was logical and reasonable. That not only heightened his indignation, but also left me feeling saddened that we couldn't connect. Eventually, I learned that staying silent was the most prudent approach, which is what I'm doing now.

And soon enough my brother's tirade ends. He sits back, seemingly more relaxed, and asks me what car I'm driving these days. It's still the same Nissan Pathfinder, I say, now close to ten years old. Reto laughs, reminding me that he's never been able to relate to my vehicle preferences. Then he describes his most recent choices: the Rolls Royce, the MacLaren and, for winter driving, the Subaru.

We don't look or eat like brothers, either. Even though we both grew up in the same household, Reto gravitates toward the fleshier cuts of meat, ideally served half raw. Just a few minutes ago, he startled our waitress by ordering a one-kilo serving of beef tenderloin, admitting that it wasn't on the menu but insisting that he'd accept nothing less. I ordered trout. Occasionally, when the whole family gets together, Mami expresses concern about Reto's weight, while she scolds me for being too thin. That's when, as brothers, we come together and tell our mother how inappropriate it is to lecture her long grown-up sons.

There are things we have in common. We both detest hypocrisy, political correctness and government overreach—what sets us apart is really style, not substance. And, sharing the same sense of humour, we can laugh together, too.

Tonight, we end up talking about the generational gift we've both taken advantage of: the ability to reinvent ourselves as often as we like to. Like me, Reto didn't do well at school. Instead of heading to university, he took a job in a chemical factory and learned to process and dye textiles. Hating the tediousness of that trade, he became a computer programmer, briefly working in Canada and the United States for IBM. For more than twenty years now, he's been independent. Unable to fit into the committee culture of large corporations, he offers his computer technology insights to one of the major Swiss banks. "The employees do the debating, while I design and implement the systems," he explains proudly.

We talk about our father's and grandfathers' generations. Being entrapped by a professional identity chosen early on, staying on the same track until the onset of old age, then being expected or even mandated to retire—it's a course neither of us can imagine.

FLAVIA AND I have taken a long walk together and now we sit in her garden, blossoming bushes and budding flowers all around us, waiting for Urs and the kids to join us. She's asking me how we're doing. I'm not sure how the question is meant, but it makes me reflect on the progress of the past three years.

I tell her we're managing, that we may have emerged from all the chaos stronger, both as a family and as individuals. We've redefined ourselves, I explain, each in our own way.

John has left the highly regarded labour law firm where he was a partner, and become a successful arbitrator. Melissa took on huge new responsibilities as Managing Director at the bank, then called me in Colorado one morning, completely distraught. She could no longer relate to the institution she was working for; amidst the most serious financial crisis in years, she felt the bank's senior executives were more interested in generating corporate revenue than they were in protecting the clients' interests. I tell Flavia what that meant to me—how proud I was of Melissa when she stood up for her beliefs, even though it cost her job, and how pleased I was when the bank was forced to pay her a huge compensation.

"And what about you and Caroline?", my sister asks. I tell her that Caroline is regaining her balance as well. Determined to find peace through self-inquiry, she's been drawn deeper into her spiritual practice and is spending a lot of time creating pottery. As to myself, I've decided to do less planning and more living. I'm learning that I can't project everything by spreadsheet and control outcomes.

Flavia nods, but I'm not sure she can relate. Convinced that all happens for a reason and will turn out well, neither she nor her husband have ever felt compelled to plan ahead. Perhaps they don't need to: both have secure jobs, the same ones they've had since they started out in their early twenties.

Nina drifts in first; she's close to 17, polite and awkwardly shy like her dad. Roman, who's been playing soccer with some friends, arrives next. Outgoing, lovable and talkative like his mother, he quickly makes himself the centre of attention. Finally, Urs and Christian emerge from the house, carrying trays of food ready to be grilled.

I end up talking to Christian most of the evening, aware that it may offend his siblings. We've shared a year together, a year of promise and tragedy, a year of exploring potential. I try to remember Christian when he arrived, gentle and innocent, and eager to learn. I look at him now, more mature, close to the end of his studies. But what I really see is Christian ten or fifteen years down the road, the agent of change he'll be in his next role in life.

TWO YEARS AGO, Melissa and John invited us to a family holiday in California, where we spent most of our time in and around Ojai, exploring the stunning white-walled, red-tiled historical town that's somehow managed to avoid development, and the orchard dappled valley surrounding it.

Now it's our turn. I'm at the airport, welcoming the whole family to Switzerland. Waiting at the arrivals area, I see the grandkids first, excitedly looking for me amidst the crowd. Then Abigail spots me and the three of them come running. Melissa steps down the hallway next, looking dopey; when we hug each other, she tells me she took a sleeping pill as the flight took off and just woke up. Finally, Caroline and John emerge, each pushing a cart loaded high with suitcases.

We drive off to my favourite pizzeria where we have lunch, then onto the hotel, overlooking Lake Zurich. The children don't notice the spectacular location—they're overjoyed that they have their own room, something they never expected.

Tomorrow, we'll start with memory-building. During the next three weeks, we'll see cathedrals, castles and dungeons, take lake tours, ride cable cars to mountain tops and careen back down on alpine slides, play with cows and goats and ride in my brother's Rolls Royce. We'll visit my class mates Brigitta and Caspar and their daughter Lea, who spent several seasons with us in North America and who's now married and a mother. There will be family get-togethers, too, at Flavia's place and in Herisau.

Everyone loved the Switzerland trip. Being away on 'neutral' territory made for a nice balance. Even though I had planned everything, there was plenty of opportunity for each of us to put our own imprint on how we lived each day. We all agreed there will be more such adventures in the future.

For me, the only negative was to see Mami struggling with her health. She'd suffered from a rare form of fibromyalgia and, not long ago, had recovered from a difficult hip replacement.

She was in less pain now, but the progressive loss of her eyesight was undeniable. At meals she frequently knocked over her glass, unable to distinguish its outlines against the white tablecloth. By the time we left I'd convinced her to start drinking her mineral water out of a tea mug, but was wondering how long she'd be able to live by herself.

Caroline's parents agreed to take the big leap last year. Both of them had started to fall and had trouble remembering to take their medicines. Caroline and Bob helped them move into a multi-level care home, where they have their own ground level suite with their own garden. Given their age—Mike is 97 now, Nellie 87—they're doing remarkably well.

NOW IT'S PRIME cottage season. For a couple of years now, Caroline, Melissa and John have asked me to consider a renovation of my favourite retreat. On sunny days, our small building serves us well, with most of us spending at least half the day on the wrap-around porch or on our sizable deck at the beach. It's different when it rains. No matter how hard we try, having four adults, three kids and now Marley, Melissa's new puppy, inside an 800 square-foot cabin, makes for a challenge. We get on each other's nerves.

Still, so far I've steadfastly resisted any suggestion of change. For me, the cottage is sacred ground. I've been emotional, to the point of writing a poem entitled 'No More Fairies", a reference to my favourite pastime of looking for the mythical creatures with Caroline and our grandchildren, even building fairy houses with them and placing them in the forest covering much of our property. Giving up the old cottage appears equivalent to the loss of the serenity and innocence I've always attributed to it.

Worse, when we recently had an exploratory meeting with an

architect, it became clear that renovation is not an option. Without a foundation, the cottage, now 53 years old, sits on piles of natural rocks. The walls are slightly crooked and the floor isn't quite level. Remove the roof or any wall and the building is likely to collapse.

Caroline, sensing my pain, agrees to postpone the decision. For now, we'll make the outbuildings more user-friendly, converting the 'play house' we built for the children into a small sleeping cabin and building a pottery studio, a 'clay house', for Caroline.

CURIOUS WHERE A new, much larger building would stand, I've been staking out the area, taking inventory of the trees that would have to come down if we built. Only a few weeks have gone by since our talk with the architect; there have been several meetings since with Marshall Black, the son of neighbours on our bay and one of the most promising local builders.

Not far from me Steve Blundy, Marshall's retired cousin, is framing the new pottery structure. Steve is a perfectionist. His work is so impressive that I've asked him to also build two wood-sheds. Even better, he's taken it upon himself to appoint Cameron as his assistant. Watching the two is a delight. While Steve saws and hammers away, Cameron gets to pick up the scrap pieces, load them onto a wheelbarrow, move them to the firepit and feed them to the flames. Steve and I both keep a close eye on him. He's only six.

A few days before Labour Day I announce my decision to Caroline. If she agrees to take charge of the design of the new cottage structures and supervise the building process, I'll be on board. The challenge will be to inject the sanctuary-like simplicity of the place I've enjoyed for more than three decades into two structures—a main cottage and a guest cabin—that will together be nearly four times as large. If anyone can marry such seemingly contradictory objectives it's my wife.

Caroline consents, but wants to make sure that if we do this, I won't complain. It'll be my decision, she explains, not my compromise. I think I can live with that, hoping that our new, more spacious place away from everything will be as much of a haven to the kids and grandkids as it has been for me.

IT'S THE LONG weekend when we reveal our plans. The mosquitoes and deer flies are long gone; we're sitting under a stand of young maples and cedars behind the cottage, on Adirondack chairs I've arranged in a circle. Not far from us is the crude table where we work on our art projects together. A few of the leaves above us have turned as fire-engine red as the colour of our chairs.

Our explanations meet with questions. Melissa and John politely inquire whether their new quarters will have a king sized bed, while the girls, who've just come back from their camp, want to know whether they'll still have the bunk-bed they've come to love. Cameron weighs in too. He's attached to the sleeping loft I built with his mummy, accessible only by a wall-mounted ladder from Alexandra's and Abigail's bedroom. Will he still be able to see down onto the girls bunk?

I try to get everyone to understand that if we rebuild, things won't be the same and, gradually, the conversation veers away from sleeping arrangements. Caroline and Melissa start talking about the grandiose kitchen we'll have and the culinary delights they'll be able to produce. John and I look at each other, smiling.

We know we'll miss out on next year's summer season and can't quite imagine what it will be like, but we're very excited.

FALL PROVES PHYSICALLY exhausting, but emotionally energizing. By October, when we close for winter, 41 trees have been felled, the brush burned and the logs stacked. There is no going back now.

In the past, I've always taken one of my axes to the wood and split it into burnable pieces, cutting enough wood for a few weeks ahead. Now, with enough firewood for a couple of decades, I realize that it's time for a change. When the new buildings stand, I'll buy myself a hydraulic splitter.

Mike has died. He was taken to hospital after his heart failed him. The pacemaker the surgeons inserted worked for a while, although he suffered significant memory loss. Caroline, who flew back from Colorado, stayed with him and ensured that he could return to his new home, where he received around-the-clock care. He surprised us one last time, starting to eat again and even getting up to walk a few steps, but in the morning hours of a gloomy March day, he slipped away.

What a life he lived. Growing up as one of many children of a tenant farmer and his wife in a very impoverished Ukraine, suffering through the years of the Great War, the Russian Revolution, then coming to Canada during the Great Depression—abuse, food shortages and deprivations I cannot imagine. Who could have imagined that these kinds of odds could lead to a life of wellbeing and plenty in one of the world's most stable countries? Poverty and harshness turned into riches and contentment—to me, a fairy tale life.

But was it to Mike? Did he see himself as the beneficiary of countless blessings? He loved his family, but never stopped worrying about them. Letting go and enjoying didn't come easily to him.

I guess his conditioning was that you never knew what came next, and life reinforced that imprint.

I grew to love Mike, always wanting to hold him and reassure him that all was well, that the era of dictators and economic hardship was over, at least for now. Sometimes I succeeded, at least for a few moments. In Cuba, on our family holiday, I tricked him into having a Rum-and-Coke; he sipped at it, squinting at the setting Caribbean sun, and his face relaxed. I saw the same when he looked at a crane suspended over a high-rise construction site or contemplated a newly built highway. For a few moments, life was good then.

Whenever I summon Mike's memory, a favourite image comes up. 'Topless', wearing only shorts, he stands on our patio in Colorado. His face and body are deeply tanned, as he looks at the mountain range across our narrow valley. Mike is 93 years old but his chest is that of a man in his fifties.

I always admired Deborah and David. Like few of the original hip-pies in the Aspen Valley, they lived by the laws of the universe. To them, the earth was always a place of plenty—plenty of fun, plenty of food, plenty of opportunity. They'd travelled the world, living in places like Bali, guiding treks to the Andes and the Himalayas, and while doing that, doing photography shoots for the Patagonia catalogue. Their daughter, Alison, had journeyed with them, being home-schooled.

Whenever we met them, they expressed gratitude for what they had. When they built something, they asked if someone knew where a few used windows left over from a remodel might be found, or which construction site might be left with surplus roofing shingles. And before long, a building would take shape, Deborah and David working alongside their contractor friends, who loved them enough to sacrifice their weekend to help.

They gave back too, most generously. When we lost Krista, they invited us to their hide-away in Hawaii, which they'd built themselves and where they hosted spiritual retreats and yoga weeks. They vacated their favourite rooftop room for us. It was there, surrounded by lush tropical gardens and palm trees whose leaves turned a deep rust when the sun sank, that David and I talked about life.

"What do you do when you face a fork in the road?" I asked, and he said that he let his mind work through the possibilities he could identify, but then sat back and waited until intuition showed him the way. I was dumbfounded. It's what I would have answered, and yet, we had led such completely different lives. "And when a way forward reveals itself, I sometimes consult the I-Ching," David added.

Now I was curious. With my Toronto friends, I had tinkered with the I-Ching during my early twenties. We asked it questions and were *invariably intrigued by the elegance with which it avoided actual predictions, but instead provided insights into our present situation.*

"Let's have an I-Ching session one evening", I suggested, and David agreed.

A COUPLE OF *nights later, as David placed his well-worn book on the wooden floor between us and laid out three Chinese coins next to it, I asked about working with Melissa. What would it bring?*

We had already decided that we would work together, Melissa and I, a solution that seemed perfect for both of us. If we kept the size of our client base unchanged and divided up the workload, it would mean that each of us gained a few hours a day of spare time. For her it meant that she could spend more time with the girls; on my side, it would help me transition to a better balance between financial work and my other interests.

How, I now asked, would things work out? David's first response was that much depended on the intention Melissa and I entered our arrangement with. Then he turned to the I-Ching, adding that the book's answer might be more cryptic than I expected. Next, he threw the coins six times, each time recording the combination of heads and tails. He then consulted his well-worn guide and gave me his interpretation.

The reading wasn't ambiguous at all. No matter how long Melissa and I ended up working together, we'd learn a lot from each other and contribute to each other's growth.

When I look back, that is very much how it played out. We immediately noticed that our investment styles were quite different, which triggered intense debates. Yet, before long, I saw that my particular approach could benefit from some modifications. Melissa exposed me to the idea of considering the prevailing consensus opinion, something I had rarely done. Why let the talking heads on TV influence the conclusions my research produced? The hosts were more interested in controversy than substance, while most of their guests were at best deeply conflicted, and at worst shamelessly self-promoting. Besides, hadn't I produced excellent results over a period of decades, without paying attention to TV personalities?

Melissa concurred with my assessment, but pointed out that media exposure could materially boost an investment we believed in—so why not pay attention to the narratives served up on the most popular shows? She was right, which didn't mean that I'd have to watch TV—that was her job.

There were other advantages that arose from our cooperation. Melissa was the queen of financial and consumer stocks, areas in which I'd often underperformed; my expertise was in the natural resources and utilities sectors. Merging our specialties has a favourable impact on our performance.

Melissa also focused me on some of my entrenched personal habits. She was particularly critical of my practice of constantly updating dozens of Excel spreadsheets. I was defensive at first, then examined the need for each of the daily or weekly updates, and eventually tossed a good half of my spreadsheets overboard. Why had I meticulously maintained them for so many years? Most had provided some marginal value to our investment activities, but that was a side issue. I could see what the real story behind the constant spreadsheet updating was: recording every detail I could think of gave me the illusion that I could control the chaos all around me.

THERE WAS ONE more thing that working with Melissa taught me. After our performance for the client accounts improved even more, I thought that she might want to completely take over the firm I had started, which had only a few clients left but had an excellent reputation and could *easily be rebuilt. I'd convinced myself that this was the most desirable outcome and I expected Melissa to jump at the chance.*

When she replied to my proposal with a resolute no, I was taken aback. But when she explained her reaction, I could easily relate. She absolutely detested administration and didn't particularly like client contact; what she really enjoyed was the investment related work. Now I saw things differently. Why should she clutter up half her day with tasks she disliked? And besides, didn't she join me so she could have a half day to herself?

Her answers were the ones I would have given. What I'd learned was that what my ego wanted for my children and grandchildren wasn't the same thing that my heart wanted.

As it turned out, Melissa and I worked closely together for a few years, then interfaced less frequently, as my clients of several decades gradually died off and the size of the business shrank.

Up the street in Snowmass Village lives my neighbour and fellow memoirist William Turner. Bill, long retired, had a distinguished career in management consulting; he is the only person I have met who's visited more countries than I have—74 versus my 72. The difference between us is that Bill has looked at the world through a somewhat different lens than I have. While I routinely visited the same dozen countries as an executive or on vacation, I experienced the rest as a backpacker on five dollars a day. Bill Turner, in contrast, travelled wherever there was a major bank merger taking place and, typically, lived there for a few months or sometimes years. And while he was in the neighbourhood, he dashed into as many of the surrounding countries as possible, always on a generous budget.

Still, we have many things in common. We've both had deep insights into the institutional dynamic and come to see how it can corrupt. Having lived in many places, we've both learned to see our culture through the eyes of others.

Like Bill, I've always been good at walking away from things. Once I opened myself to the possibility of quitting my financial career, events that made an exit easy quickly materialized. For a while, I turned to financial journalism and, once again, I was very successful. But disappointment and frustration soon followed, because I was not being true to myself.

In stages, I withdrew from the financial world and surrendered my identity to something that is much greater—instead of doing what I thought my world expected me to do, I decided to align myself with what would come naturally and easily, what would be a delight and not a weight.

In other words, both Bill and I deliberately withdrew from the professional world, happily surrendering the identity we took for ourselves, in an attempt to let ourselves be reinvented.

IN HIS MEMOIR, *Bill defines the five segments of his erstwhile career in a way that not only resonates with me, but perfectly describes the stages I went through. With Bill's permission, I'm substituting my name for his:*

Stage 1	*Who is Peter Cavelti?*
Stage 2	*Get me Peter Cavelti*
Stage 3	*Get me a Peter Cavelti type*
Stage 4	*Get me a young Peter Cavelti*
Stage 5	*Who is Peter Cavelti?*

Not long ago, I heard about Peter Hug's sudden death from cancer, at age 69. Just three weeks earlier I'd seen him give the kind of interview that provided insights and indisputable value to the viewer. It left me with admiration and pride. Here was the boy I'd first met when he was a busboy at the Um-Pah-Pah restaurant in Toronto, the university gradu-ate who asked me for his first full-time job, the young man I trained to be Guardian Trust's chief trader, now in his late sixties giving sage advice to the investment world.

The obituaries and industry tributes that popped up within days of his death were equally impressive. The consensus was that Peter would be sorely missed—by his co-workers at the institution of which he was the head of global trading, by peers in other corporations, by the people in the financial media who'd regularly interviewed him.

Seeing all these accolades gave me pause. For a day or two, I allowed my mind to explore where I'd be if I'd stayed the course like almost all my peers in the financial industry. I'd still fly to the New Orleans investment conference once a year to give my keynote address. I'd run into fellow speakers and panelists there, have dinner with them and reflect on how we'd first met. And I'd be on TV often, just like the people I worked with long ago. My grandchildren would be deeply impressed and, eventually, my death would be widely reported, like Peter Hug's.

My mental discourses continued. Did my peers, who were still follow-ing the routines they'd followed decades ago, lack imagination? Or was I one of these people who just couldn't follow through on anything? The two propositions, I concluded, weren't mutually exclusive.

After a day or two, I ended up where I should have gone immediate-ly. I allowed myself to visualize my presence at a major investment con-ference, speaking on a timely topic. And as I did so, I asked myself what emotion that evoked. Giving the actual speech left me with a good feel-ing; I always enjoyed communicating my views and offering perspectives the audience may not have considered. Envisaging the interviews that usually followed left me less buoyant; there were few journalists, radio or TV hosts I respected. But when I contemplated the intense logistical demands that came with the public profile I once had, I felt alienated.

I knew I'd made the right choices.

How fleeting, almost surreal, many of the images from my past are—like one of those midnight displays of Northern Lights I occasionally get to witness at the cottage: blurry-edged, dreamlike constructs moving across the horizon, to be remembered forever, but always with a dose of doubt whether they were real or imagined.

They come out of nowhere, gain definition, then leave me in a trance-like state of fascination, where for a few seconds or minutes, I'm in the past, its smells and feels undeniably real.

One of the grandkids tip-toes up to our bed at dawn, lifts the sheets and climbs in, before wordlessly snuggling up against our bodies and falling asleep again. Or I find myself standing next to Papi in our Herisau kitchen. Everything is in glossy detail: the light-blue cabinetry, the black-and-white speckled Formica counter with the toaster oven and the portable transistor radio on top, and the tiny gas range next to it. Before heading off to work, my father says a few kind words to me and I smell his aftershave and the coffee on his breath.

Not all my reveries involve people. Sometimes I have glimpses of our Colorado courtyard, tall mint-coloured grasses interspersed with purple columbines and yellow cone flowers swaying in the snappy mountain breeze, the trumpet vine carrying a hundred orange blossoms threatening to break loose from the solid wooden post its trunk is attached to. I hear the chirping of robins and the soothing murmur of the fountain, except when an occasional blast of wind drowns them out for a second or two.

And then the phone rings. It's my long-time assistant Christine Morgan who wants to ask me a question, and as I listen my day-dream dissolves in swirls of implausibility.

THE IMAGES OF the grandchildren are ever present. I don't have to let my mind wander, don't need to be relaxed to summon them. They are there all the time, hundreds of them, like tiles on a mosaic floor I stand on. I can see them all at once or choose to focus on one or the other.

It's early morning at the cottage, all three of them are sitting on the floor, mesmerized by the fire I've lit to warm them up. Abigail is petting a black-and-white speckled hen at Sustainable Settings, the Aspen Valley farm we visit whenever the kids are here, her hand tentative before she boldly reaches past the bird's crown and strokes its long neck. Someone's knotted her light brown hair into pigtails.

Another image: Abby on my lap, giving me directions on what colour or shade I should apply to the wooden duck we're painting. Dozens of other memories of being close and doing things together crowd in. Cameron is pulling my mustache and I give a little squeak, with my mouth closed, convincing him a mouse lives in my facial hair. He's fascinated and wants to do it again and again. Alexandra, wearing a Disneyesque princess costume wants me to come trick-or-treating with her, and there she is again, underneath Caroline on the yoga mat, the two of them in a Downward Dog pose.

Other tiles in my favourite mosaic depict us swimming, skiing and even horse-back riding together, each of the grandchildren wearing a helmet. A soundtrack comes along with the movie of our steep ascent toward the meadow just below West Maroon Pass where we'll be overnighting. I hear the kids talk to their new companions, addressing them by name: Abby's and Alex's mares are Butterscotch and Jake, Cameron talks to Mouse. And late in the day, all of us are calling Cameron's name. He's missing from the tent he and his cousins shared. Alexandra reports that he's gone to the close-by creek, looking for something. We're terrified: it's getting dark, and it's June, which means the water flow in the creek is at its highest, carrying a torrent of ice-cold water along its rocky bed. When we find Cameron searching the banks of the stream for an ideal entry point, he explains that Mister Wade, our guide, told him that prospectors used to come up here to look for gold. He was hoping to find some.

HOW RICH MY life now is, in ways I never could have expected or even imagined. My days aren't free of challenge or the occasional disappointment, but it's easy to escape negative emotions. All I have to do is invoke the effortless smiles of my grandchildren and joy surges through me. □

Caroline, editing my first novel.

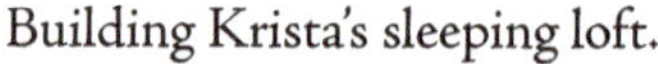

Building Krista's sleeping loft.

Theophane the Monk.

Melissa's wedding.

Alexandra observing.

Krista's Wedding Day.

Skiing with Caroline.

Caroline, helping with
Cameron's birth.

Krista.

Melissa and her girls.

On Georgian Bay, with Christian.

One last memory: Cameron with Mummy Krista.

Walking the beach
with Cameron.

With Nick and Cameron
in Colorado.

Family time in Zurich.

Precious moments: Papa, Cameron and Alexandra.

Precious moments:
Alexandra.

Precious moments:
"Papa Claus" and
Abigail.

Precious moments: the mouse in the moustache.

Gratitude

*A*t *dinner a few weeks ago, I told Caroline that I was struggling. Not with life, not with my health or tempestuous financial markets, but with this memoir. How was I going to tackle the challenge of dealing with the past decade or so, a period when everything in my life seemed uncharacteristically calm and predictable?*

It's not that there is nothing to report. On the contrary, the intensity of what I've experienced could easily make for another lengthy volume, the bulk of which would probably deal with moments shared with family and friends. There are trips to be reported on, as well as cherished recollections from carefree days at the cottage or in Colorado, and the occasional adventure. Finding my way through chaotic traffic to a parking garage in Venice, dependent solely on a GPS app on my mobile phone, would qualify as an adventure of sorts. Miraculously, I made it and was there for Caroline as she arrived from a different part of Italy. Taking Cameron to the CN Tower and walking the world's highest ledge was a few notches up on the adventure scale. The experience of our bodies suspended backward over 356 meters of nothing, the only support our toehold and a harness, might fill several suspense-packed pages.

The question on my mind, I explained to Caroline, was whether I should stay true to the terms I had set forth when starting this project. If I felt it hadn't profoundly affected me and influenced the course of my life, I'd leave it aside.

Caroline offered me much-needed perspective. Perhaps, she suggested, my perception that there is more tranquility in my life is due to my having achieved a more balanced existence. To her, I look as busy as always, but the tasks and events that fill my day seem to be more agreeable than they once were.

I've been thinking about that. For a few years now, most of my days have followed a fairly disjointed course. I arrive at my desk with an agenda of must-do tasks and boldly project they will take no more than two or three hours. The intention is to spend the rest of the day doing what I like best: reading, contemplating, writing and engaging in some outdoor activity. But that rarely happens. By early afternoon I'm still caught up in the morning work, slightly bewildered by the lack of progress but far from frustrated. On my way home I often think about how life routinely interferes with my plans.

Some days there are hard reasons. A long-retired client wants to discuss a readjustment of his financial affairs. Or a friend phones; after exchanging uplifting or even exciting news, we end up discussing the sad state of the world or our respective ailments in too much detail. Then there are the 'keeping-up-with-technology' days. Microsoft releases a new office suite update, which interferes with my Apple operating system, and hours are spent trying potential fixes.

Sometimes, the unforeseen can be wildly agreeable. One of the grandchildren drops by the office, suggesting that I listen to an exciting new track of Hip-Hop or Rap, after which I insist on playing a blues track by Lightnin' Hopkins or a rock classic, ideally by Pink Floyd or CCR, for them. Amazingly, they put up with my outlandish attempts to musically re-educate them and an hour or more goes by.

Caroline is right. Reinventing myself has made for a far more tolerable life.

ANOTHER COMMENT CAROLINE *made is that I should think not only about the world around me, but also what's going on inside me. After all, isn't that what defines me and what influences the course of my life? It's hard to disagree with that.*

I reflect on how complicated life is, and yet how simple. The simple part is that everything comes and everything goes. It's taken seven decades to realize, mourn, and eventually accept the inevitability of this. Everything arises and falls back, grows and recedes—like the cycle of the moon, the pattern of the surf, the snow crystal born of the cold and melted by the rays of the sun. The rhythm of life.

I think of tasks that seemed insurmountable when assigned, but were accomplished a short time later. Marks at school and insignia on the lapels and epaulettes of my uniforms and, later, a flurry of ever more impressive titles on business cards, once the focus of all ambition, now gathering dust in the museum of my past. The careers I made for myself, the identities I created—whole histories of human interplay and logistical challenge, and all brought to an end seemingly long ago when the only relevant question arose: who are you, Peter?

The loves and friendships of a lifetime march through my mind like soldiers in a parade, and again I take note of how many have come and gone. And then, most painful, I listen to the laughter of the loved ones I've lost—once clear as crystal bells, now no more than a memory, the accuracy of which is questionable.

There are times when I wonder if they've hardened me, these many years of living, like fire hardens metal into steel. No, I conclude, they haven't. If anything, I'm softer now. In my youth I would have sacrificed myself to change the world, and boldly slain those I considered evil, or so I think. Now I know too much. In the middle of my life I had convictions; now I'm no longer sure of what is true. Come to think of it, that's what I've learned: there is no truth, and that knowledge is sometimes difficult to bear.

I once had plans for myself, the earth mine to conquer and shape, and the future my unmistakable ally. Now I'm interested in finding calm in the moment. I've tried to understand the past and given up, and my aspirations for what is yet to come are dulled.

It's not that I'm disinterested in the future, but my relationship with it has changed. I now realize that my projection of what may lie ahead is merely part of the narrative I've created for myself. Like in a mathematical algorithm, the input information makes for minute changes in the outcome. As I experience each day, my storyline changes—imperceptibly during the course of a week, but from year to year enough to be noticed. It took me a while to appreciate this mesmerizing dance, and a lot longer to accept that ultimately, it is without relevance. The future, no more than an illusion, will not be dictated by any story I come up with, or the adjustments I make to it.

CURIOUSLY, SUCH MUSINGS and the insights they bring aren't leaving me tired. I find they calm and often reinvigorate me. Instead of vigilantly watching everything that goes on around me and reacting to it, I seem to contemplate at a more unrushed pace, inviting different perspectives to what I see. Perhaps that's the reason why the past few years seem so deeply satisfying.

Whenever we agree to build something, I quietly withdraw and let Caroline do the job. The reason is that I can't handle being caught up in a construction project. To me, it is an erratic and annoying process with far too many moving parts. I'm also uniquely inept at visualizing. Caroline can look at an architectural drawing and see the completed structure, inside and out. It's a skill I totally lack. And, finally, I've learned that the management techniques I'm accustomed to don't work with contractors. In my business, when being pitched on a project or delegating one, I invite time and budgetary projections, then generously adjust both to safeguard against unexpected problems, but insist that the revised targets be met. With contractors that doesn't seem to work.

I've had a glorious summer in Colorado, spending a major part of each day playing tennis, hiking, and tending to our spectacular garden. I'm stunned by the variety of produce our few berry bushes and small vegetable patch have produced—carrots that are white, mauve and even black; green and pale yellow beans, some adorned with purple and grey patterns; plump, juicy heritage tomatoes; raspberries and currants of a sweetness that reminds me of my childhood days in my grandparents' garden.

Caroline, meanwhile, has shuttled back and forth between city and cottage, sometimes staying over at our neighbours' cottage, at other times at a motel in Parry Sound. Like she did in Colorado a few years ago, she's spending a lot of time on the construction site, watching the new buildings take shape, making slight adjustments to where windows are placed, adding a door, or adjusting the length of the kitchen counter. As she did in Snowmass, she's picked the perfect builder. Both she and Marshall enjoy viewing their project as a work in progress that will only benefit from ongoing adjustments.

NOW THAT IT's mid-October and I'm back, I finally get to see what they've accomplished. The layout is practical and deeply pleasing; my fears that a much larger main building would inevitably lose in character were misplaced. The massive, raw hemlock beams holding up the roof, the simplicity of the layout, the way the large sliding glass doors and windows draw in the natural beauty around us, leave me awed. With Marshall's help, Caroline has managed the impossible.

Yet, regarding my belief that construction projects are inherently unpredictable, I feel vindicated. Several months ago, on his first visit to the site, the building inspector decided to halt the project. Even though the township had approved our plan, he ruled that the main cottage would exceed allowable height limits. In a series of phone conversations, Caroline and I weighed our options. We could take the issue to court, which would cost a lot of money and keep everything on hold, without knowing what the eventual outcome would be. Or we could completely redesign the cottage and seriously delay the building process. In the end, we chose a third alternative: we'd slightly lower the structure into the ground, which called for the foundation to be altered and the property around the cottage to be regraded. The extra work would blow our budget and meant that we'd lose not only the current cottage season, but also half of next year's.

When we made our decision, neither of those consequences overly worried me, but now that I'm on the property I'm deeply troubled. On the one hand, even though our new cottage is far from finished, I can recognize the beauty of what will, sometime next summer, be reality. What torments my mind is the terrain surrounding both cottage and guest cabin. Where there was dense vegetation, there is now an expanse of sandy dirt that resembles a moonscape. Marshall is confident that additional regrading, the construction of pathways and some planting will result in perfection, and he knows just the right people who can get us there. I'm too disoriented to embrace his vision. Caroline urges me to keep an open mind and let the experts do their job, but I can tell she's concerned too.

When Stephanie lived in Toronto, the walls in her apartment were like a continuously evolving exhibition. As she became an accomplished printmaker and eventually one of Canada's best known artists, her large, bold collages, laden with codes and metaphors, not only afforded a preview to the next show at the museum, but created an ambiance of dreamlike wonderment in which, for an hour or two, everything seemed possible.

Lately, Stephanie has been shuttling back forth between Toronto and Maine, where she's settled down with her husband Jim Weaver. She started work on the 'Boat of Eternal Return', her latest creation, in 1998. Now, in 2012, it's nearing completion. It's thirty feet long and the cello head at its stern stands nine feet high. There are many components to the boat, including hand-worked glass bones, an antique ruler and the pelvis of a mare, but among its most distinguishing features are thirteen pairs of moose ribs.

Long ago, Stephanie told us how she came upon them—in the necropolis of a wilderness park, as she put it. Later we got to look at the bones and feel them. They were clean, the decomposing flesh that had still clung to them when they were found, long gone. Over time, we saw other elements that would eventually contribute to the boat, in a garage friends let her use. What comes to mind first is the five-foot long rectangular black frame containing the score to Mozart's Requiem, Stephanie called it the bier—the enclosure holding a coffin on its way to cremation or burial. The bier exuded somberness, perhaps even more so after we learned that the Mozart score rested on a layer of DNA sequencing gel that Stephanie had been given by a friendly scientist.

Caroline and I looked at each new part to the creation, fascinated by the insights we were offered, but wondering whether the actual Boat of Eternal Return would ever be completed and seen by an audience.

TWO HOURS AGO I fell off a step ladder and landed on my knee. Now, aching and limping, I'm walking up to the steps that lead into the Peel Art Museum, Caroline helping me along. A large crowd has gathered for Stephanie's official opening. On the way in, we meet mutual friends—writers and artists, mostly—and once we approach the main exhibition hall, I recognize members of Steph's family, most of whom I haven't seen for decades.

It's not the first time Stephanie's art has been shown in a museum. Her collage *Solar Boat* adorns one of Toronto's museums; another, *Galileo's Eyelid*, ended up in Zurich. For years now, she's refused to sell any of her major pieces to private collectors. But as spectacular and stirring as those earlier works are, this is different. The scope of the exhibit and the strength of its expression are extraordinary.

As we enter, I notice how hushed the conversations among the guests are. Perhaps the music, an array of timeless chants and cello laments, is responsible. Along the walls are large panels that

Stephanie has described, but we haven't yet seen. They provide perspective to what inspired the artist and supply keys to understanding what she wants to communicate. In the middle, on a masterfully crafted platform, floats the boat. It is intimidating, magnificent in both its grace and power.

The curator says a few words and introduces me. I talk about the Rayner family first, Stephanie's father, Gordon Rayner—he who held court in his stone castle at the edge of the woods, which he built all by himself, overlooking that deep primeval, meteoric pond. How Gord, when not holding court, retreated into his tower, complete with curved staircase, and painted, painted, painted, one spectacular canvas after another. Kathy was there, too, and between Steph and her sister, there was always a flood of tales of the dark woods and of scary moments at the pond, stories of encounters with the otherworldly matched by accounts of star gazing and exploring nature. I touched on Gordon Rayner junior, too, "Snoon" as we called him, who veered off on his own, in every sense of the word, but most importantly, in terms of his art, which could not have been more different than his father's.

When I first knew Steph, I explain, she was struggling, trying to find out how she wanted to express herself. She knew she wanted to be an artist, of course. But imagine: with that kind of competition from within your family, how do you find the confidence to do so? And even if you succeed, how can you distinguish yourself from those who've already established themselves? Encouragement from the masters might have helped, but her dad could not imagine his daughter, a woman, matching his skills, a view that was fairly common in the small circle of North America's top illustrators he had graduated from. These were the realities for Stephanie, and probably for most female artists at that time.

When I touch on what the boat has come to mean to me I know

that no words can do justice to the creation before us. "I am in a twilight zone," I say, "its serenity quieting and its undeniable energy keeping me attentive and focused. I'm left to rest and observe, rest and observe. And that, I believe, is what we are meant to do, because the Boat of Eternal Return transcends what to us humans is known and knowable, and what is forever beyond our grasp."

STEPHANIE AND JIM are living in Maine. Not long ago, after we spent the fall preparing for the upcoming cottage construction, they invited Caroline and me to visit. Their house, set among rolling hills and forests, but only a short drive from the ocean, offered us much-needed tranquility. On a cloudless November day, our friends treated us to a railway trip to historic Rockland, where we visited the Farnsworth Art Museum and admired the work of another distinguished family of artists, the Wyeths.

On the way back we dropped by at Richard and Noriko Moore's country place in Connecticut. More rest, more invigorating conversation with friends.

The barge is here. It's the length of two eighteen-wheelers. How it could have navigated between the shoals and banks in our island archipelago is a mystery. The driver effortlessly lowers the wide metal bridge onto our sand beach and the unloading begins.

Kirby Hall, who's taken on the regrading of our property, supervises. Before long, loaders and backhoes bring a couple of hundred massive granite plates onto shore, then head uphill to the flat area behind the cottage. That's where Marshall's crew put the tons of sand from the excavation last year. Gradually, the major part of the twenty-foot high mountain disappears from our property and is recreated on the vast deck of the barge.

All along, Caroline and I talk to Karl, the man who'll be on our site for weeks to come. He explains how he'll build an entrance to our basement, where the granite pathways will be, where culverts will allow rainwater to escape. I find it hard to imagine what he describes; to me, the area around our new buildings is still a disaster zone. Caroline, in contrast, asks intelligent questions and offers suggestions.

Inside, meanwhile, Marshall and his helpers pick up where they left off last fall. With the framing complete, the attention is shifting to installing floors and walls, electrical lines and plumbing, building a fireplace and installing appliances. It's late April and the cottage will be finished by summer. When in summer we don't know; it depends on the weather.

Caroline has asked for the guest cabin to be finished first, so that we can stay there and keep an eye on things as the project nears completion. I look at the construction equipment and imagine the noise, not sure whether I'll want to be around.

A FEW WEEKS into the process, I can finally see the potential. Bit by bit, Karl converts what I've come to call a moonscape into an area of unpretentious beauty. Skillfully placing granite steps and pathways around the cottage, with just the right balance between precision and randomness, he manages to create the illusion that what emerges has always been there. My deep-seated fear that the simplicity and serenity I had always found at the old cottage would be lost forever, is finally receding.

Marshall and his helpers are accomplishing the same inside. Like she did in Colorado, Caroline has managed to find stunning antique cabinets, cupboards, shelves and counters, which are now effortlessly integrated into a functional, contemporary design.

By early July, appliances are being installed and walls painted. Outside, shrubs and native flowers are being planted. Karl is busy building a nature path that loops through the forest. He came up with the idea when he learned that the bargers were going to charge us to take the sand away. "Why not keep a couple of tons and use it here?" he suggested. I was intrigued but felt we'd taken down too many trees already. How could we build a path through the forest without losing more?

Karl came up with the solution. Together we entered the dense woods behind the cottage, carrying a tape measure and construction tape. We knew roughly where we wanted the path to go, but we thought we'd let nature decide its exact course. It would go in whatever direction the seven foot wide backhoe could be moved without destroying anything. We were both stunned by the outcome. We ended up with an uphill-downhill, nearly kilometer long loop taking us first through densely populated oak, maple and pine forest, then along the shoreline back to the cottage.

CAROLINE AND I are both living in the completed guest cabin. Roman, following in his brother's footsteps and spending time in North America, sleeps on the floor in the one finished room in the main cottage. He reports that his nights aren't peaceful ones. The porch isn't screened in yet, and animals go in and out: mice, chipmunks and racoons scurry around. At breakfast the other day, Roman explains that he went outside to check on a series of loud noises and thought he saw a bear. We can tell he's terrified—in Switzerland, nature doesn't encroach the way it does in Canada's cottage country.

The terms of Roman's stay with us are different than the ones I hashed out with Lea a decade ago and replicated with Christian a few years back. The plan for both of his predecessors was that they'd work with me and accompany me wherever I went. More independent-minded and perhaps less interested in my financial work, Roman spent the winter with us, but checked into a student hotel and attended a three-month college course, after we returned to Toronto.

Now, for the final weeks of his stay, he's helping at the cottage. The tasks are demanding and unpleasant. As Marshall's crew gradually empties the large basement of appliances, tools and building materials that were stored there through winter, we turn to the possessions we kept from the old cottage, opening bins filled with tools and books and emptying plastic storage sheds containing deckchairs, beach toys, tarps, ropes and cables. Without exception, the containers are covered with mouse poop; behind them carcasses of mice and moles who'd been hiding there, cover the floor. Cleaning it all up is nauseating, ghastly work.

Occasionally, we take a break and explore the new nature path, where we encounter other manifestations of nature—the summer of 2012 marks the worst bug season I can remember. While the mosquitoes and swarms of deer flies leave me mostly alone, something I ascribe to my daily helping of B-vitamins, they relentlessly assault Roman. After a few days we decide on a new routine: we work morning and afternoon, and in between hop on the boat, motor out onto the bay, where we anchor and have lunch. Roman likes that.

Even so, I'll have to find a way to reward him for his sacrifices and I think I know the way. I'll let him stay at our Toronto loft for a week or two and organize a roof-top party for his student friends before his return to Switzerland.

AS THE LAST July weekend nears, we're getting ready for the arrival of Melissa, John and the grandchildren. A couple of days before our official opening date, scaffolding still reaches to the living room ceiling, but it's now being used by the cleaning crew. Painters and carpenters still deal with last-minute touch-ups and fixes, while other cleaners mop up behind them.

When the family gets to explore the new place, it becomes clear that expectations are vastly surpassed. We now have a get-away that will sustain our need for quiet and togetherness for many years, perhaps generations. Everyone is overcome with gratitude for what Caroline has created.

We've never been at the cottage together for more than a few days, but under sunny skies we end up staying for two weeks. The children love their new rooms and play at the beach, but nothing excites them more than the new nature path. At our outdoor art station they paint signs, which they later place in the woods: Abigail's reads "Acorn Alley", Cameron's "The Lorax Path", and Alexandra's, which turns out to be prophetic, says "Beware of Snakes and Poison Ivies." We encounter more rattlers than we've seen in years, and soon after the family leaves our bichon pup Hansli decides to explore a patch of noxious weeds. Caroline, who hoses him down, ends up nursing two badly infected arms.

THE FIRST LEAVES are turning colour when Marshall has a surprise for us. One of the architectural publications wants to profile our cottage. We invite the magazine's photographer and its senior staff writer and spend most of the day with them, but have no idea what to expect.

It's spring again when we pick up a copy of *Our Homes* and see our place on its cover. Inside is an eight-page spread; the photography is exceptional and the story of how our new cottage came to be is masterfully told. Not only has Caroline managed the impossible, almost on budget and almost on time, but now there is a record of it all.

Marshall will benefit too. Within a few years, he'll become the go-to builder for quality projects in our area.

Hansli, almost eleven, is not just a close friend, he's long become an integral part of our family and our lives. He picks up on our emotions and readily shares his. If Caroline and I have an argument, he sulks; when a thunderstorm passes he communicates his distress, whimpering and shivering until we cradle him in our arms. We communicate telepathically. We are each other's pack.

We were on our way to the kids' house when we first saw him, a third of the size of the other two dogs. As we drove up Bayview Avenue, there was Melissa with Marley, her three-year old white doodle and Guinness, the reddish girl doodle she'd just adopted. And tagging a little behind was the sad little thing Abigail was to name soon after. "I wonder what Melissa is doing with a third dog," Caroline said. "John won't be happy about that."

What we soon learned was that Melissa had taken her doodles for a walk in Sherwood Park, where she came across a group of people huddling around an abandoned puppy, stripped of his tag, tied to tree. It was a cold mid-November day. There was debate among the concerned bystanders as to what should be done. Melissa took charge, volunteering to take the distressed creature home.

Now, sitting in the living room and taking turns petting and holding the trembling pup, we debated what exactly should be done. Predictably, John announced that he wouldn't have yet another animal in the house. I wasn't sure whether he was posturing or whether he meant it, but one of the girls took the cue and suggested that Nana and Papa should adopt him. That prompted me to state that the last thing we needed was a dog. With all our travelling it seemed a ludicrous and utterly unfair proposition. We decided to call the Toronto Humane Society and get some guidance. Their response was sensible: there was a shortage of shelter space and if we could keep the puppy for a few days it would greatly help them. In the meantime, they suggested, we should visit a veterinarian and make sure he got examined and vaccinated.

While we adults debated the logistics of doing that, the girls focused on other practicalities. Abigail insisted we give the puppy a name, suggesting it be Hansli, after a toy dog my sister Flavia had given her during our recent trip to Switzerland. Hansli, she knew, was Swiss for "Little Hans"; it seemed a perfect choice. Alexandra's mind, meanwhile, was on the design of the Lost notices that we needed to post in the park and the neighbourhood.

MOST OF THE *people who first see Hansli comment on his expressive eyes; many have called them soulful. I thought of them as sensitive and trusting, especially during those first days. Still, I'd find myself repeating to Caroline that we couldn't shoulder the responsibility, and that I'd only agree to have him in our lives if she committed to being the primary caregiver. I'm not sure what made me think of that term, but it came naturally. And while I recited the complications that would arise if we adopted Hansli, he parked himself at my feet and looked up at me imploringly. "I trust you; please let me live with you", his oversized black eyes seemed to plead.*

Not much later, I felt compelled to make rules for his and our family's behaviour. Deeply concerned that Melissa, John and the girls would allow him to jump on top of couches and easy chairs, as was the custom with their dogs, I had a sign made, advising against any such indulgences.

Over time, I became Hansli's greatest enabler. Halfway through the night, when he got tired of sleeping in his doggie bed and crouched to the side of ours, I invited him up. Before long, he started joining us without an invitation, confidently hopping up whenever he felt the need of our company.

John keeps saying he wants to make his next earthly appearance as a dog. He'll tie himself up in Sherwood Park, so he can spend winters in Colorado and summers at the cottage—and always have a spot on a king-sized bed available to him.

IN A SHORT-STORY *she wrote, Caroline recalls her reaction to the idea of adopting Hansli. "The last thing I needed, or so I thought, was a dog. At least not yet. I'd occasionally mulled over the characteristics I would desire in a dog, if or when I ever got one. I was quite clear on my requirements. It had to be non-shedding, small enough to take on board a plane, but big enough to enjoy hikes in the mountains with. It had to be intelligent, loyal and loving, as well. It seems the universe heard the part about dog and characteristics, but not about the if or when."*

Caroline talks about the blanket of grief she was wrapped in after Krista died and how Hansli, in his knowing way, slowly chipped away the shell in which she had encased her heart. He taught her to be open to the possibility of love, even though it can really hurt at times. He showed her how to play and laugh and see the world through his eyes. "I had the idea that a dog was the last thing I needed, when actually it was exactly what I needed."

HANSLI IS BOLD *and assertive. At the cottage, he's been known to chase mature stags; in Colorado, we have to watch out for coyotes and bears. So far he's been lucky. Animals that could easily kill him with a kick or a swipe of the paw—or in the case of coyotes, lure him to their pack and devour him—have routinely run away when charged by this ferociously barking white creature they can't make sense of.*

But Hansli's favourite prey are small creatures: squirrels, chipmunks and other rodents. In seafaring days, bichons were a sailor's best friend;

they made for great company and were skilled ratters. Not that our pooch is a bichon—Caroline and I have come to call him a bichon mutt. A DNA test we commissioned categorized him as 50% Bichon Frise, 25% Shih Tzu, with the rest made up of another few breeds, including Irish Wolfhound. Maybe that's where the notion that he can prevail against a moose or a bear comes from.

Yet, when a storm passes, the Wolfhound is conspicuously absent. Long before the first distant drumrolls of thunder reach our human ears, Hansli comes begging for shelter, whimpering and his eyes desperately pleading. We take him on our laps then, or lie on sofa or bed with him, holding him tightly and feeling the tremors that rack his traumatized body.

It wasn't always like that. I think he was three when Caroline and I stood on our cottage porch watching a serious storm pass. Hansli sat on the ground, content to be near us but by no means panicked. Then lighting struck, no more than 150 meters from us, cutting a massive jack pine into two. The crack was deafening and deeply unnerving. Within seconds an acrid smell reached us and bluish-yellow flames shot up around what was left of the trunk, but long before then Hansli had jumped up on me, somehow managing to claw at my five foot-high shoulders, crying and torn by violent shivers that racked his small body for the better part of an hour.

A COUPLE OF *years ago we nearly lost our companion. After spending some time with Abigail, I drove her home. Caroline was in Colorado, Abby's parents and sister away. I parked the car and opened the back door as I always do, knowing that Hansli would jump out and bolt across the lawn and down the driveway to the side door of the house, confident that we'd follow and let him in, so he could visit with his cousins Marley and Guinness.*

As Abby opened the door, Hansli looked back to check if I was com-ing along, and that's when he saw a chipmunk on the other side of the road. What followed in the next second or two was traumatic. We saw him dash between parked cars and managed to shout "Hansli" and "No", before we heard the screech of a car brake and a loud thump. It was a sound that haunted me for days afterwards and made me wonder how Abby could deal with the memory.

Whimpering, Hansli managed to limp back across the sidewalk and onto the lawn, where we caught up with him. When I lifted him up, I thought we'd lose him. His belly was split open and his spine seemed twisted. There was no time to lose.

I briefly talked to the young driver of the Toyota who'd hit him, giv-ing him my phone number. He was as distraught as we were. And then, we hurriedly walked to the animal clinic, trying to make the two-block journey as gentle as possible. When we got there it was ten minutes to closing time.

After stitching up Hansli's abdomen, Ruth Weintrop, the very vet-erinarian that had looked after him since he first came to us, gave us the diagnosis. Miraculously, there were no broken bones and his belly rupture would heal. However, given the severity of the impact, which had split the vehicle's fiberglass mud guard, internal bleeding was more than likely. The best course, Dr. Weintrob recommended, would be to take Hansli to an animal hospital where he'd be under close supervision throughout the night. The only negative, she explained, was that they would not allow me to be with him. I took one look at our friend and decided not to go that route. To him, I knew, the most important thing was to be with me, to be held by me.

Late at night, at our condominium, Ruth unexpectedly called, asking if she could come by to check on Hansli. When she dropped in and saw him lap up bits of water from the bowl I held up to him, she felt I'd made the right decision.

HANSLI HAS MADE *a full recovery. For a few months, his spine was out of alignment, but in time some chiropractic treatments took care of that. There are no indications that he's learned to look around before going after a squirrel or a chipmunk, which leads me to believe that he's long forgotten. Abby and I, on the other hand, will never be able to purge the sound and visual memories of that fateful November afternoon.*

We were supposed to be in Morocco two years ago, but a series of terrorist attacks on foreigners convinced us to delay the trip. Instead, we opted for a three-week road trip to France, which took us to Provence, the Luberon and the Drôme regions. The latter was our favourite; we mingled with potters and artisans living in the area, hiked through lavender fields, and enjoyed exceptional meals and local wines, often perched at the edge of dramatic gorges. Our base was Le Poët-Laval, a small town devoid of cars and even streets. The hotel we stayed at, Les Hospitaliers, was integrated into a 12th century castle built by the Knights of the Order of St. John of Jerusalem.

Now we're visitors to a different kind of castle, the Kasbah, which towers above the Berber village of Imlil, high up in the Atlas mountains. Last night, I wondered whether our plan for today's seven-hour trek that would take us toward North Africa's highest peak, Toupkal, was realizable. My knee has been badly swollen ever since we arrived in Morocco, my torn rotator cuff has kept me awake most nights, and on top of it I have a stubborn chest cold that's been with me since we left Canada. Caroline has been joking that she's now indisputably the strong one. Yet, once we started our steep uphill hike, I started to feel better than I had in weeks.

The trek was tough, taking us from 1,800 to 3,200 meters, but the scenery was stunning and the cultural insights we gained made for one of our most memorable mountaineering experiences. Few people visit the Atlas Mountains at this time of the year. Luckily, it's been an exceptionally dry November, or there would have been solid snow cover. As it was, we had to traverse only the odd ice patch or snowbank and hiked mostly on dry scree or rock. At our destination, Toupkal's peak still towering above us and inaccessible to any but the most experienced technical climbers, our guide Abdul conjured up a surprisingly civilized late lunch. We could feel the intense African sun on our faces, but despite our many layers of clothing we soon started to shiver.

On our hike down we got to know Abdul, and with him the mindset of the North African Muslim male, a lot better. Abdul has a sweet disposition and is considerate, but has none of the traits of subservience that tour guides in Rome or Jerusalem might display. Like the sardars and their sherpas in the Himalayas, he has the imprint of the ruggedness of his native mountain terrain. He's not shy, but seems reluctant to open up.

Still, when Caroline asked him during our descent whether he was married, her inquiry triggered an enthusiastic response. He described how fortunate he'd been. Not only had he been able to observe the virtues of his neighbour's teenage daughter, but her father had given him permission to marry her. She'd proved to be an obedient and industrious wife, unlike most of the other women, who were known to be scheming and meddlesome. As we descended from the barren mountain scape to the lushness of the valley, Abdul talked about the mosque and his Imam, whose teachings he fervently observed. We realized that the Imam must have a very limited and warped understanding of almost anything.

We ended up in a village below Imlil and our Kasbah. A quick hike back up, and the simple comforts of our room were ours again. The night would be bitter-cold, but after our strenuous workout a warm shower in the communal bathroom and a solid meal seemed outrageously luxurious.

BEFORE HEADING TO the mountains we spent a week in Marrakech's Medina, the centuries-old walled town that is accessible only through several ancient portals.

When we first got out of the car that had taken us here from the airport, we felt bewildered. We'd booked a luxury suite in a well-reviewed *riad*, and here we were wheeling our suitcases around muddy puddles and dodging bits of animal droppings. The city's bustling car traffic had been left behind, but the labyrinthian array of crowded dirt alleys that faced us was shared by pedestrians, mopeds, bicycles, dogs and donkeys. Luckily, it was only a few hundred feet to the non-descript wooden door the driver guided us to. We'd never have recognized it as the entrance to a hotel or guesthouse, but he was certain we were at the right place.

The sensation of stepping across the threshold to our riad was momentous—on one side a sordid, noisy and polluted alley, on the other a quiet, mysterious, candle-lit hallway. As we stepped into the light at its end, we faced a stunningly serene courtyard in which lush trees hosting flocks of songbirds were reaching for the open sky. To the side of the courtyard were sitting alcoves, some with rough, whitewashed walls, others tiled or adorned with mosaic, filigreed plaster or meticulously carved wood.

When we ascended a steep, colourfully tiled staircase we arrived at our accommodation. We'd booked a suite, but what we got was an array of rooms worthy of a sultan and his retinue. Through the windows and from the balconied walkway that led us here, we could see down into the courtyards or up to the wide-open, clear African sky.

After settling in, we explored the rooftop, where we could hear the voices of two competing muezzins, each calling to prayer.

THINGS GOT A bit more difficult when we ventured out into the Medina, which we did for several hours each day. Apart from dodging the bicycles and mopeds and breathing polluted air, there was the challenge of fending off overanxious guides and bazaar merchants. To me, the contemporary bazaar culture seemed strikingly different from 40 years ago, when I last toured North Africa and the Middle East. There was only foot traffic then, and the sellers made what they sold on their premises. Much of the merchandise here was from India and China and of low quality. Caroline managed to find a few things of exceptional beauty, but at prices higher than they would be in North America. In the end, we bought natural goods to bring home—spices, blocks of fragrances, and oil and other products from the argan tree.

We found the Moroccans a gentle lot. The merchants did their best to make a sale, but the kind of relentless hustling that is typical in much of North Africa, the Middle East and Asia, was absent here. On the contrary, more than once we were invited to a friendly chat, after making it clear that we weren't buying anything. Moroccans also seem to be pleasantly unhurried: whether in the bazaar, in taxis or in a restaurant, everyone seemed to have time for us and each other.

Even so, the tensions between the old and the new, the effort to manoeuvre through the maze of alleys, and the strain to deal with hundreds of impulses and sensations we weren't used to, made it difficult to relax. Thank heaven for our palatial quarters. With its 8-foot long bathtub and our oversized bed and the seductive chants from the nearby minarets, it felt exactly like the place we needed to be to celebrate our 25th wedding anniversary—even if we were a year late.

WE SPENT SEVERAL days more with Abdul, mostly trekking deep into Berber country. The contradictions here were as evident as they had been in Marrakesh. We'd hike amidst dense juniper forests for a while, encountering flocks of goats grazing in the occasional clearings, and next, we'd struggle to circumvent the massive pile of garbage that frequently marked the entrance to a village. Abdul explained that the locals had always dumped their trash outside the walls, where it gradually deteriorated. Unfortunately, contemporary packaging materials didn't degrade.

Inside these settlements, the only people we ever saw were elders and small children. A few times we tried to take pictures, but as soon as the villagers saw a camera they covered their faces. Their reaction, we were told, was anchored in superstition and misinterpreted Islamic teaching.

Curiously, the Moroccans weren't hostile toward all technology. Most people over the age of ten had a cell phone. As we trekked, Abdul repeatedly made calls to friends and family, which at first we found surprising. Used to Colorado and Northern Ontario, where vast areas are without any cellular signal, we found it hard to comprehend the sophistication of the Moroccan phone system. Before long, our amazement gave way to annoyance.

By now, an elderly mule driver who seemed to follow us and whom Abdul seemed to know, was constantly yapping on his mobile as we struggled up a steep incline. When I hinted to Abdul that this interfered with the serenity of these remote areas, I was told that the mule driver was calling his sick mother because he was worried about her. Abdul added that he'd personally programmed the mule driver's phone, using symbols instead of names for speed-dialing, to make it easy for his illiterate companion to connect.

Fortunately, a couple of hours later, we once again found ourselves in an oasis of peace, inside a sheltered courtyard filled with vast rose gardens, pools and tasteful architecture replete with history. We came to the conclusion that the Morocco of yesterday was a less complicated and more peaceful place—as long as you belonged to the privileged class.

FINALLY, WE ARE headed to Morocco's Atlantic coast, a drive predicted to take four hours that ends up taking twice as long. En route we stop at Tin Mal, still in the High Atlas, where one of the world's oldest mosques stands. Built in 1156, it is manned by a charming 18 year old who opens up and shows us around. He says we are his first visitors in several days. The mosque has not been in operation for centuries, but its simple majesty inspires deep peacefulness and tranquility.

Soon the narrow mountain roads turn into highways and the temperature rises. Along the roadside we see goats high up in argan trees, looking for seeds. Apparently, the only way argan oil can be harvested is if the seedpod has been digested and expelled by a goat. We're convinced no one will believe us and take pictures of the robust animals balancing themselves on the sturdier branches.

When we get close to the city of Agadir and the coast, we are treated to a spectacular sunset, but shoddy mass developments of condominiums and townhouses spoil the experience. Apparently, we are looking at hundreds of unsold leftovers from the pre-2008 real estate boom. Abdul explains that the builders hope to sell these properties to Moroccans, now that the French and British are no longer interested.

We fear Essaouira, our final destination, will be like that too, but what we find is a very manageable mini-version of Marrakech. The Medina is traffic-free, uncrowded and clean, and our accommodation is palatial, but in a charmingly forsaken way. Outside our window we hear the ocean roar and when we look out, we can see the monumental waves crash against the seawalls.

Essaouira by day turns out to be even better than its night-time manifestation. Also known as Mogador, it was known to the Carthaginians as early as 500BC and continued to be regarded as the best anchorage on the Moroccan coast, attracting the Romans, the Portuguese, the Spaniards, French and British. Walking to the harbor we get the impression that little has changed in the past two or three hundred years. The fortifications are medieval, the boats on anchor are made of wood, and the fish sellers along the seawall display their merchandise the way they would have centuries ago.

Inside the Medina, we find that the bazaar is to our taste too. It's smaller than Marrakech's and the merchants are relaxed, even playful. On one of her excursions, Caroline finds an artisan community, where elder craftsmen teach the traditional ways. We return there together and finally find something of great beauty that we can bring home: superbly finished inlaid boxes that will make a repository for Melissa's jewelry and for our grandchildren's treasures.

We spend three days in Essaouira and vow that, if we are to revisit Morocco, we will make this our key destination.

I'm on my motorbike, the fire-engine red Honda CB750 I've been riding for close to ten years. Fall is my favourite season: the last tourists left on Labor Day, the leaves are changing colour, and the air is crisp.

At first daylight, a few hundred meters below our house, I nearly got rammed by a neighbour's car backing out of his driveway. Now, nearly an hour later, I feel calm again. The sun is rising, bathing the fields around me in soothing light.

I'm headed toward McClure Pass, knowing that the straight road ahead will soon turn curvy, then climb in a series of perfectly engineered switches. I also know that my mind will take me back to my army days. It's the hour of the day and the complete absence of traffic that do it. And the certainty that I can rev up my bike to any speed I desire and lean into each turn as deeply as the laws of physics allow. What magic!

Halfway up the pass I've submitted to a completely natural rhythm, entering the turns at about 45 kilometers, then speeding back up to about 85 on the straight portions. My breathing has joined the pattern—navigating each bend equates one leisurely inhale and exhale, the stretches in between allow for two breath cycles. Only when I ski can I lose myself in such harmony.

As I effortlessly glide out of one of the turns near the top and reaccelerate, I see a black line that stretches across the road. I scan the terrain above, wondering whether I'm looking at the shadow of a pole or a dead tree, but that's not it. And then I'm into my next breath, halfway through the straight part, still motoring along at brisk speed and now rapidly approaching the line. I gear down aggressively, cutting my speed to about 40, when I realize what lays ahead. It's a gap, about three feet wide spanning the road in a lazy zig-zag pattern. Worse, I'm too close to bring my bike to a stop. My brain shuts down and instinct, aided by skill and experience, takes over. I hit the brakes, but not too hard, slowing me down to about 20 and when I'm at the edge of the gap I pull my handlebars up and aggressively hit the gas. The result is that I jump across the chasm and miraculously land on the back wheel, before stabilizing myself and stopping. My breathing no longer follows any pattern. The last time I attempted anything similar was in the army, when I was twenty.

I lean the bike on its stand, take my helmet and gloves off and walk back to see. There is only one explanation: an earthquake must have created the crevasse I'm looking at, and it must have occurred minutes ago, or others would have been gathered around the site. I also see where my rear tire landed; a black rubber mark extends about six inches, starting at the very edge of the gap. If my leap had been a couple of inches shorter, I would have badly crashed, perhaps been trapped in the chasm, along with my bike.

As I contemplate what could have happened and consider my good fortune, I hear engine noise below me that, within a few seconds, grows in intensity. The rapidity of gear-shifts tells me that there are at least three motorcycles coming my way, and judging by the high pitch of the motors they're smaller bikes.

I take a few steps back, run toward the gap where I judge it to be least wide and easily land on the other side. Looking down the hillside to the road far below me I can now see that there are five riders headed my way, all on brightly coloured machines, travelling at high speed. I run a bit further downhill and position myself. Once the first bike comes around the nearest corner, I start desperately waving. Alarmed by my appearance, and perhaps that of my parked Honda in the distance, the first bike stops. The others slow down, look at me curiously, then start accelerating again. When they realize what's ahead there is a scramble. Two of them fall as they wrench their machines sideways to avoid the gap, but fortunately no one is seriously hurt.

We talk for a while, debating what should be done. All five are kids in their twenties; they all carry cell phones, but we're out of range. They decide to turn back, promising to frequently stop and try to phone the authorities.

I hop across the chasm once more and get on my bike, knowing that in less than an hour I'll be in Paonia, a town situated in a lush river valley where much of Colorado's fruit is grown. The peaches should be at their peak. I'll pick up a dozen or two, but not before stopping in at the local police station.

As I ride downhill, I find it hard to find my stride. The interval between switches and straights is the same as on the way up, but my smooth rhythm is gone. I'm too guarded, even afraid to lean into my turns. Not far from town, a traffic guard is standing next to a barrier, preventing vehicles from entering the road. We exchange a few words. I learn that tremors are quite common in the area and that a crew will soon be on the way. He also explains how I can get back to Snowmass, the long way.

In Paonia, I'm suddenly hungry. I buy coffee and a power bar, sit down on a bench, and reflect on the morning's two near-accidents. By the time I start looking for peaches, I've convinced myself that I need to sell my Honda. I'm sixty-five, after all. Motorbikes are for young people.

A MONTH LATER, I've found a willing buyer. Paul, a Canadian pharmacist who arrived in the Aspen Valley decades ago to become a ski instructor, is five years older than I am. He feels he'll ride for many years to come.

Considering that Caroline's mother and father were together for 65 years, Nellie coped with Mike's death quite well. She continued to occupy the spacious room at the old age home, mingled with other inmates, as we called them, and attended religious services. Emotionally and physically, there wasn't much to worry about.

More recently, we've noticed changes. Nellie is often confused and she's started to hoard muffins and bananas, which she's been hiding under her clothes. The muffins simply dried out, but the bananas turned into a mushy mess. When we left for Colorado at the beginning of winter, we were concerned.

When Melissa and her family visited us on March break, we learned that Nellie had lost a lot of weight. And a few days ago, back in Toronto, Melissa called Caroline, urging her to come back if she wanted to see her mother alive.

HAVING DROPPED CAROLINE off at the Aspen airport, I'm driving back to our house. It's late March; I marvel at the deep blue sky, wondering if the weather will be as favourable when I'll follow Caroline in a few days' time.

Minutes after I settle down in my office, the phone rings. It's Flavia, telling me that Mami was rushed to hospital. The diagnosis is grim. Apparently, her bowels have ruptured and the surgeon would like to have some guidance on whether he should operate. He can't get it from our mother, because she's unconscious. When Flavia asks me what my opinion is, I suggest that I call the hospital and get more details. That's when she tells me that she'd prefer it if I made the decision. I promise to call her back.

The surgeon is a model of professionalism and empathy. He explains that he can operate, but that the chances of success are low. Even if Mami survives the operation, it's unlikely that she'll live for more than a month or two. He'd feel better if he had some input from the family, but if I felt uncomfortable to make a decision, he'd understand that.

I ask him what his choice would be, but he dodges the question. One option, he says, is to make her passing as comfortable as possible. If he does that, Mami is likely to slip away in the next twenty-four hours. The alternative is to subject her to the trauma of a risky and lengthy operation, but we might be able to have her in our lives for a bit longer.

I think I know what Mami's choice would be and explain. He tells me it's how he'd choose if it were his mother. A few hours later I'm on a flight to Chicago; by evening, I'm on the plane to Zurich. "Hang in there, Mami," I keep repeating over and over. "I want to be with you when you go, and I'm on my way."

MY MOTHER'S DECLINE has been consistent, but her death has come unexpectedly. When Melissa and I met up in Switzerland two years ago, we felt she was doing well. Yes, Mami was close to blindness now, but we didn't feel she needed special attention and happily embarked on our cross-country journey.

Not long after our return home Mami had a serious fall, which convinced her that she could no longer live alone. How she handled the transition moved me deeply.

My childhood friend Urs, who'd been Papi's doctor and had caringly looked after my mother for many years now, had made some calls and secured a large south-facing room in Herisau's best home. Several of Mami's acquaintances were living there too.

When I arrived a few days after her mishap, her face badly bruised and her jaw fractured, she told me what should happen next. "Take what you want, except for a table and three chairs and two or three paintings, and sell the rest," she directed. "It's all I'll need from here on." Given that her two adjoining condominiums were filled with antique furniture, dozens of valuable paintings, etchings and oriental rugs, all of which she was deeply attached to, this adjustment to reality left me stunned.

I've visited my mother three times since her move and found her well-adjusted to her new circumstances. Her health, unfortunately, has steadily declined. The last time I saw her, confined to a wheelchair which Flavia and I pushed through lush late-summer gardens, she was in much pain.

AT THE ZURICH airport, I call my sister and learn that Mami has died while I was somewhere above the Atlantic Ocean. Flavia and the surgeon were with her when she briefly regained consciousness. When told about her ruptured bowel and the options available to her, she said, "Well, in that case I have to move on." They were her last words.

Inside the hospital chapel, I spend an hour with my mother. She looks at peace; sunbeams penetrate the stained glass windows, illuminating her face and bathing it in gentle shades of colour. I touch her cold hands, kiss her forehead, talk to her. How brave she was; what a good mother she'd been.

The days following Mami's death are taxing. Organizing a get-together for her friends and caregivers, disposing of her belongings, dealing with authorities—all to be completed within a few days. Still, after the first difficult days, I find two or three hours each day to go for walks, look at sights and visit places I once experienced with my mother, and converse with her.

WHEN I RETURN to Toronto, Nellie is still alive. She's been without food for more than two weeks and is hardly recognizable. Caroline, her brother Bob, and Melissa and John and their girls, have all been visiting daily. The doctor is in disbelief; the family is exhausted. A few more days go by before Nellie quietly slips away one early morning.

As life slowly returns to its normal pace, Caroline and I reflect on our journey. We've both gained an appreciation for the caregivers who looked after our mothers. We got to know them well and were awed by their ability to perform a difficult and often unpleasant job with grace and sensitivity.

There is something else we learned. Fellow residents, staff and even the doctors commented on the happiness our mothers had brought to them. Obviously, what others saw as unusually positive traits had been taken for granted, and were perhaps not even recognized, by us.

The initial part of my journey through the charitable universe was not unusual. Like most people, I learned by observing my parents.

Papi's way of giving back fit his temperament, his business and the general climate of post-war Europe. As a young dentist, he often came home with a crate of apples or a couple of hams —things he'd been given by farmers who couldn't pay their bills. More than once, I overheard Mami calling him a bad businessman, then quickly revising her complaint when she noticed we children were listening. Looking after the less fortunate, she then told us, was an imperative. Her style was to send twenty or thirty francs to the organizations she felt needed helped: the Franciscan monks, the blind, a bird sanctuary and a dozen or two other good causes.

I was more attracted to my father's style of giving—his spontaneous generosity inspired me. And like him, I struggled to make a living at first, but soon succeeded on a scale I could not have imagined. Within a few years of arriving in Canada, I earned what seemed to me enormous sums of money. Yet, when I started to support charities I followed Mami's example. I gave a small percentage of my income away, five percent at first. I knew little about the organizations I supported, nor was I in touch with them or understood how exactly my donations were used. What mattered was that, each year, I could write an ever greater number of cheques. It made me feel incredibly good. I thought I was making a difference.

Other dynamics kicked in. It was my mother's voice I frequently heard when I received a charity solicitation or became aware of some humanitarian crisis or social injustice. "Noblesse oblige," she used to say—privilege infers a responsibility to act with generosity and nobility toward those less fortunate. That I was privileged far beyond any expectations or hopes I may ever have harboured was clear.

Having been exposed to the monks at the monastery school, and more recently Brother Theophane, made me think of yet another rule: if you give of yourself you shall receive back ten-fold. It's a concept that always fascinated me.

I WAS AROUND *fifty when I met with Doctors Without Borders and started to understand the impact my annual donations had achieved. I wondered how other charities stacked up and was appalled to find that I'd supported some highly unworthy organizations. That, I understood, had not only channelled money to undeserving causes, but deprived the worthy ones of my support. I changed my approach.*

In 2011 I started a family foundation. Having seen numerous wealthy clients pass away and leaving money to charitable causes, I wondered whether I should do the same. I started reading about philanthropy and, more importantly, what constituted charity. For a decade or so, I'd given away ten percent of what I earned, but there was room for a lot more. Should I crank up the percentage now or copy what my clients did and leave a large bequest in my will?

That question led me to explore what the consequences of either approach would be. The key difference, I determined, was that giving money away now constituted a definable risk, while deferring the act of giving past my death didn't. I talked to a couple of my clients, who confirmed this sentiment. "You're a very rich man," I'd start the conversation. "Why not grant the bulk of your annual account appreciation to your favourite cause?"

The answer was always the same. They couldn't do that because they, or someone in their family, might get sick or need money for an emergency. They felt they couldn't take the risk. When looking at their portfolios of many millions of dollars, I found it difficult to relate.

My alienation only grew after I talked to Michael, my accountant. He told me that if I donated 75% of my income each year and continued with the tax-deductible contributions to my retirement plan and to the grandchildren's education savings plans, I'd be virtually exempt from paying income taxes. I decided to do just that and accept what my clients saw as a risk. If anything went seriously wrong and we needed money, I could always go to the bank and borrow against our properties.

It took three or four years for our foundation to build up a size-able capital base, but Cameron was with me from the beginning. When visiting my office, a place which always intrigued him, he often looked through my pile of incoming mail and asked questions. That's how he came across the International Activity Report of Doctors Without Borders. The pictures fascinated him and he wanted to know the sto-ries. Here was Fati, a woman from Burkina Faso whose four-year old girl was dangerously malnourished; and there was Ablo, a boy in Mali who'd suffered from Malaria. I quickly realized that Cameron's mind was on his mummy Krista. After each report, he wanted to know wheth-er the patients would have died if the doctors and nurses from Doctors Without Borders hadn't been there to help.

One story fascinated him more than all the others: that of Bestman, a ten-year old who'd come to the Monrovia hospital with tuberculosis. Each time he came to the office he wanted to read Bestman's account to me:

"I WAS VERY sick when they brought me here. I couldn't even play with my friends any more and I was sweating and coughing so hard. My mother was worried. She thought she would have to pay a lot of money, but my family doesn't have money to pay. But everything here was free. After two weeks in hospital I had to come back once a month to get medicine. Now I can play with my friends again."

THREE YEARS INTO *the life of the Cavelti Family Foundation, I thought the time was right to involve the family. Not sure what would come out of it, I started by bringing all three grandchildren to my office, promising them a real business meeting and telling them I needed their help.*

"Do any of you know what charity is?" I started out. Alexandra, the eldest, now twelve, told me that she'd participated in a fundraiser for the Cancer Society, organized by her school. Cameron, in fourth grade, reported that some of the older kids in his neighbourhood had raised money by selling lemonade.

"But what do you think the word 'charity' means?" I probed. Abigail provided the answer. "That's easy, Papa. Charity means being kind." I was touched by the irresistible simplicity of her assessment, concluding that we were off to a good start.

At our second meeting, we discussed the complexities of giving money away. When I provided an overview of the different types of charities and asked how they felt about each, I was taken aback. I knew humanitarian relief organizations resonated with Cameron and Doctors Without Borders was on top of his list. It was the girls' notion of who should benefit from our foundation that surprised me. Social engagements like food banks or after school program left them unenthusiastic, and so did environmental initiatives. They wanted to help animals. I hadn't expected that.

As time went on that changed. What made a meaningful difference was my exposing them to Charity Intelligence, Canada's top rating service for charitable causes. I wondered whether introducing them to sets of data would dampen their enthusiasm, but it did the opposite. Gradually their focus widened. The girls were still passionate about animal welfare and Cameron's heart was still close to Doctors Without Borders, which he now expertly called MSF, for Médecins Sans Frontières. But sitting at one of our oversized computer screens and studying what happened to the donations various organizations received focused them on new possibilities.

"Look Papa," one of the kids would exclaim, "here is a charity that pays way too much in salaries." Or, "I think I've found one we should support—76% goes to the cause!" How much of the money an organization collected was spent on actual charitable activities (as opposed to administration or fundraising) was one of their favourite metrics. Before long they produced elaborate spreadsheets, detailing each charity's merits and shortcomings.

The next step was to give each of the kids a small allocation they could grant to the causes of their choice. Questioning their decisions was always a highlight for me. Without exception, their decisions were well researched.

I also invited them along to meetings with groups we supported or considered adding to our list. Cameron came along to Doctors Without Borders several times, often surprising me with his intelligent questions. Melissa became involved too. Like her daughters once did, she felt the animal kingdom was where much of her allocation should go. By now, Alex and Abby were a lot less dogmatic.

Early this year, I decided to ask each of the grandchildren for input on how we should divvy up the year's allocations. They're in their late teens now, reluctant to engage in anything that isn't related to their social life. Still, each one of them came up with a proposal. Even better, their ideas were remarkably similar. It made me realize that the foundation will be in good hands once I'm gone.

THE FAMILY FOUNDATION has taught me a lot. I've learned that many of the skills I learned during my business career, particularly writing and public speaking, can be applied to purposes other than corporate success. For years now, I've been an unofficial advisor to MSF, mostly on the fundraising front, usually addressing high-level donor groups. Sometimes Kate Bahen, the Managing Director of Charity Intelligence, without which my ongoing search for worthy causes would be much harder, asks me for input. There are other organizations I'm involved with as well, and invariably the outcome is as gratifying to me as it is beneficial to them.

I've also come to appreciate that not all charities put their stated cause first. Some shamefully hoard money instead of putting it to work, others spend far too much of their donations-generated revenue on salaries and fundraising. A few are outright frauds. Like corporations, governments or other institutional constructs, charities attract idealists, as well as bureaucrats and sociopaths.

It's taken me a while to identify a dozen or so causes we can confidently favour with the bulk of our annual grants. In the process, I've found new friends and built countless memories, both for myself and our family. Attending a charity presentation is always interesting. But being invited to look behind the scenes and brainstorming with those committed to make the world a better place is an incomparable privilege, as is the experience of meeting the beneficiaries of charity.

Over time, my journey through the charitable universe has allowed me to sit down with nurses returning from war zones, huddle with kids who not long ago spent their after-school hours on the streets and were now cooking nutritious meals for themselves and others, and play with distressed animals before their rehabilitation into nature.

How much better can it get?

Death has made repeated appearances in my life. Over and over, the passing of loved ones has caused me to examine the magnitude of what I've lost—my father passing on much too early, then Kurt, Gaby, Krista and Mami, all leaving unexpectedly, depriving me from being with them one last time. In each case, allowing myself to sit with the agony of loss and longing was an important part of the grieving process. Later, once I managed to let go, bitter-sweet memories of cherished moments surfaced, often along with regrets over missed opportunities.

The other night, in my dream space, I had an insight I didn't expect. Why don't we pay more attention to the living?

That question wore Melissa's face. For most of the night, episodes portraying her played out. Here she was, when I first got to know her at age 13, defiantly telling me I was nothing more than her mum's boyfriend. Then consistently principled Melissa made an appearance, rebuffing her father when he tried to convince her not to take a summer job with our firm, promising her a Caribbean holiday with the same pay I'd offered. Persuasive, not-ever-letting-go Melissa came next. Eighteen now, she convinced me to buy her a double bass built by the renowned Giuseppe Testore in Milan during the 1760s, determined to pay me back one day.

There were examples of silliness, too—Melissa's habit of saying snarky, grand-standing things she didn't mean, some pure fluff intended to be instantly dismissed, others provocative, getting under my skin and tempting me to react.

Then, more recent incidents came up, leaving me in awe of what she's capable of. Still deeply traumatized from attending Krista's final moments in the hospital's resuscitation unit, there was Melissa witnessing a car crash and running into the intersection to attend to the fatally injured, heavily bleeding elderly driver who soon after perished. Big-hearted Melissa.

And finally, Melissa the doer, sewing hundreds of designer masks after the Covid pandemic struck, and selling them at boutiques around town to raise money for the symphony orchestra of which she is a director and performing musician.

The morning after re-living these dream-induced scenes, I thought of John too, how he saved two lives in one day, not that long ago. Rafting down Costa Rica's Balsa River when it was at its most turbulent, he pulled me back up after I'd gone overboard and was headed toward a rocky chute. Minutes later, in a calm stretch of water, we beached our vessel and went for a swim. As we adults waded back to shore, we noticed that Cameron was in trouble. His scrawny ten-year old body couldn't resist the current, which fervently pulled him toward the waterfall that was no more than thirty meters downriver. Without hesitation, John jumped back in, swam in Cameron's direction, managed to grab him not far from the abyss, and struggled to get him back to safety.

The grandchildren know how precious they are to me, but have I told Melissa and John? Probably yes. Do I tell them often enough? Most likely not.

Being in a rainforest is a magnificent experience, but also a profoundly intimidating one. Both in the Amazon and in Asia's Golden Triangle, danger seemed to lurk everywhere. Even though I couldn't see them, I knew poisonous reptiles and dangerous cats lurked nearby. Besides, had I not been in the company of a local, I would have easily lost my way, perhaps never to return to the safety of a human settlement.

Experiencing a rainforest from above is quite different. Suspended between a deep gorge and a dramatic tree canopy, we're riding in an open gondola to a mountain top. The trees are higher than any I've ever seen and many host a dozen or more other tree and plant species. Symbiosis is ever present.

All around us, we hear the distinctive bark of Howler Monkeys. Occasionally, the operator stops our 'sky-cab', so that we can observe the creatures swinging from branch to branch or leaping through the air into what seems to us impenetrable foliage. There are sloths, too, as well as snakes, toucans and countless other creatures.

We're in Costa Rica and this is the day we set aside to ride one of the world's longest ziplines. At the top, after due instruction, we are sent off on two short trial runs, followed by consecutively longer descents. Each one of us gradually learns to control our gliding speed and form, and when we get ready to tackle the longest cable, which is almost one kilometer long and sees us zip along amidst the tree canopy at a terrifying pace, we all look like actors pulled off the set of an adventure movie.

John, who at the top reminded us that he's afraid of heights, comes careening down toward the target area much too fast, his face distorted by terror or exhilaration, I can't guess which. His stretched-out legs hit the mattress that's been strapped to a couple of trees for just that eventuality. Caroline and Melissa both look elegant, a bit scared but totally in control. What I find most remarkable is how fearlessly the children tackle the challenge. Alexandra is only twelve; Cameron and Abigail are ten.

I notice that I've been more concerned that something could go wrong with us adults than with the grandchildren. It's a sentiment I'm not yet used to, something I first realized a few months ago when skiing with the whole family. I'll feel it again in a few days' time, when we're on our rafting adventure.

When we finally arrive at Costa Rica's Pacific coast and embark on a snorkelling excursion, Cameron puts it all into words. Swimming up to me as I come up for air and a glimpse of the sky, he asks me if I'm okay. He knows that I start feeling disoriented or even panicky when I have my head underwater for too long. Now he offers help. "Here is what we'll do, Papa," he declares confidently. "Let's push back down to the reef together, and if you start getting uncomfortable, I can take your hand and guide you to the surface."

At the cottage, seemingly a long time ago, we helped four-year old Cameron build a monument, a cairn made of weighty shore-line boulders, placed on a flat piece of land protruding into the lake. Krista had camped there with one of her high-school friends one summer. When we ordained our creation, we sprinkled some of Krista's ashes over it. Then we held hands, Caroline and I and our grandchildren, watching the breeze carry fragments of white dust away onto the open water, confused snowflakes on a summer day. Caroline said, "We miss you, Krista," and the girls quietly repeated it. Cameron suggested we call our creation the Mummy Rock. He made a map of the cottage property, detailing its exact location. Our monument was three feet high when we erected it, visible to anyone canoeing or swimming past our property. Now, due to steadily rising water levels, it's below the surface.

We took some of Krista's remains to our courtyard garden in Colorado, too, where she'd loved to sit, but we knew all along that the true home of Krista's spirit was the ocean. She'd loved her time as a scuba instructor, adored her encounters with underwater creatures, and even had the image of a dolphin tattooed on her ankle, long before tattoos became fashionable.

When Caroline returned from a visit to Hawaii, she knew where Krista's remaining ashes should be. She described the undeveloped shore of Southern Kona, where she'd stayed with our friends Deborah and David, how she'd watched humpback whales with their calves migrate North, sometimes surfacing only partially to blow water out of their lungs, and sometimes exploding out of the sea, displaying all of their majestic bodies. She talked about the pockmarked black lava beach, broken up by sandy inlets where she'd snorkelled and where dolphins came to play.

Two years later, we flew there to part with the last bit that was left of our physical Krista. The time was right to let go.

BEFORE DAWN, WITH *a few close friends and the Hawaiian priestess we had asked to join us, we walked to the edge of the ocean, a plump, orange full moon guiding our way. It sat right above the spot we headed for—a craggy, narrow inlet carved into a lava cliff atop which we decided to stand. Five or six feet from our perch was the ocean, swelling high with the morning tide and its surf thundering against the rock.*

We stood for a while, trying to balance on the bumpy surface, awed by the forces of nature enveloping us. Caroline spoke of the gifts Krista had brought to our lives and what she had been here to teach us, and we evoked her form and her spirit. I remembered her eyes—glowing with rebellion, or sparkling with mischief—and talked of Krista's determination to live life fully.

Then we walked to the abyss, Caroline offering the ocean Krista's ashes and me tossing plumeria and hibiscus picked before dawn, a handful of blossoms for each who loved her—one for Cameron, one for each family member, one for each person dear to her.

When Caroline smashed the urn she had built and threw it into the roiling surf below, the priestess raised a large conch shell to her mouth and the deafening sound this brought forth momentarily dominated the world. And at that very moment, a magnificent wave came toward us, higher than any before. It rose against the cliff side and emptied itself over us, its crashing sound drowning out even the call of the conch. And then the wave receded and everything of Krista's and in Krista's honor was taken back to sea.

Moments later, right at the mouth of the inlet and very close to us, a baby dolphin surfaced, all by herself, tossing and showing off atop a cresting wave—at play, in union with the universe. How could this not be Krista! And a couple of minutes later her family came into view, a school of adult dolphins, cruising along, looking for their missing child.

We lingered by the ocean side a while longer, watching the moon sink into the water. And then, as we turned to walk back, a new sun rose above the horizon of Hawaii's gentle, volcanic hills. We passed the ruins of a roofless old church, its stone altar invoking the generations of beings who congregated here to worship and celebrate birth and death.

WE'VE HIKED UP the narrow path uphill to our spot for years since, always on the same September day. Sometimes it's dry and brittle and sometimes the rain or sleet makes it slick and treacherous. Late September in the Colorado Rockies is like that.

Now we're sitting on the fallen trunk of a once mighty aspen, the black markings where branches once grew still distinct and gritty against the smooth, silvery bark. Below us flows a tiny creek, its surface constantly changed by the objects it carries: fragments of wood, autumn leaves, some bright yellow or green, others discoloured by disease or the onset of decomposition. We can see only a small section of the stream; thick bushes block out its origin and the path forward. The floating bits come into view, sometimes briefly mingle and sometimes cluster together more determinedly, and then they're gone.

It is the same with the clouds above. Through a modest opening in the tree canopy we can follow a small portion of their seemingly endless journey, fragments of moisture travelling independently for a time, either to be eaten by the hungry sun or finding protection by joining a larger structure.

Caroline and I are here to think of Krista, as we do every year, trying to remember the vivacity of her eyes, the sound of her voice, melodious but edgy, picturing her healthy dark hair blowing in the wind. We reach out to her, through the gurgling water below us and the sky above.

Krista was the leaf that would have braved the floods alone. She was the cloudlet that would have stayed independent, preferring to be burned up to being swallowed whole. We feel her presence and let it surround and envelop us.

"Ladies and gentlemen, we're circling over Toronto," the captain announced as we approached our home city. "Those passengers sitting on the right can see the CN Tower and a bit to the side of it is the Air Canada Centre, home of the Maple Leafs, who last won the Stanley Cup in 1967."

Despite their team's less than stellar track record of recent decades, Toronto's hockey fans have not only remained loyal, but are eternally hopeful that the cup will soon be theirs again. Unlike them, I've long given up—not only because I don't share their vision, but because the atmosphere in contemporary sports arenas no longer agrees with me and ticket prices have more than five-folded since my Guardian days, when I was a frequent spectator at playoff games. That was about 35 years ago.

Now I'm holding two $200 tickets in my hand. John, who is out of town, has asked me if I'd take Alexandra to the game, an elimination-round contest between the Maple Leafs and the Boston Bruins. John also explained that, thanks to his special status, we could access the arena through a special side door. Better yet, if we went 90 minutes early, we'd be able to check into the Hot Stove Club and have dinner there. No lining up, a lavish dinner and a two hundred dollar stadium seat? I looked forward to the experience.

Alex, knowing her way around, has led me through a long tunnel and found the VIP entrance without difficulty. No more than a dozen others walk through the inconspicuous door ahead of us, but once we're inside it's evident that there is a line-up. Two security guards are asking people to place any metal objects on a tray and raise their hands; a couple of spectators with back packs are asked to open them for inspection. I'm stunned and mutter something unpleasant, but when it's my turn, submit to the unwanted ritual. Once we're on the stairs to the dining room, Alex speaks up: "Papa, is something wrong? You seem a bit upset." I try to convey to my granddaughter why being searched before a hockey game is offensive to me, but struggle for words. My explanation of why what we've just gone through is wrong meets with disbelief. "But Papa," she counters, "whenever you go to a public event, you have to be searched." I realize that what to me is an unnecessary intrusion into my private sphere, is to her the baseline, the utterly normal.

Dinner for the two of us sets me back three hundred dollars, but the food is superb and spending the evening with Alex is special. The hockey game is enjoyable too, but I find it hard to focus on the play. Each time the referee whistles, the electronic boards all along the stadium walls flash messages, accompanied by sound effects that are deafening. I notice that none of this bothers the thousands of spectators around us—their attention is as much on the snacks and small meals that are being offered by vendors as on the game. They all know that if they miss a particularly juicy episode or even a goal, close-ups will be shown again on the huge console suspended over the centre of the rink. I yearn for the simplicity of the hockey experiences that meant so much to me during the 1970s and 1980s. Yet, whenever I look sideways at my granddaughter in her oversized Maple Leafs sweater, I see only one thing: infectious excitement. Unlike me, Alex has no basis for comparison, only appreciation for what is.

FOR WEEKS ON end, my mind keeps returning to that evening. My acute revulsion and Alex's effortless tolerance of being searched as a precondition to attending a hockey game is instructive. It reminds me that a lifetime of experience has brought me perspective, but that it's come at a price. I'll never be able to 'accept what is' the way Alex can. The insights I've gained continuously force me to evaluate, compare, then judge.

What's equally on my mind is how vulnerable my grandchildren are, how easily the young can be manipulated by the narratives served up by those in power—more so, I think, than was the case with our generation. Technology is the major reason. To my grandchildren it's an irresistible source of entertainment and information; to corporations and governments a surveillance tool and a means to shape public opinion.

When I think of the consequences my hope for the future dwindles.

Something I never expected has happened. My well-ordered world, the life I learned to control so well, the balanced pace that routinely and contentedly led me from hour to hour and day to day, have all been shattered. Relentlessly, my mind keeps returning to the two electronic messages I received.

The e-mail I first received seemed benign enough. The subject line read Doctors Without Borders, and all it said underneath was, "Hallo Peter." I never answer messages like that, except this one was signed by Christian Zangger.

'Chris', as I called him, was the fellow Swiss immigrant I'd met on the Cape Town bound airplane and with whom I'd spent the first few nights at the Millroy Hotel, drinking Chivas Regal and smoking cigars—an indulgence he could easily afford, but which ate up the most of the cash with which I'd arrived. For a short while, I'd shared a room with Chris and, halfway into my time in South Africa, we journeyed to the Etosha game reserve together.

His one-line message brought back these and countless other memories. I tried to recall his face and remembered both how much fun Chris could be and how often he sought out confrontation, especially when he drank too much. Still, I thought, why not respond? "Chris from Cape Town, five decades ago?" I asked. "What's the connection with Doctors Without Borders? I'd love to know what you're up to."

A WEEK PASSED; the lengthy response I received left me bewildered. Zangger started out saying that he'd read several of my published articles and noticed that none talked about South Africa. He then resorted to a number of metaphors and obscure statements. Like any good card player, he explained, he wasn't going to tell me whether he'd drawn a good or a bad hand—so what was I expecting when asking him what he was up to?

The next paragraph stated his life philosophy: let sleeping dogs lie. Looking for a mutually rewarding and balanced solution was so much better than delving into the past. He went on to quote Karl Lagerfeld, who apparently said that anyone deceiving him should know that forgiveness was not part of his vocabulary. The ending was moderately softer, but equally unnerving: "Perhaps I'll hear from you again. Or you from me. Wishing you and your large family all the best."

I read the message several times, trying to make some sense of it. My confusion gave way to annoyance, then anger. I started typing a reply, demanding clarification. What sleeping dogs? A mutually satisfactory solution to what? I looked at the paragraphs I'd written and considered hitting the Send button, then deleted it. Why should I engage with someone who'd clearly lost his mind?

On my walk home, I tried to relive my time in South Africa,

focusing on my interactions with Chris. Clearly, he held a grudge against me; now I was trying to figure out why. When I couldn't come up with anything that would justify the kind of message he'd sent, I wondered if his hostility was fuelled by something unrelated to Cape Town or our trip to Etosha. Perhaps he resented me for succeeding in business or for having a loving family, things that may have been denied him. No matter what the impetus for his communication, he'd succeeded in getting under my skin.

Once at home, I read the message to Caroline and asked her for advice. She felt there was no point trying to understand Chris' communication logically. With someone who was clearly operating from a position of deep antagonism, that would never work. She suggested that I simply ignore him. Grateful for Caroline's unemotional and prudent input, it's what I decided to do.

NEARLY TWO MONTHS have passed and here it is, another e-mail. "Hallo Peter. No answer to my last mail. Do you want me to wake the sleeping dogs? Think about your lovely family."

This is as clear a declaration of war as any. Even worse, the bastard is putting me into an impossible position—unless I respond, telling him to explain himself or lay off, he may escalate the confrontation. The insinuation that my family may be affected leaves me distressed.

Once again, Caroline urges restraint. To her, provoking Chris is a treacherous path. Besides, she points out, to be acknowledged and know that I feel uncomfortable is what he really wants. Curious what a psychologist might think about my dilemma, I call Stephanie's husband Jim. As a psychologist, he may see things that have escaped me.

Jim listens patiently, asks a couple of questions, then surprises me by offering fairly definitive conclusions. He explains that the messages reveal a person who is deeply insecure, and probably always was. Jim also feels that Chris' life must have gone terribly wrong, or he wouldn't spend energy on some perceived injustice that occurred literally half a century ago. He adds that I have no choice but to take this seriously.

When I ask Jim what he recommends, he sounds ambivalent—both responding to the latest message or ignoring it carries obvious risks. I relate Caroline's feelings on the matter: is it likely that what he really wants is to be acknowledged? Jim completely agrees. People with Chris' profile always demand recognition, the only question is how far they'll go to get it. For the moment, he concludes, it may be best to do nothing, except to tell everyone in the family what is going on. After a night's sleep I decide to go a step further. I call my friend Markus Schultz in Switzerland.

Markus and I have helped each other on many occasions. He's a distinguished and highly connected lawyer and, in addition, a judge. I got to know him at Cavelti Capital when he introduced several clients to our firm. In turn, I referred some of Camafin Trust's administrative and legal work to him. Over time the Schultz and Cavelti families grew close.

When I explain my dilemma to Markus and tell him that all three messages were sent from 'bluewin.ch', one of Switzerland's most widely used internet providers, he assures me that the chances of tracking down Chris Zangger are excellent. It's an unusual name and knowing both his approximate age and his e-mail address will help. Once he's located him, he'll talk to the police.

A FEW DAYS later Markus calls me back. Apparently, Chris lives in Ticino, is retired and has no criminal record. By sharing what's happened with the Cantonal authorities, Markus explains, he's made sure that there is now a police file, without officially accusing Chris. The police may even call him, advising him that he's on their radar.

I've never heard from Chris again, but every now and then I remember how his communications triggered me, and for a few minutes I'm back to that feeling of profound unease.

✧✧✧

The grandkids are visiting, without their parents. They flew into Eagle Airport, a couple of hours' drive from Snowmass, where we picked them up. Seeing them strut toward us, pulling their suitcas-es behind them, grinning with confidence, reminds us that they've travelled the world since they were babies.

Alex preannounced that she wouldn't be skiing this winter. She's sixteen now, eager to define herself, so we've accepted her latest whim. We've found other ways to bond with her. On days Caroline doesn't ski she's taking Alex food shopping and cooks with her; whenever I have an hour or two available, I take her to some of the village's more challenging backroads, preparing her for her upcoming driver's exam.

But most days I'm on the mountain with Abby and Cameron. Both are exceptional skiers. Abigail has mastered all but the most challenging double-diamond runs. As she follows me down steep fall-lines, I hear her chanting, "Pole-plant aaaand turn around". Cameron is more interested in speed than technical acumen. I frequently have to remind him that losing control means he may hit a tree or another skier. Only when we venture into wilderness terrain does he rein himself in. For the first time ever, I'm taking him down the legendary Hanging Valley Wall.

At the end of our time together I realize that I'm having far more fun skiing with my grandchildren than with any of my adult ski buddies.

The contrast between city dwellers and country folk has always fascinated me.

In rural Herisau, whether I entered one of the few stores or restaurants, or whether I bought a train ticket at the railway station, I was immediately placed in the context of my family and the family's standing in the community. "How is Jack?" the people who knew my dad well would ask. Others, while handing me my change, might say, "Good thing you are here…it reminds me to make an appointment with your father." Whenever I interfaced with another Herisauer, there was a subtle reference to who I was. It was comforting because my parents were looked up to; it would have been disheartening if my family had been unpopular.

When I first came to Zurich, a town of a few hundred thousand, I quickly realized that no one knew who I was. The much larger cities I lived in later, Cape Town and Toronto, offered an even greater degree of anonymity. Even though being anonymous brought me no tangible advantages, I fell in love with the notion of freedom it promised.

It wasn't until I bought the cottage that I thought much about disadvantages of city life. When I tried to insure my cabin, I was asked where the nearest police and fire stations were. I explained that Parry Sound, the nearest town, was a twenty-minute boat ride away. Now the agent wanted to know if I or one of my close-by neighbours owned a fire pump. That question surprised me. I'd come to rely on big city's support systems. In Toronto, if the power goes, you report it to the utility; if there is a fire or a sewer overflows, you dial 911 and sit back. Adversarial things are taken care of by others.

Over time, I've learned to do things by myself. In summer, I take inventory of dying or dead trees, especially ones that are likely to fall on a structure. Fall is the time that I take them down, cut them up into fireplace-sized logs and get busy on my splitter. Only occasionally, when a particularly tall tree needs to be felled, do I engage a professional. Self-reliance has become a big part of how I define myself.

ACROSS THE INLET to our bay the rising water level has killed a stand of young pines. Stripped of their needles, their trunks and branches have taken on an unusual hue—taupe when the clouds move in and distinctly purple when it's sunny. Stephanie, who's visiting for a few days, has captured it all, first using a gesso-laden knife to capture the texture of the barren trees, then tinging the emerging shapes with bits of pale colour.

As the painting comes alive, I think of how dramatically our view has changed. A few years ago, on our side of the water, there was a sand beach wide enough to play volleyball. Now the water reaches far into the vegetation, drowning not just the pines across the way, but the healthy sumac, irises and lilies that lined our shore.

Not only the plant world is affected. The ducks now use our docks to rest; the soft, pine needle covered banks that gave them shelter are far under water. The heron that lived at our point and paced the shallows is gone too; so are the dozens of frogs and hundreds of sunfish that fed him. And as we navigate the bay, we drift past countless submerged docks and numerous flooded cottages.

For now, the water rules and vegetation is in full retreat. Not long ago, it was the opposite.

IN NEWFOUNDLAND, REMINDERS of nature's authority are everywhere. Outside St. John, the capital, few structures are level, few mooring posts straight. Forceful and unpredictable ocean currents, ever shifting sand or rock bottoms, gales uprooting trees or blowing off roofs—nature's pageant of experiments is relentless. John and Melissa, who've been here before, have told us as much, describing the Newfies as a sturdy, upbeat and loveable lot. They've invited us along so that we can see for ourselves.

In Toronto it was summer; here the skies are a menacing grey, the wind is harsh and tempestuous, and the temperature bone-chilling. Bundled up in windbreakers, scarves and knitted hats, we hike along stretches of foggy coastline, admiring fishing villages and lighthouses, occasionally warming up with a rum toddy in badly-lit, friendly pubs.

We journey to nearby Cape Spear, too, North America's easternmost location, where more lighthouses and an array of World War II canons await us. The guidebook Melissa bought us says that, if we travelled across the Atlantic in an easterly direction, we'd end up in Ireland. A quick latitude check on my iPhone suggests that that's untrue—we'd find ourselves near Brest, on the coast of Bretagne. Still, Newfoundland's links with Ireland seem ever-present. As we talk to locals, a distinguishable Irish lilt appears nearly universal. The last time I saw a society of such uniform background was in the more remote Swiss valleys, a long time ago.

On our last day in the capital we embark on a whale and puffin spotting tour, but half an hour into the journey, Caroline and John are starting to feel nauseous. Neither Alex nor Melissa say much, but they both look uncomfortable. Only Abby appears unaffected; she excitedly points at a colony of puffins that passes over us before disappearing in a wall of dense mist.

I feel a bit woozy, too, but evoke my self-image as an experienced sailor. I'll be the adult who's there to support the rest of the family. That sentiment soon reveals itself as delusional; thinking back to my sailing adventures on Georgian Bay, I realize that I always threw up when first hitting the turbulent open water.

What keeps me from getting sick is my fascination with what reveals itself. My perception of space has changed completely. As we push through the swirling fog, we seem headed into unknown territory. For a few moments, as another swell rises before us we see nothing but a grey wall of wet; then, as our vessel briefly crests, we're offered a murky glimpse at the watery peaks and valleys ahead. What adds to the sense of drama is the utter monotony of all we see: the violent waves, the blustery fog, the bits of sky and land we occasionally see—all tinted with the same drab ashen wash, immersing us in its inescapable dampness.

An announcement interrupts my contemplation; it's the captain informing us of a medical emergency. Apparently, one of the heavy breakers relentlessly assaulting our boat has sent a passenger sprawling across the deck. We're headed back to harbour.

ONCE WE START our drive northward, the weather gradually improves, and by the time we cross into Terra Nova National Park, we're actually starting to feel warm. We lunch in a hamlet called Happy Adventure, where Melissa threatens to 'park' us during our retirement. Caroline and I love the place and readily agree with the suggestion, on condition that we get to keep our bank passwords. The place is quaint, the surrounding scenery dramatic and the fresh seafood exceptionally tasty.

As we move further up the coast, our appreciation for the real Newfoundland grows. The scenery and the settlements are invariably rugged and charmed with a simplicity that leaves us stunned.

We're starting to see the white specks that we know to be icebergs far out at sea, but the whales most tourists come to see have so far eluded us.

Twillingate is our Northernmost destination. Heading back on the water, we're prepared for any climatic extreme. It's frigid, but the seas are unruffled and the sky is clear, turning our five-hour excursion into a wonderful experience. We pass several odd-shaped icebergs, wondering what they'd look like closer up. Then, a far larger structure looms in the distance and before long we notice that the captain is heading straight toward it. As we get close, the temperature sharply drops. Our vessel is soon close enough that we can study the iceberg's complex shape and texture.

Grey-brown markings run across its side, bits of ocean floor that remind us of how the massive formation came to be, when long ago a shelf of ice broke off a glacier and sank, before resurfacing in its current appearance. When we look into the water, we see the frozen mountain's outline protruding toward the hull of the boat; it's easy to understand how even an experienced sailor could misjudge. Staring upwards, taking in the iceberg's multiple peaks and the steep chutes leaves me intimidated and deeply awed. The captain, surely knowing that we can't get enough of witnessing the miracle before us, backs off and closes in again, each time from a slightly different angle. And with every new approach, the way the light falls makes for an entirely new experience.

Eventually we head back toward Twillingate. The sun is arcing lower now; we're standing close together, shivering.

ANOTHER LONG DRIVE and we're in Gros Morne, in many ways the high point of our trip. Shaped by colliding continents and grinding glaciers, the area provides a deep glimpse into geological history.

One moment we wander across the Tablelands, literally walking on top of what was once oceanic crust—the earth's mantle. Next we drift into a bay where spectacular cliffs and imposing waterfalls skirt the icy water.

The settlements within Gros Morne are as unique as the natural surroundings. We stay in Norris Point and visit Rocky Harbour, communities as homogenous as they come. The villagers, mostly composed of fishermen and people running the handful of inns, restaurants and stores, would far more easily fit into Sligo or Galway than Canada. The small cemetery tells us that the Irish have ruled this place for a long time.

We spend our last evening walking along the deserted shore, watching the sun set and the ocean turn dark, soaking up the serenity that only places this far away can give.

✧✧✧

A few weeks ago, while in Colorado, I turned seventy. I dismissed the event as unimportant, a chronological marker reminding me of the fact that, in statistical terms, I was now indisputably old.

My big day would be like most others, except for the rituals Caroline and I had adopted during our thirty-plus years together. These included my favourite breakfast (a limp, moist omelette, as we jokingly call it, filled with feta and spinach, accompanied by half a dozen roasted asparagus, washed down with several cups of Peet's Sumatra coffee blend), an early afternoon Pavlova with bits of Kirsch sprinkled on top of the whipped cream, and dinner at one of Aspen's better restaurants. In between, I'd take calls from family members and friends and answer a few congratulatory e-mails and text messages.

The actual event turned out much like that, except we also skied for a couple of hours and took Hansli for his daily walk on 'Labrador Lane', an off-leash path not far from our house. I was pleased with how my birthday unfolded. With Caroline's help, I managed to make it special without attributing too much significance to it.

Yet, within a week, the reality of my being seventy years old started to mess with my brain—at first randomly, then with a persistence that left me bewildered. The most urgent message broadcast by my mind was this: since it was indisputable that I had a limited amount of time left here, I needed to focus on how I wanted to use it.

I faintly remembered that a similar thing occurred when I entered my sixties, but there wasn't much urgency to it. Now I felt challenged by the severity of my thoughts. Every now and then the spectre of my father, skeletal on his deathbed, popped up. He'd just turned seventy.

I DON'T FEEL my age, of course. I can still easily outdo kids and grandkids when skiing, and I delight in seeing them slow down when we hike up a mountainside while I motor ahead, my breath as steady as if I wandered along a city street. I allow other images of my physical prowess to arise; for a few seconds they make me feel invincible. Then the realities brought on by my big birthday crowd out such musings and the one relevant question reasserts itself: do I allow enough time for the things I cherish?

I reflect on the things that are most precious to me, reminding myself that each segment of time well spent fills a vast space, both in terms of my perception of it and the memory that persists. In contrast, how quickly do the hours, days and weeks of attending to routine tasks pass, only to appear dull, even irrelevant, when remembered. Even if I think of my life as nicely balanced, I still spend too much of my time completing spreadsheets, answering e-mails, updating operating systems and downloading software releases, absorbing news stories and performing handyman tasks, all at the expense of vivid, meaningful moments of living.

The challenge is obvious. How do I retreat from what's become perceived necessity and make an even greater part of my remaining years less dominated by responsibility and, by extension, more wholesome and resonant?

FOR DECADES NOW, I've constantly been on the move, never in one place long enough to maintain the type of ongoing deeper connection I prefer. The combination of turning seventy and writing about my adult life has refocused me on the rich tapestry of people I once knew well and have lost touch with. The idea of reaching out to them holds appeal.

A few weeks ago, I started with Charlie Campbell, with whom I paddled through half of Quetico forty-five years ago. An online search revealed that he was still alive. Charlie's web-page referred to his distinguished career as a litigator in quest of social justice, made reference to his interest in attending and writing plays, and featured his photo-essays. We recently met at his downtown Toronto condominium and talked for a couple of hours, then moved on to a noisy Italian restaurant where conversation was difficult. When we parted, we both vowed to get together again. The only hitch: I was leaving for my winter in Colorado soon. Then the pandemic hit and what would have been a gap of a few months turned into more than two years.

Next, I decided to contact the people I'd worked with at Guardian

Trust, most of whom I'd last seen more than three decades ago. The internet was of little use, other than to guide me to the obituaries of some of my considerably older colleagues. Still, with the help of Julius Gryguc, one of our senior foreign exchange traders with whom I still did business, we managed to get a small group of ex-employees together. They were the young ones—in their twenties back then, around sixty now. Yet, I recognized them all as, one by one, they trooped into the crowded pub.

With combined forces, we managed to reach out to a few others and met a second time, this time for a four-hour dinner at a fashionable uptown eatery. This time, Rino Rinaldi joined in. Finding him took dozens of phone calls, which made me wonder how I could have lost touch with one of the most upbeat and generous people I'd ever worked with, the man I'd asked to be a witness at our private wedding. Yet here he was, a bit more hunched over than I remembered, but within minutes of his arrival at our table, the indisputable life of the party.

Our dinner together made for a bitter-sweet experience. There were the long-forgotten stories that come up at any reunion, leading to joyful laughter and a sense of newly gained intimacy. But inevitably, the conversation returned to the treachery that brought our collective journey to an end. It turned out that all my co-workers had found contentment in their private lives, but none had ever again found as stimulating and supportive a working environment as the one at Guardian Trust. The human cost of the heartless takeover by Les Coopérants was colossal; the gullibility of those who made it possible still lingered.

Close to midnight, on my walk home, I felt enormous gratitude to the people who made the Guardian miracle possible. Many of our co-workers couldn't be there, but among the ones who attended, there still was an unmistakable connection. Within minutes of being together, we'd effortlessly returned to the space of openness and companionship we had once shared.

SOME ATTEMPTS TO revive old friendships have produced mixed results. After my father and my brother-in-law Kurt died, I wanted to be there for Mami and Gaby. With regularity, I visited Switzerland once or twice a year. That meant that I stayed in touch with several of my closest friends.

After Mami died, the frequency of those contacts suffered. My regular get-togethers with my school mates Caspar and Brigitta ended. On one of my visits to Herisau, I found Roland's leather goods store closed, neighbours telling me that my childhood buddy had mysteriously disappeared to a different part of the country. Even my get-togethers with Martin, which always involved a walk to the places we attended Kindergarten and grade school together, followed by dinner in the building where our families had been apartment neighbours, were no longer realizable. Even so, the two of us stayed connected and have recently started a new routine: a monthly Zoom session, during which we swap old stories and discuss contemporary problems.

Most recently, Martin made me an unusual offer—he, the ultra-successful academic who'd become the Dean of one of Europe's top business schools and was now the Chair of the International Board Foundation, was asking me, the school drop-out, to join the ranks of his organization's highly accomplished partners.

For a moment I was at a loss, not sure whether I should accept. After all I'd resigned from all my corporate board seats nearly twenty years ago. Then I recognized what Martin was doing. He was inviting me to extend a friendship that had transcended our childhood and adult years into old age. What a generous thought!

After discussion of how I could make a meaningful contribution, we agreed that I'd be the designated resource for the governance of charitable institutions—something that helps Martin and an institutional engagement I can feel good about.

I'm in a state of contentment, despite the fact that so much has changed. The Covid pandemic is upon us, leaving people the world over in a disoriented state. Caroline and I are stuck in Colorado—have been stuck here for months, the U.S.-Canadian border having been closed long ago.

Initially I felt off balance. Not only had the freedom to determine our comings and goings been annihilated, we also had 15 year-old Abigail with us. Her parents were in Hawaii, not sure when they could get back home, and her sister Alexandra was at home alone. She'd been left behind because she was to leave on her graduation trip to Cancun, which got cancelled. Chaos was everywhere. The conventions we'd become used to over a period of decades were challenged or had entirely disappeared, some overnight. Governments, corporations and individuals started behaving in unpredictable ways. I could cope during the day, somehow intellectually rationalizing the behavioral disparities I saw all around me. Nights were a different story. I was caught in endless, circuitous dream loops—standing in a lineup at customs looking for the right documents but never finding them, or being in a deserted hotel, aimlessly trying to open a hundred doors because I'd forgotten my room number.

After a couple of weeks of that, things shifted. Abigail got back to Toronto, where Alexandra picked her up at the airport. Melissa and John made it back the next day. And Caroline and I, still in Snowmass Village, experienced the unimaginable: the ski mountain was closed and the tourists left, construction ceased, car traffic came to a halt, shops were shuttered, people stayed indoors. There was no silence, though. Birds, in multitudes never seen by us before, chirped excitedly throughout the day, while at night the coyotes howled louder and ventured closer to our house. The stars and the moon seemed brighter, too. And I slept well again, untroubled by vexing dreams, spending eight and sometimes nine hours in a deep, restful state.

WHAT OUR KIDS, *grandkids and friends report from Toronto sounds chaotic and dystopian—a vast array of rules of behaviour to be observed, parks closed but sidewalks open, restaurants and shops inaccessible, large numbers of people working from home unless they've lost their jobs altogether. What we hear about the big American cities is even worse. The laws enacted by different municipalities and counties often contradict each other or are in conflict with state or federal statutes; big-city dwellers are locked down in their apartments unable to step out; hospitals struggle to deal with the load of the sick and dying; and healthcare workers are unable to get protective masks and gloves. Predictably, frustrated and disillusioned citizens are taking to the streets to protest and riot.*

Life in our mountain resort is far more bearable, even though evidence of the pandemic persists here too. Some people are determined that 'masking up' is an imperative, even if they're out hiking or biking along a deserted trail. Others demonstratively venture out without a mask, even when they visit crowded places like shops or the post office. There is tension between the two groups, but it doesn't affect us.

I'M DOING MY *morning work in my office, frequently glancing at the ocean of aspens outside, all interconnected through their root systems, part of the largest living organism on earth. Higher up, across the valley that's less than a kilometer wide, I see forests of conifers. Above them are ridges and peaks still covered in snow, and higher still rests the clear Colorado sky.*

In the afternoons I sit outside at the courtyard table, doing my writing. And throughout the day I take breaks in the garden, often with

Caroline—a garden that gives us enormous joy, constantly revealing new secrets. The climbing clematis is showing off its first two blooms, each a deep purple; the vines snaking their way up the posts of the pergola are growing new shoots, a tender light-green colour still. Hundreds of hollyhocks, each more than four feet tall vie for attention with other flowers, some wild and native, others like the Hudson Bay roses and the Siberian sage, brought in by Caroline twenty years ago.

This morning, taking a break, I noticed a luna moth sitting on a patch of cat-mint, its lime green wings sharply contrasting with the Prussian blue of the flowering stalks, its wingspan bigger than the width of my hand. I thought of getting my camera, then vowed to simply observe, which proved rewarding. Within seconds I noticed a few smallish bees darting in and out of the plant; some collided with the resting moth, which appeared completely untroubled. Next, several hefty bumble bees appeared. As I followed their path and watched them busily navigating their way from one seed pod to another, I realized that the smaller bees crashed into them as well. I was in disbelief, then overcome by awe. Here were three species, one using the plant for a peaceful rest, the others nurturing themselves while contributing to the plant's reproduction, all happily tolerating each other's presence and occasional clumsiness. If only humans could behave this way!

I try to process all this and feel overwhelmed. Not only am I escaping the Covid hysteria; I'm doing so in paradise.

I REFLECT. I have a loving relationship with my wife, based on countless shared adventures and unfathomable tragedy, which in turn led to mutual respect and the appreciation of togetherness. My time with Caroline now makes up roughly half of my lifespan of more than seven decades.

I'm part of a deeply connected family and feel secure that my love for all is reciprocated. Although I know many people, I have only a handful of friends, but I treasure their company and, when needed, their objective input and sometimes criticism. I get to do my favourite things in my most preferred places: I ski in Colorado, drift in the canoe and explore the woods on Georgian Bay, walk the streets of Herisau where I grew up, or dash to a Caribbean island haven when Toronto gets too dark and cold. I'm healthy, too. My doctor, Vera Kohut, routinely praises me for maintaining a perfect weight and tells me that no patient in my age group has a more impressive pulse rate and blood pressure. She frets that my twenty-plus drinks a week are at least five too many, then adds, "But you're used to it." And I'm financially well-off, by most people's standards even wealthy. I have everything I want and need.

I know I feel this way because I'm in a space of good balance. The hours I spend on my financial work and those devoted to writing and other creative pursuits are nicely matched, and there is still enough time left to share at least two of my daily meals with Caroline, communicate with my siblings, nephews and niece in Switzerland, and to get together with kids and grandkids in Toronto. Even better, I manage to get in several daily walks and have time to read or evening-binge on a TV series, all without feeling overwhelmed.

Of course, it's not always like that. Usually, when I realize that my life has been in graceful balance for a few weeks or months and congratulate myself for such a wondrous achievement, things are on the verge of slipping. One moment I behold the enthralling mirage of flickering Northern Lights on a moonless summer night, fully aware of how privileged I am to witness such a miracle, yet already cognizant that after another few minutes or hours, it'll be gone again. And then, as perfection recedes, I start getting frustrated and soon feel sorry for myself. Sometimes, it's the burden of too many possessions that forces me back to a less balanced state, and sometimes an unexpected crisis intervenes. Yet, somehow, after a few troubled weeks, I always find my way back.

HOW DID I get to this enviable state? Caroline frequently points out that my gratitude for the blessings I have received is a major contributor. I agree, but still wonder if other factors were at play.

To what extent has the course of my existence been determined by solid planning? When I look back, my life looks like a patchwork of seemingly irreconcilable episodes that somehow led to where I'm now. Setting myself small goals and meeting them helped me evolve on a micro-level, professionally and emotionally. But when it came to the serious, fork-in-the-road decisions, I usually let intuition determine in which direction I should proceed.

Some of my friends dismiss intuition as over-rated when I try to explain this to them, arguing that it's just another word for cumulative past experiences translated by the brain into a conclusion. I disagree, firmly believing—or perhaps knowing on a deep level—that intuition is not of the mind at all. But, having said that, I can't deny that actions are to an extent influenced by the body of our experience. And when I turn my attention that way, I can see that all kinds of events and people have left their mark on my belief system.

Looming large in the people category are the gatekeepers who, at crucial moments, knowingly or unaware, held open portals I was briefly allowed to see through. Their invitation was implicit: I was free to enter or stay away.

My parents gave me invaluable gifts. Even though their relationship was troubled, I felt loved and well taken care of. And later, when I was ready for independence, they let me choose my own way, never once trying to influence the decisions I struggled with. Others might have preferred guidance; I would have viewed that as meddlesome and rebelled.

Once I was away from home, truly on my own, I ran into an enthralling array of characters who showed me possibilities and sometimes opened doors. Some were colourful and pompous, while others were gracefully understated. Some offered me ways to engage through *hard work, others tempted me with nefarious schemes, and a third group simply inspired me with their example, wanting me to become more like them.*

What made my first boss in Zurich, Herr Von Arx, delegate the supervision of his department to me whenever he took time off? Me, a school drop-out not even twenty years old, whose expectations of life had just been decimated? I'll never know, but what Herr Von Arx showed me was that giving someone a small chance can pay off in a big way.

And what about Fred Hirschler, my first boss at Deak's, who always made me and his other employees feel special by acknowledging each of us in a personal way? Later, as an executive myself, I made it a habit to do the same with my staff. I wanted to know their circumstances, where they lived, whether they were married and had children. That motivated not only my employees, but also me.

When I ended up in charge of his Canadian operation, I dealt directly with the patriarchal Mr. Deak. By then, I'd built up enough confidence to confront him with new ideas, which he appreciated and even respected. When I pitched him on my idea that we should have a currency trading desk, he responded positively. But when I asked him what budget I could count on, he countered that if it would generate the profits I foresaw, I didn't need a budget. It was the first time someone challenged me to engage in an undertaking of my own conception, where results would be clearly measurable. An important portal was opened and I decided to step through it.

Howard Kelly was another gatekeeper I needed to meet. By giving me the freedom to build a serious enterprise, but frequently reining me back in and thus causing me great frustration, Howard made me realize that there was only one place where no superior and no board of directors could interfere in the destiny I sought for myself: my own company.

BOSSES WEREN'T THE *only people who taught me powerful lessons. James Sinclair, in the space of the only meal we ever shared, taught me something completely different: that financial compensation and impressive corporate titles should never be an ambition. Don't make plans for world domination, he explained—instead set yourself a realizable next goal, small as it may be, and articulate a generous time limit to get there. Everything else will follow. And so it was in my case, and in the case of the many employees I passed this bit of wisdom on to.*

Then there was the legendary James U. Blanchard III. Confined to a wheelchair since his teens, he opened countless doors for me and many others. Thanks to him, I ended up managing one of the world's largest gold funds. But money management mandates, no matter how prestigious, come and go. Jim's enduring gift was to expose me to the cast of highly accomplished and resourceful people he invited to his conferences, from academics to bankers, broadcasters, writers and philosophers. Their thinking greatly enriched me and encouraged me to define my own path. And even though I'm not nearly the socialite Jim Blanchard was, his example motivated me to introduce exceptional people in my orbit to each other.

Others influenced me not by offering advice or explaining their thoughts but simply by example—some in a positive way, others negatively. By the time I left Guardian Trust I'd met enough people in elevated social positions to know that the rich couldn't easily be categorized. There were those who understood that their privilege was to a large extent the result of good fortune, and there were others who were convinced that their brilliance had got them where they were. There were the spendthrifts, insecure and always in need to project an image of opulence, and those who managed to stay humble. I met extremely wealthy people whose only goal was to add to their hoard and who defined success purely in monetary terms. And I met scions of the financial aristocracy who commuted by bus, while generously supporting others.

I CAME ACROSS *indisputable thieves, as well. My sheltered childhood and adolescence left me unprepared for the boldness of their schemes, even though I found them consistently intriguing.*

When I worked at Deak's, one of Canada's better known labor leaders came to see me. His proposal was extraordinary. "What if I sold you a few hundred South African Krugerrand gold coins that looked and weighed exactly the same as Krugerrands, but weren't?" I was amused and pointed out to him that if the false coins contained anything other than pure gold and weighed the same, then their size would have to be slightly different. "But which of your customers would notice?" he responded. "Whether they buy one coin or ten coins, they have nothing to compare them to." Evidently, the man was serious. When I resolutely dismissed his idea, he took the concept a step further, telling me he could see that I had reservations doing this with gold. But how about us buying a load of fake foreign currency? We could both make big money.

My potential partner in crime reminded me of the some of the shiftier characters I'd encountered during my travels; he struck me as crude and his intention was immediately transparent. In contrast, the more sophisticated fraudsters I was to meet throughout my banking career blended into the corporate world with a perfection that stunned me. It took me years to spot their intended scams and even then I managed to do so only half the time.

The inimitable Lothar Arzt, with his pretend stutter and put-on inhibition, was a master of deception. Hansjürg Engel, my school mate who'd worked as an executive at Canada's UBS subsidiary and had brokered my first appointment with Guardian Trust, turned out to be equally sophisticated. I learned that when, on his way to Switzerland, he stopped over in Toronto and asked me to join him for brunch at the Four Seasons Hotel. Our meal turned into a three-hour affair with copious amounts of champagne, Hansjürg at his most charming, entertaining me with lots of stories about his time in Canada and his imminent transfer to Saudi Arabia. Then, gracefully charging the breakfast to his room, he asked me for a favour. His Amex card was maxed out and he wanted to bring his fiancée Yvonne De Beers a gift. Since we were in fashionable Yorkville, surely there was a decent gallery around, at which he could find a small painting or etching. "Being from an illustrious family," he joshed, "she has expensive taste."

I enthusiastically declared that I knew just the place. "The Arthur White Gallery has an exhibition of etchings from Picasso's Volard Suite," I explained. "I went there last weekend and the pieces are not exorbitantly priced." Hans settled for an unframed etching that cost just under $3,000 and I paid for it. The understanding was that he'd initiate a transfer to me as soon as he got to Zurich. Months later, having asked for repayment a number of times, I finally threatened Hansjürg that I'd discredit him with his employer. I reminded him that I had access to UBS's Chief Executive, Nikolaus Senn, who had grown up in Herisau just like me. I got my money back.

Others were less lucky. In time, Hansjürg would embezzle tens of millions from the Cellere family, the owners of one of Switzerland's largest construction firms, and go to prison. A few years after his release he was found guilty of defrauding several wealthy seniors and jailed once more.

Then there was Jan Soels, the head of one of the large Dutch banks in Pittsburgh, introduced by one of the top executives at the Toronto Dominion Bank. I was surprised when he opened a briefcase containing half a million dollars and wanted to convert it into German Marks but, on the strength of TD Bank's assurances, I authorized the transaction. A few weeks later he returned, this time with two million dollars. When I asked him about the origin of the funds, he explained that he acted on behalf of a rich Latin American family. When I refused to accommodate him, Jan Soels got up and left with a smile every bit as engaging as Hansjürg Engel's.

That wasn't the end. Within a year I received a polite letter, sent from a U.S. federal prison. Soels reported that he'd been charged with money laundering. He'd made terrible mistakes, he wrote, and it was tragic that his son now had to bear the consequences. The good thing was that Jan had taught him to trade commodities—if I wired ten thousand dollars, his son would have the capital to open an account and, with the trading profits, not only quickly repay me, but also cover his tuition.

Criminals were not an uncommon presence in the banking business, especially during the 1970s and 1980s, when know-your-client legislation was sketchy. Both Deak & Company and Guardian Trust were in the foreign exchange business, which seemed to be a magnet for resourceful money launderers. One huge advantage of going on my own and confining my activities to money management and consulting was that I no longer had to pre-judge every client relationship.

Still, the unsavoury characters that I met in my banking years helped my evolution as much as the people I looked up to. They too were gatekeepers of a sort, except that I chose not to enter through the door they held open for me.

NOT LONG AGO, our family was a hub of shared creativity. Part of Melissa and John's living area transitioned into the music room. Like their mother, Abigail and Alexandra practiced their skills on multiple instruments—piano, recorder, cello, double bass, trombone. Melissa had taken to the harp, as well.

At the cottage and in Colorado, Caroline taught the girls how to make pottery, while I kept them busy with painting and calligraphy projects.

Melissa and Caroline also benefitted from each other's gardening skills. The outdoor patio at our new Sheldrake condominium, used by our predecessors mainly to barbecue, was converted into a haven of tranquility, its sitting areas sheltered by decorative trees, potted hydrangeas and banks of irises. Melissa's garden was home to the world's largest heritage tomatoes; indoors, she grew lemons and oranges.

Wherever, whenever we all met, culinary explorations unfolded. Caroline even took Alexandra to Italy, where they expanded their knowledge of Tuscan food. Melissa and Abigail were the family's much-appreciated bakers, while John profiled himself as the meat expert. I've never been part of that dynamic, except at the savouring stage.

Meanwhile, Cameron and I worked on our geography project. Having learned about countries, their flags and capitals, and even some of their anthems, Cameron was now moving on to geographic and cultural attributes, capturing his knowledge in countless spreadsheets. The aim was to create an online game. We named it 'Wheel of the World' and even registered the domain name. Once we composed the first set of one thousand questions and answers, we called up Richard Moore to learn about design aspects. Then we connected with a top app designer in California, learning that to get our game fully designed and onto Apple's distribution system would cost $70,000 or more. Cameron surprised me by suggesting that we lay off—we'd had a lot of fun and learned a lot, why spend all that money?

Even on the construction front there was mutual inspiration. Using Melissa's and John's contractor, Caroline managed to make our Sheldrake condo into a masterpiece of contemporary, practical design. That, in turn, inspired Melissa to redesign parts of their house.

WHERE HAS ALL that collaborative family dynamic gone? Much of it has to do with the grandchildren entering their teens. Alexandra now giggles when I call her by her name; she wants to be Alex. Abigail has transitioned to Abby. They're still eager to play board games or poker when we're all together, but we're seeing each other less often. That is largely a consequence of their busier social life and, more recently, the frustrating restrictions the pandemic has brought on.

At times, all my hopes are centered on my grandchildren's generation. They are, after all, the future. Humanity won't change, of that I've convinced myself, but perhaps I've influenced the course of Alexandra's, Cameron's and Abigail's life sufficiently that they'll make a difference. As I started believing somewhere in my twenties, if each of us can profoundly affect the beliefs and behavior of five other human beings, we'll end up with a better world. I'm not without hope, but that doesn't mean I'm unconcerned.

It's November and I'm sitting at my desk, reflecting on the events of the past three months.

After being stranded in Colorado, joyfully so, we finally returned to Canada, heading straight to the cottage for our mandated 14-day quarantine. Melissa had filled our fridge and freezer to the brim and John had made sure there was enough wine and booze to entertain a platoon of hardened soldiers. The health authorities called every few days to make sure we hadn't left, occasionally asking us sly questions.

"Describe where you are," a male officer with a strong Quebecois accent asked. When I answered that we were on a lake, he asked how near our closest neighbours were. I told him there were no neighbours; our property was on a peninsula jutting out into a body of open water that was speckled with islands. He didn't give up. "Would you mind describing what room you're standing in right now and where the person closest to you is?" When I countered that I wasn't standing in a room, he thought he'd tricked me, saying that I wasn't allowed to leave my place of quarantine. I explained that I hadn't done anything like it; I was standing on our spacious screened-in porch, breathing the fresh Georgian Bay air. He gave up, noting that what I was describing sounded incredibly healthy and congratulating me on my good fortune.

We spent most of the fall up North, enjoying the outdoors just as we had in the Aspen Valley. When we visited Parry Sound to buy food, we found most of the locals to be fairly relaxed. Many were mask-less now, at least when outdoors. By mid-October, when we closed the cottage for winter and headed back to Toronto, even the city dwellers had calmed down. For a very short time, the Covid scare faded.

Now all that has changed again. Municipal, provincial and federal authorities have invoked harsh new measures, many of which seem utterly senseless. Mega-stores like Costco and Walmart are open, but smaller businesses have been ordered closed. I was lucky to get a haircut before the stylists were shut down. The young Iranian refugee who looked after me was devastated; unlike the other employees at the salon, he is ineligible for government compensation. Apparently, his wife, who works as a helper in a restaurant, will be without income too. I gave him a hundred dollars, three times as much as he was owed, and left him my phone number.

AS I DO every morning, I scan the headlines, first in the New York Times and the Wall Street Journal. One is shamelessly to the political left, the other gives me a one-sided perspective from the right. I adjust their offered opinions, knowing their inherent biases and considering my own—all in the hope to arrive at a balanced conclusion.

If there is a global news topic I need to analyze, I go further afield. In Britain, the Guardian provides liberal input, the Telegraph supplies the conservative viewpoint. Sometimes I go further afield, looking at what Germany's, Switzerland's or France's media have to report.

What's been fascinating me lately is the coverage of Covid or, better put, the way pandemic information is manufactured by corporate interests and their subservient governments, then obediently disseminated by the media. Being in the business of data and news analysis and having often been interviewed, I've observed narrative manipulation for most of my adult life. When America unleashed its Forever War, the U.S. media quietly stopped using the term 'armaments industry' and replaced it with 'defense industry.' Those who questioned America's military adventurism were accused of being friends of terrorism.

Similar media-assisted transitions occurred in other areas. Chemical giant Monsanto became part of the agricultural industry, with opponents of yield-boosting and earth-ravaging fertilizers being accused of not appreciating world hunger. In the financial industry, manufactured consent has been the norm longer than anywhere. A country's central bank, the treasury and the financial industry can be counted on to collude. When reckless speculation by banks and brokers results in disaster, massive coordinated support operations and bail-outs are virtually assured. Unsurprisingly, the story-line served up to the citizenry is that it's all done to protect the economy and thus the public's welfare.

Now, it seems, it's the turn of the pharmaceutical complex, which is being reinvented as the health industry. The signs of manipulation are present everywhere. An open discussion of alternative approaches to the management of the pandemic has become impossible. Those who dare criticize the schizophrenic lockdown provisions or ask relevant questions about the vaccines that are hurriedly being introduced—under emergency statutes, without peer review, and with a blanket liability exemption for the manufacturers—are portrayed as anti-scientific, no matter what their credentials are.

I've been trying to escape the Covid frenzy, but keep failing. On the one hand, constantly changing regulations demand that I inform myself, because they affect everything, from the financial markets I need to navigate, to whether I can meet a client at my office or go to the gym to exercise. Yet, as soon as I start reading up on this morning's pandemic-related news and editorials, I feel my body tense up. As I have for the past week, I remind myself to limit my exposure to the Covid-topic to twenty minutes a day.

An hour from now traffic will intensify, but right now only few vehicles are on the road. I'm walking the twenty minutes from our city home to the office, as I do whenever the weather is clement. I'm not alone, either: some people are walking their dog and others, probably headed to their place of work, carry backpacks. It's still dark, which amplifies the red glow of the traffic light at which more than half a dozen pedestrians are waiting.

For a couple of weeks now, I've subjected my fellow city dwellers to a test, which I now initiate once again. I walk slightly ahead of the group of people standing at the edge of the sidewalk, step into the road to be crossed, and demonstrably look left, then right. Clearly, no cars are visible. Then I turn back to the group with an inquisitive glance, before decisively stepping forward and doing the unimaginable: crossing a road when the light is red.

Once I'm on the other side I peek back once more, this time to check if anyone is following me. Unsurprisingly, today's experience is like yesterday's. They're all still standing there, patiently waiting for the light to change, determined to be good citizens. Occasionally—I'd say every third day or so—someone decides to follow my example, recognizing either the opportunity at hand or the futility of obeying traffic signals when there is no traffic.

I'VE BEEN THINKING about my fellow citizens a lot. It seems that the vast majority isn't remotely interested in independent thought, but prefers the easy-to-embrace storylines dished up by government or its servants, the media. In the context of the Covid pandemic, the mantra is that people keep dying because a few trouble-makers have decided to question the government guidelines.

It's astonishing to me with what ease the authorities have spread this narrative and have managed to create a public enemy. Even worse is the complacency with which the average person embraces that message.

The parallels with the situation I left behind me in apartheid-era South Africa come to mind almost immediately. No matter how brutal the regime's tactics were, most people agreed: if there was anyone who interfered with the attainment of paradisical conditions in this blessed country, it was the non-white trouble makers. Even worse was the view that many young immigrants from Western Europe embraced—stay the course until you are, say, thirty years old and you can be the owner of a house, a swimming pool and enjoy the help of three or four servants—provided you show up at work and stay out of trouble.

In a way, I'm back at the stage I was when I left Cape Town, unable to relate to the vast masses of people who can't see the injustices perpetrated in front of their eyes, or more likely, choose to ascribe them to necessity and therefore ignore them. I gave up on humanity back then, convinced our species as a whole was a failed experiment and would eventually self-destruct. But I also learned that one-on-one relationships with individual human beings could be deeply satisfying.

What I never thought would happen was that a situation like the one I encountered in South Africa would make a second appearance in the country I once deeply admired and chose as my home. There are colossal differences, of course, at least on the surface. Apartheid-era South Africa was a racially abusive construct, while contemporary Canada pretends to be the opposite. But is it? The rhetoric advanced by Prime Minister Justin Trudeau and his circle suggests the opposite. He's calling the unvaccinated extremists who don't believe in science, while labelling those critical of his authoritarian edicts enemies of the state, revealing that his image as a champion of equality is nothing but a convenient mirage. And dutifully, the once-beloved CBC and other major Canadian media outlets not only echo such judgments, but suggest that most people agree with them.

The question that lingers is why my pessimistic conclusions about humanity at large faded into the background for the better part of life. Was I, like most of my fellow citizens, taken in by the warm embrace of the economic wellbeing of the past half-century, foolishly allowing myself to take my eyes off the progressive corruption of the monopolists and their corrupt lackeys in government?

AT DUSK, ON my way home from the office, I trudge through a blanket of early snow. Plugged in, I'm listening to a compilation of Swiss military marching music that I selected a few days ago. I was curious how many tracks I'd still recognize and what listening to them would do to me.

The result is stunning. The instant the Schönegg March starts up, I find myself in a state of extreme vigilance. My spine straightens and my arms start to swing. It's as if our dreaded colonel, forever looking for signs of weakness or inattention, was watching me. Unexpectedly, I also find the marching music uplifting, perhaps even more so than the Supertramp and Abba tracks I listened to earlier.

Still, every now and then it's hard to stay in step with the band. Perhaps the patches of ice are throwing me off, perhaps my flashbacks to the Covid topic are responsible. I'm thinking of the family. John is confined to his basement because his arbitration hearings now have to be conducted online, while Melissa is unable to attend her orchestra practices. Besides, what's the point of rehearsing when the concert halls have been shut down?

The children come to mind. If the new realities are stressful for adults, how about them? Earlier this year, Alex saw her prom and her graduation trip cancelled at a few days' notice. Now, after working hard to get into McGill University she's in Montreal, a city renowned for its vibrant party scene—in a residence apartment she's not allowed to leave, attending classes remotely. Abby is confined to home too, unable to see any of her friends, trapped with her parents twenty-four hours a day.

Only Cameron seems to have stayed ahead of such adversity. Back in spring, sitting in his room and looking into the neighbouring backyards, he noticed that most adults no longer went to the office. He correctly assumed that some would soon want to upgrade their new working environment and designed a pamphlet, offering an array of fence and deck maintenance and upgrade options. A few months later, he had three employees and a respectable amount of money in his new bank account.

I'm on the Covid topic again, this time writing a market update for our website. My commentary focuses on the army of self-styled 'experts' offering their particular perspectives on the pandemic. Their opinions are badly contradicting each other, yet they all claim to have 'the science' on their side.

"What is an expert?" I ask myself, and my mind immediately settles on an episode a few years ago, which followed a fairly relaxed inter-generational doubles match. The four of us players had left the tennis court behind and were headed to the clubhouse. Gaines Norton and I were the young ones, both in our early fifties;

Mel Spira and Jim Heywood were more than twenty years older.

Mel, the distinguished surgeon and Professor Emeritus at one of America's top teaching hospitals, complained about the incompetence of his financial advisors. I knew exactly what he was talking about, because not long ago I'd analyzed a stack of his brokerage statements, each showing between 50 and 70 monthly transactions. Once I explained to him what had happened, he transferred his assets to our firm.

"As if making a fortune churning my account wasn't enough," Mel now complained, "they actually managed to lose money." I pointed out to him that the transaction volume was inexcusable, but that incompetence was not unusual. "You mean in your industry," Mel countered.

I challenged that, turning to the other two players. Jim had been the Chief Research Engineer at Ford Motor Company before retiring. I asked him whether incompetence was a factor in the automobile industry. He chuckled, saying that the history of automobile manufacturing was a case study of failures, interspersed with the odd major success. That's when Gaines, who'd worked with the Internal Revenue Service before becoming Bill and Hillary Clinton's tax advisor (and eventually testifying against them during the Senate Whitewater Investigation), chimed in. "Hell, in the accounting industry it's as bad as anywhere," he drawled in his pronounced Arkansas accent.

"Now everyone," I pushed on. "Out of ten practitioners, how many are exceptional, how many mere average, and how many complete duds?" I offered that in the investment management profession there was a 1-8-1 rule: for every ace, there were eight average operators and one complete failure. Gaines and Jim agreed that sounded about right. Mel was more resistant, muttering something about not wanting to make his peers look bad, but eventually agreed that the odds of finding a first-class surgeon were much the same.

For a few minutes we debated why that was and all came up with the same answer. The health industry, the automotive business, banking and finance, and even accounting, were institutionalized constructs that attracted professionals of a wide range of talents and ethics. And as long as they brought in patients, clients or consumers, middle-of-the-road performance was readily tolerated.

My attention swings back to the Covid-related essay I'm writing. What is an expert, really? Probing several possible answers, I conclude that it's someone who's diligently studied a given topic, then looks at a problem and comes up with a judgment. Evidently, opinion and truth are very different things.

Humility would be a good start for those who profess to know. But it's not what is being taught at our learning institutions. Nor would it, in most cases, work for the institutions our experts serve. In the health arena those are mostly medical schools and national health authorities, along with the pharmaceutical complex, which generously supports them both. What we end up with is heavily influenced expert opinions at best, and grossly manipulated information at worst.

Fortunately, there is a bright spot in all this: if we can't trust the experts, we have to take responsibility for ourselves.

A few weeks ago, at Christmas-time, the Province of Ontario ordered a complete lockdown, prohibiting visits to any other household. When we discussed the situation with Melissa and John, we all agreed that we should break the law. We were going to celebrate like we always had. Driving to their place on Christmas Eve was an eye-opener. As we arrived, we noticed half a dozen other families emerging from their cars, carrying presents, ringing doorbells and hugging their loved ones. Law breakers, all of them!

Stalling free movement within the city was not the only government objective. Next, the federal authorities attempted to keep Canadians in Canada. They stopped short of enacting legislation, but engaged the media in a campaign to vilify travelling Canadians as uncaring and selfish. When that didn't work, they suspended all flights to popular holiday destinations. Steadily, the tension escalated.

By the time Ontario Premier Doug Ford ordered police to stop people stepping out of their residence and ask them to prove that their outing was essential, we were back in our mountain paradise. From afar, we watched events in Canada in disbelief, then felt elated when police forces in several cities refused to comply with the hapless Premier.

Still, Canada's apparent slide toward despotism troubled us. The path the government was following was identical to the one I'd studied in numerous African, Asian and Latin American dictatorships—exploit an emergency by passing legislation to amass power, then use that power to undermine personal rights and freedoms. And while you do that, create scapegoats who can readily be blamed for the adverse conditions and you have a split society, allowing for a divide-and-conquer dynamic to take hold.

Will Canada's bungling stab at authoritarianism fail? Some of our friends and acquaintances boldly declare that they're ignoring most of the rules. But others fervently believe that the pandemic would long be over, were it not for those resisting government dictates.

Every now and then, when infections drop and a few restrictions are lifted, social tensions lessen. What I fear most is that with each new wave of Covid, divisions will flare up anew and anger and anxiety reach new highs—allowing the authorities, their puppet masters in the corporate world and their servants in the mainstream media to expand their power base even further.

I've also given thought to why exploiting the Covid emergency is such a boon to the corporate and political rulers. For a couple of decades, I've written about the illusion of stability citizens of the Western democracies are being fed—all while unsustainable policy platforms virtually guarantee the inevitability of broad collapse. I've watched the dramatic escalation of income and wealth disparity, especially in the United States, wondering when social unrest would broaden into a more dramatic popular uprising. Now I know that it won't. The inescapable fallout of half a century of misguided health, education, economic, monetary, environmental and defense policies will be attributed to the unforeseeable arrival of the pandemic. It won't be the doing of politicians, central bankers or their corporate ventriloquists—it'll all be the fault of a virus.

IN COLORADO LIFE is far more agreeable than in Canada. Rules limiting restaurant capacity and mask mandates were lifted when the ski season ended, restoring most pre-pandemic conventions.

Still, when we attend a social function, Covid talk abounds. Worse, there are always a few guests eager to profile themselves as law abiding and compliant and by extension, shaming others. Most days, more than half of the top-ten news stories are pandemic related, invariably offering a one-sided perspective. The propaganda is now inescapable and its reach has become global.

I try to shrug it all off, but not a day goes by that something vaguely related to Covid stealthily tip-toes back into my brain. It can happen while I'm doing my financial work, while I'm reading a novel or during exercise. Worse, since we've set a preliminary date for our return to Canada, the pandemic has found its way into my sleep, as well. It's not nightmares or even bad dreams that plague me, just annoying reminders of an inescapable topic. Once or twice a night my bladder comes to the rescue, signaling that it's time for a bathroom visit. When I return to sleep, I try to relax and work on slipping into more pleasant reveries. Sometimes that works.

Even my writing has been affected. Just a few months ago, in my state of unmatched contentment and gratitude, I was overwhelmed by the perfection of it all—imagine being able to finish my recollection on such a high note. Now, with the Covid dynamic complicating life with such intensity, I feel frustrated. How inconvenient that I have to integrate such maddening complications into my narrative!

Putting my woes into context can help. After all, I've had to endure far greater aggravations than this. Besides, the complications Covid has imposed on me are far more benign than the anguish millions of others have endured.

WITH SOCIAL INTERACTION *at a new all-time low, Covid-stress has become the baseline in our society. Mental illness, suicides and marital separations are at an all-time high. When we talk to our friends we notice an edginess that wasn't there before. Some appear anxious.*

Caroline and I squabble more often. Among other things, ever changing travel restrictions have brought uncertainty into our well-ordered lives. How and when will we get back to Canada? Will I ever get to see my Swiss family again? Sometimes we listen to opposing perspectives on the reliability of reported infection data, proposed treatment options, or the vaccine itself. On both sides of such arguments, some of the views offered seem entirely logical, while others sound far-fetched. What's terrifying is how aggressively the government line is promoted and how quickly critical views are suppressed, their authors finding themselves banned from social media and seeing their internet postings eliminated.

A few times our quarrels have escalated into something bigger. One morning, emboldened by the fairly relaxed Aspen Valley regime, Caroline vows that once in Canada she'll refuse to wear a mask, even though she'll violate the law. Making a determined stand will be her imperative. She's been listening to webinars and checked out renowned scientists who confirm that the widely used surgical masks prescribed in much of Canada and the U.S. don't afford any protection against the minute aerosol particles through which the virus propagates. I've examined the reliability of her sources and found that most are solid, but refuse to go into open rebellion mode. I know it'll upend my overall perception of bliss and balance, and create negative energy for me. I boldly state that if I have to dress up in a mask to maintain the contentment that still dominates much of my day, so be it. Yet, as I say that, I can't help wondering if that makes me a coward.

One day, as we argue, Caroline says the inevitable: "We need to be away from each other." And I, without giving it any thought, respond that, yes, that's what we should do. Under different circumstances, Caroline would have booked herself into a retreat or I would have flown to Switzerland to see my family, only to miss her within a few days of being apart. Yet, given the pandemic's harsh realities, those options don't exist.

We spend much of the day apart, wondering how badly things have deteriorated between us. Later, when over an afternoon cup of tea we compare notes, we agree on the principal causes for the periodic flare-ups of our discontent. We both feel that the relentless load of pandemic information is far greater than our capacity to process and understand it, at least in the time we are willing to devote to it in the course of each day. We also realize that we've never spent two consecutive years together. What's made our relationship so special is that we've grown together, often sharing tasks, goals or adventures, while also encouraging each other to evolve as individuals.

Our talk ends with resolutions. We agree to set limits for pandemic related discussions, and decide to devote as much of our time left in Colorado as possible to the outdoors. We'll also delay our re-entry into Canada.

From our courtyard, we've been watching a well-hidden nest full of robin chicks high up on a beam. Only a week ago, we had to patiently wait until one of their parents arrived with an offering, before we could see the tips of their open beaks. Now, they crane their necks high above the rim of their cradle of twigs and dead grasses. Both elders restlessly flock in with juicy fresh worms and, seconds later, flutter off again. But only one of them carries away a load of white fecal matter after each food delivery. Caroline and I debate whether it's the female or the male whose job it is to keep the nest clean. We're also taking bets on how long it will be before the chicks are prompted to leave their nest forever, hoping we'll be here to witness it.

Every now and then, we get up to work in the garden, trimming back old growth on wild rose bushes, or helping clematis, wisteria and other vines start their audacious climb up nearby posts and walls. The abundance of growth around us is hard to process. In disbelief, we place ourselves next to wild grasses seven feet high, caress the hundreds of hollyhocks, all of which came from the same few handful of seeds dropped more than twenty years ago, and reach down into the rich patches of lavender, rubbing bits of purple between our fingers and inhaling the invigorating scent.

BEING OUTDOORS KEEPS us sane. Two or three times a week we go hiking, Caroline, Hansli and I—taking on steep mountain trails that lead us up through spectacular forests of aspen or evergreens, and later loop back down across rich meadows speckled with lupines, bluebells and columbines.

Like millions of others, we try to eat healthily, drink a bit too much and get our eight hours of sleep. In the evenings we read or watch an episode of a favourite TV series. Sometimes we crank up our karaoke setup and sing songs that were popular forty or fifty years ago. We see fewer people face to face and spend more time on the phone and in Zoom sessions.

We've found our own way of coping, of keeping out the negatives and focusing on what we still have. Most of the time it works.

Our time in the mountains has come to an end. Worse, the airlines have changed their rules; with Hansli no longer welcome on board, we'll have to drive back. A thirty-hour trip that will take us through Nebraska, Iowa, Wisconsin and Michigan lies ahead. Our friends in the Aspen Valley offer their perspectives: a seemingly endless drive through flat, tedious terrain devoid of any topography is how most describe it.

I'm fretting about my leg, which has for some time given me trouble on car trips exceeding three or four hours. How will I manage ten-hour drives? Still, without a better option, we start packing. Our old Volvo easily accommodates three suitcases, a cooler, two backpacks and an array of bags Caroline is determined to take along. I remind her of our five-week Himalayan adventures, which we had to tackle with a backpack and a small duffel bag, and we laugh.

The trip unfolds much as predicted by our friends. The landscape is uninspiring until we reach Wisconsin and Michigan, where bright blue patches of lake water can be seen between sturdy conifers lining the highway. My fears of leg-cramps prove unfounded; I end up driving the whole way while actually enjoying it. The back cushions Caroline ordered keep me as comfortable as I was in the army or on my journey through Africa, when long hours behind the wheel were commonplace.

Still, as we approach the massive bridge that separates the American and Canadian parts of Sault Ste. Marie, I'm starting to feel profoundly uncomfortable. I reflect on my backpacking years and explain to Caroline how excited I used to be when I approached a border, always looking forward to the new culture that awaited me—distinct behavioral traits to be observed, a new native languages and its dialects to be listened to, different artistic expressions to be studied, and unique culinary offerings to be savoured. Even when I travelled as an executive, often visiting the same handful of countries, border-crossings never failed to stimulate and excite me.

It all started changing after the 9/11 terrorist attacks, when countless new search and examination protocols were introduced. Seemingly overnight, border guards became more irritable and inquisitive, keeping the traveller on the defensive. With the advent of Covid it got even worse. In recent weeks, changes in entry requirements have been relentless, as if the various governments deliberately wanted to keep us off balance.

What adds to my unease today is that the Canadian border guards are on strike; I've been fussing over the delays we may face. Finally, with pandemic restrictions constantly escalating, we've been wondering when we'll next be able to return to Colorado. The air around us is muggy, the sky above hazy and lifeless, echoing our sentiments. Silently, we roll toward the only open gate, coming to a halt behind waiting vehicles. A large sign reminds us that even while inside our car we must wear a mask, something that strikes us as absurd.

Two hours later, after being briefed on our quarantine rules by a nurse and ordered to officially import our Colorado-plated car—an unexpected complication that involved a lengthy registration process—we're finally on the way to Parry Sound and the cottage.

AFTER THE FAIRLY relaxed climate in the U.S., nothing could have prepared us for the Canadian experience. The rules for our quarantine and the two mandated at-home Covid tests are contradictory and, in some aspects, unrealizable. We're told to have the government-owned courier service pick up our samples. When I explain to the health official that couriers don't operate boats, I'm instructed to take our packages to the Parry Sound drop-off point. But wouldn't that be a violation of our quarantine, something that carries a $5,000 fine, I ask? I'm told that someone will get back to me, but that never happens.

Meanwhile, Caroline and I are required to call the authorities once a day to file our symptoms reports. We're also frequently called by Health Canada, reminding us of our obligations. The government end of these communications is conducted by a computer that impersonates a sweet-voiced female who mostly recites the many hefty fines and consequences of not being fully compliant.

When I share my feelings with Melissa during one of our phone conversations, she surprises me by saying that she thinks it's great that the government finally clamps down. I'm bewildered. What to her is worthy of applause, is to me is a page straight out of Kafka. John's view is a bit different; he feels that only the endless repetition of threats will get people to obey the provisions of the law.

THE COTTAGE PROVIDES solace. Escaping the Covid-theatrics is as difficult as ever, especially with two, sometimes three daily messages from the government coming in. Still, we feel blessed we can be here, listening to the wind and seeing it ripple the waters, taking Hansli for loops on our nature path, hearing the excited voices of children playing at a distant cottage. Very occasionally, a boat glides by. A couple of hours each day, I work outdoors, throwing dead branches onto the firepit, trimming dead wood off the wild blackberry bushes or power-washing one of our many deck surfaces.

With annoying regularity, my conversations with Melissa and John keep coming up. How can they not recognize the steady subversion of our personal liberties? I tell them about my upbringing in post-war Switzerland. Government must never get the upper hand, as it had in our neighbouring countries, we were told again and again. The tales of overreach that had turned into unimaginable abuse lingered for years, if not decades, fortifying the concept of a decentralized state.

I think they understand that part, but cannot see the parallels, don't understand that Europe's fascist leaders were widely admired for their ability to enforce laws which, at first, focused on broadly popular initiatives, then used their newly gained power for far more nefarious purposes.

Can I expect the kids to see the world the way I do? Of course not. Their journey has been different from mine. I see government as a construct to be distrusted, while they see it as a place of benign incompetence. And our grandchildren, Melissa points out, are different again. To them the baseline includes being interrogated and searched when travelling or attending a public event.

There have been few times when I've felt utterly disoriented by what's going on around me. Krista's death left me in a state of incomprehension. So does the pandemic. Several times a day, I feel like I'm waking up in an alien, incomprehensible world. What baffles is not just the way government is using the Covid crisis to advance its powers, but also the inability of the people to see through it.

A year ago, at one of our weekly Whiskey Summits, Larry Gaudet inquired about my work in progress: this retrospective. I told him I was getting close to the end. And how old was I at this stage, he asked? Somewhere in my sixties, I replied. The other two participants, Richard Moore and Steve Cornish, snickered.

Larry didn't give up. As an author of several books and a reader of countless memoirs, he seemed seriously interested in how far I intended to push this. His next question startled me: "I mean, where and how will you end it, Peter?" It was something I had never given any thought to, assuming that I'd find a way to finish my project if and when I sensed the joy of process was ebbing away.

That hasn't happened yet. But now, a few months after Larry brought up his penetrating question, I'm at the point where this written account of my life has caught up with the present. Both in these pages and in the context of my sitting in my Snowmass Village office, looking out at the last bit of sun tinging the apex of Garret's Peak a ripe yellow, I'm 73 years old. Miraculously, the events of the past decade have been recorded.

All I need to do now is pen a few more pages, which won't be difficult, because I know what the finale to my opus will look like. It'll consist of two parts. The first will capture the treasured memory of a ritual so timeless, so wonderfully descriptive of the generational dynamic, of the passing of the torch, that no other episode could rival it. Then, a task any memoirist needs to address: what have I learned from this exercise of five years, which included many more days of reflection than hours of writing time?

Cameron and I are off to an adventure. Throughout his March break holiday, he's been pushing me to ski the legendary Highlands Bowl with him. I've been stalling, because the conditions have to be near-perfect to take on the area's most challenging run, especially since it's a first for Cameron. Last night, when I checked the weather forecast, predictions were for a sunny day. But early this morning, when I looked out the window, thick grey clouds were moving toward us from the West. I thought I'd let Cameron sleep in, but before long he came downstairs, making himself a robust breakfast and wanting to know when we were leaving.

Now, a couple of hours later, we're waiting for the snowcat that will carry us to the gate marking the beginning of our climb. Having taken two chair lifts to get here, we're far above the valley. We could be standing anywhere, though; the clouds have moved in, making it impossible to see further than a few meters. I'm concerned.

Normally, getting onto the cat involves a considerable wait. But today there are less than a dozen skiers waiting. When the Bombardier vehicle pulls up and it's time to climb onto its open trailer a few change their mind, leaving Cameron and me, a group of five fit-looking young men from Montreal and a ski patroller as the only passengers.

We're halfway along the mainly flat access route when the storm moves in. An icy wet gale hits our faces. Some of the Quebeckers are pulling balaclavas over their noses; they're laughing, reminding us that they're used to this kind of weather. When the cat comes to a halt, I wonder whether we should abandon our plans or at least delay our ascent by a few hours. But then we jump onto a cushion of fresh powder and I convince myself that all will be well. Besides, if we called it quits it would have to be a decision Cameron and I made together, and I know what my grandson's answer would be. As we put on our backpacks and shoulder our skis, the snowcat turns, releasing swirls of toxic diesel that quickly blend into the dark.

Climbing the ridge to Highland Peak normally takes between 40 minutes and an hour. At the rate we're going it'll be a two-hour undertaking, at least. Intense freezing rain is now descending, icing over the steep, narrow path we're ascending. For each step we take, we first have to kick a foothold into the ice. If we don't we're at risk of slipping; if we lose our balance, we'll fall hundreds of feet down the vertical chutes that loom to our left and right.

I can see Cameron is struggling. Unlike me, he doesn't spend most of the winter here and isn't used to the altitude. We're almost halfway up when he announces that he wants to turn back. His voice is a whisper, his breath is short and laboured. "I can't go on, Papa!" he pleads.

I explain that going back is not an option. If we walked down the steep track we'd slide on the ice and crash; if we put on our skis we wouldn't be able to control our descent either. We'd careen down the bowl hitting rocks and, at the very least, be severely injured. Or, like others before us, we'd die. I tell Cameron that quitting is not an option, pointing to a spot above us where the three foot wide path widens a bit. We'll be able to rest there; I'll take off my pack and give him the oxygen I carry. I promise him he'll feel better.

At our resting spot, Cameron stretches out on the snow, thick flakes assaulting his face and melting on his overheated skin. Then he sits up and holds the oxygen dispenser over his mouth and nose. Within a few minutes, he feels better. After a while, we resume our trek upwards; I'm lugging both of our skis now, while Cameron holds two pairs of poles, one on each side, which allows him to balance himself. We can't take any chances.

At the top, I sink to my knees, not from exhaustion, but gratitude. I look down into the valley far below us, kissing the ground below me. The clouds are lifting, patches of blue showing in the sky. Cameron says he wants to take a picture. The five Quebeckers watch us and, once we're done, ask us whether we're okay. Apparently they've followed our progress and seen us struggling. One of them, who introduces *himself as Benoit, lives in the valley. He explains to his friends, who are visiting, how unusual it is to see a father and son do this together. Grandfather, I smugly correct him—in a few days I'll be 70, while Cameron will soon turn 14.*

We stay at the top for a few minutes longer, then put on our skis and drop into the near vertical bowl that's called G8. The snow near the top is moist, but a hundred feet into our descent it's at least a foot deep and perfect. By now the sun is breaking through. Before long we're hitting the tree line and ski through dense stands of evergreens. A couple of times, when we reach a clearing, we stop to look back up and absorb what we see above us: the fabled Highland Bowl, intimidating in its raw perfection, devoid of any other skiers, our fresh tracks revealing where we came down.

Later, on our way home, we talk about how a seemingly ill-fated quest turned into an exceptional and near-perfect skiing experience, as well as a cherished shared memory. Near-perfect? Yes. After climbing and skiing the bowl, having a voluminous early lunch and taking another half-dozen runs on less demanding territory, we end up in the parking lot, where an exhausted Cameron slips on a patch of ice, falls and opens up his knee.

IT'S MARCH BREAK *again, a year later. We've skied in Snowmass all morning and now, at the top of High Alpine, we're hungry. Caroline and Abigail push off, taking one of the easier runs down to the restaurant. Cameron wants to hike up to the Hanging Valley Wall. The snow conditions and the weather are perfect, so I agree, but not without bringing up that other excursion to the wall, the one when Nick wanted to ski it. Cameron, who's heard the story many times, laughs, reminding me that I took him down the Wall once before.*

Yet, once we stand at the top of the narrow chute he looks a bit less comfortable. Like I did when I stood here with his dad sixteen years earlier, I explain to Cameron where he should plan his first two turns. He nods, studies the steep, tight, chimney-like terrain below him for a few moments, and asks me if he can go first. I reassure him that his technical skills are first rate; all he has to do is follow my instructions. Then I watch him execute several flawless jump-turns and, as the chute opens up into a bowl, allow himself to gain speed. He's a tiny speck when he reaches the bottom, but I think I can see the smile on his face, as he proudly waves at me.

Now it's my turn. I do exactly what I've done many times before, but on the second turn one of my bindings inexplicably opens and I lose a ski. I push my upper body hard toward the middle of the chute, so I can avoid the rocks that line its edge, then try to initiate the second turn on my one remaining ski. It doesn't work. I fall, realize I'm ski-less now, and try to get rid of my poles, which I know can hurt me as I careen down the wall head first. Instinctively, I know that trying to dodge the bumps and snow-covered boulders that lay in my path is futile; the best I can do is make myself into ball and not resist.

It turns out to be the right thing to do. I feel myself bounce and summersault a few times, no longer sure of the direction in which I'm moving, but then I hear Cameron's distraught voice somewhere nearby, shouting "Papa, Papa," and next I see parts of his ski pants and jacket and I know this is where the terrain flattens out.

When my body is still, I try to orient myself. I've fallen a bit further than Cameron skied. I slowly roll side to side, noticing that nothing hurts, then push myself onto my knees. Cameron is next to me now, agitated and afraid, asking me if I'm all right, disbelieving when I tell him that yes, I think I'm okay. For a minute or so I have trouble breathing normally, trying to take in what actually happened. Having Cameron next to me is hugely comforting.

Next, I have to find a way to get my skis and poles back. I know they're near the opening to the chute somewhere, 150 meters straight above us, but we can't see where. When I say that I'll climb back up, Cameron stops me, saying that I'm in no shape to do so, not after my fall. I respond by bringing up his hernia, which ruptured just before he arrived here. "I had to promise your Mom you'd do nothing strenuous," I remind him. "You're going to end up in hospital." For a few meters, both of us are climbing side by side, arguing.

In the end, the deep snow makes it impossible for me to keep going. Twice his bodyweight, I keep breaking through past my knees. It takes Cameron more than half an hour to reach the top. When he comes toward me carrying my equipment, I recognize the symmetry of it all. "Remember what happened a year ago, in the Highland Bowl?" I say, drawing him toward me. Of course he does.

As we complete the run, I can see that Cameron is suffering. We are among densely spaced evergreens now, the ground steep and bumpy. His turns look forced and every now and then he loses control. When we get to the restaurant, where Caroline and Abby have anxiously waited for us, I insist that we go to the bathroom and look at Cameron's hernia. He refuses, claiming he's okay, but we both know better. Surgery is now inevitable.

What has the exercise of writing this retrospective taught me? The short answer is, far more than I expected.

When I launched this inquiry, I had only the vaguest idea of what it would mean to re-experience entire parts of my life. The process of opening myself to the past let me relive episodes of my childhood that had been buried so deeply that dwelling there a second time was agonizingly painful. I found myself crying as the truth revealed itself, at first regretful of how circumstance and the need to protect myself had blinded me, but in turn joyful that I was now managing to see things in a fair-minded context.

The rewards were extraordinary. I was left with nothing but admiration and deepest love for my parents, no longer seeing them as flawed characters unable to find each other, but as courageous, even heroic figures who managed to create an environment of stability and tenderness for me and my siblings, despite challenges that must have been monumental. When I came to the end of the segment dealing with my childhood and youth, I realized that the world I had chosen to remember and the world I saw now were not the same.

IN CONTRAST, WRITING about the years of my early adulthood didn't change the way I'd perceived them long ago. When, in my thoughts, I revisited Cape Town and once more journeyed to far-away places, I learned things about myself that I hadn't understood before, but came to the conclusion that there was nothing I had suppressed. The same was true of my early years in the financial profession. Maybe this was due to the sense of empowerment I then felt. After all, I was now truly independent and the circumstances imposed on me were mostly of my own making.

As I came to the middle part of this memoir, I started wondering to what extent the fear of losing my loved ones, and the experience of their actual death, had defined me. Revisiting little Gaby comatose in hospital or seeing the miserable bundle of life that was Reto in an incubator while being told that he wouldn't make it, took its toll. It forced me to acknowledge how deep a wound the dread of being without my sister and brother, or both of them, had left. Maybe that's why allowing myself to descend into the emotional turmoil that followed Papi's, Kurt's and finally Gaby's departure required courage.

Yet nothing could have prepared me for the agony of re-living Krista's tragic and utterly unnecessary death and its aftermath. It was the first time in my life that I experienced something akin to writer's block. I'd write a paragraph or two, then, unable to carry on, I walked away. But no matter how determined I was to temporarily forget, to switch my neural track to some everyday inconsequential matter, I kept failing. Instead of cleansing my brain, I found myself once more inescapably trapped in the throbbing anguish the loss of our Krista had brought on. Finally, after several weeks of this, my summit buddies asked me how the memoir was coming along. I shared my pain, and that helped me bust through the impasse.

Yet later, when I wrote about the process of letting go of grieving for Krista and our eventual journey to Hawaii where we surrendered her ashes to the sea, I went through a similar crisis. For days after, I could not write—in the face of the loss of such potential and the agony it had brought on, anything else seemed too trivial to report. I realized that I had never fully processed my pain, and was now reliving what had been long suppressed.

I WONDER TO what extent the close proximity to death has shaped my life. Perhaps it's helped. Maybe it's why I've never given much thought to my own demise, or feared it. Some of my elderly friends report that they find it embarrassingly difficult or even impossible to write or update their will. They can't bear the idea of no longer being here. Even though I frequently wonder what the meaning of life is and what will await me on the other side, the thought of my death has never unnerved or distressed me.

I can't be sure, of course, whether that will change and death will eventually preoccupy me as it does so many others. The advent of illness or seriously advanced age may make me less dismissive of the subject.

Some of my friends made turning 100 into a serious goal when they reached their nineties. When he was in his early seventies, Melvin Spira, the renowned surgeon, told me that health systems the world over would soon collapse under the weight of demographic trends and fiscal realities. Given constantly increasing lifespan projections, an age limit for medical care and treatment may have to be invoked. Stunned by Mel's prediction, I asked him whether he knew what that could mean for him. "Oh, if I was seriously ill and 85, I'd have no problem if they let me die," he answered, with a sincerity that made me believe him. Fifteen or so years later, I visited Mel in the Aspen Valley Hospital, as he lay recovering from a heart attack. "That was a close call," he explained, then added that he was in good hands and had access to some of the world's best surgeons. Then he announced that his setback had left him determined to live past a hundred. When I reminded him of our conversation a few years earlier and asked him whether he'd changed his mind, he paused for a moment, then said, "You know, Peter, it all changes as you get older."

Mel, staunchly believing he could die a centenarian, made it to 95. Our friend Curt Strand did it the opposite way. When he turned 98, those closest to him urged him to start planning for his 100th birthday party. Curt overruled them, setting his 99th as the right moment to celebrate. He dressed up in his favourite red dinner jacket, invited family and friends to a posh hotel, then died six months later.

In our family, pragmatism seemed to have been the rule when it came to dying. My grandparents submitted without complaint when their time came. Neither of Caroline's parents ever talked about death or projected when they might move on, nor did mine. Papi was bed-ridden for weeks, as he wasted away with liver cancer, but never talked about pain or fear. Mami's encounter with death came suddenly. When the surgeon gave her the choice of being operated on, so she could live a few more weeks, or letting her slip away, she opted for the latter. I hope I can be like them.

WHILE I CAN'T be sure about what I've learned about death while working on my opus, there are topics about which I can be definitive. Some may appear mundane, but were in fact quite transformative.

One is my relationship with the world around me.

I think I mentioned early in these pages how my recollections of being outside as a child always involve exploration under blue skies. I can't recall such a thing as a bad-weather day. Yet, during my adolescence I found myself lost. I had a few close friends and my family, but could relate to little else. The skies must have been cloudless as often as when I was a kid, but it's not what I remember. I was a harsh judge of things and people around me, then. It was my black-and-white period.

Once I left home a new dynamic took place. I started to see the world in colour again. Travelling to and living in places that were then mostly referred to as the third world was a gift that came to define me. It allowed me to not only contemplate completely different settings and cultures, but also to see myself through the eyes of strangers, from the outside in.

There were periods when, typically for a decade, I engaged in hard work and, during my weekends, played equally hard. During these career stints, I quickly fell back into the habit of living in the mind. Perhaps that even helped my professional advancement. Yet, with regularity, I felt the need to punctuate these episodes of enormous intensity with extended backpacking journeys, leisurely travel and adventure treks. That's when time slowed down again and I re-learned to see through different lenses. Over time, I got into the habit of looking at every circumstance, every discussion point or problem, from different perspectives. Bit by bit, it helped me become less judgmental.

That doesn't mean that I'm in a perpetual state of bliss or that I accept all around me uncritically. I'm passionately opposed to how most institutional frameworks operate, detest the hypocrisy with which most of our political and corporate leaders articulate their agenda, and have *even more disdain for the sycophants who pay them tribute. What has changed is that, for the past fifteen years or so, I've felt aware of what is and of what goes on around me, and been able to see things in context. I've lost hope for the large, centralized configurations toward which humanity habitually gravitates, and instead engage more deeply in smaller structures where I can make a difference and, by doing so, help change the world.*

THERE ARE OTHER *things I've learned from chronicling my life. When asking myself what the most significant incidents of my existence were, I was in for a surprise. Obituaries and eulogies have conditioned us to focus on societally admirable distinctions. In my case, these would probably be summarized as an unusual amount of travel and adventures, some extraordinary business successes, notably at an early age, a stable family life, along with a reference to my publishing triumphs and my philanthropic engagements. Looking back at my life from my seventies, I can see that these are themes rather than crucial events.*

What looms much larger than any of the things society might be impressed by are episodes of self-realization and fulfilment—shared moments with loved ones that resulted in exchanges of energy so profound that they reinvigorated me then and still do so now. Canoeing through Quetico or communicating with nomads in the middle of Afghanistan's Central Asian plain are such episodes. Staring down our board of directors to protect the jobs of my staff or opposing the ill-fated takeover bid for Guardian Trust were battles I remember with pride, but they cannot compare with the sweetness of having been able to offer stability to the two teenage girls who'd come into my life, the surge of contentment when snuggling up with Caroline in our tent after an eight-hour trek across a Himalayan pass, the rush of excitement and awe when staring up at the mountain of ice rising from the frigid Atlantic waters on which we floated, or the pleasure of seeing pure joy on our grandchildren's faces as they explored the new nature path at our cottage.

THERE IS ANOTHER *important thing that writing these pages made me realize. While my innate capacity for logic is unusually strong and has served me well, what really determined the course of my life was my reliance on intuition. I can't be sure when I first decided to trust my inner voice—perhaps it was when I quit school and left home—but before long I let intuition guide me whenever I came to a fork in the road. As I could see far more clearly when writing about it, the intuitive and the logical were usually in opposition to each other. From a rational viewpoint the decisions I took made no sense at all; but absurdly, they always led to great outcomes.*

Somewhere in my fifties I also learned not to allow myself to become emotionally attached to a projected outcome. That's not to say that I've navigated the past twenty years or so without making plans—all it means is that a desired outcome is no more than that. If it manifests, it's a reason to be grateful. If it doesn't, I've given it my best try and am free to move on to something else, without the added complication of feeling disillusioned.

NO MATTER WHAT *segment or aspect of my life I've revisited, I've learned. However, the most rewarding and least expected result of this self-inquiry is that it's helped me understand how extraordinary my existence has been. I appreciated early on that few people follow a path as erratic, eventful and rich as mine has been. But only now, having returned to each component and dwelled there for a time, can I finally see them all as one broad canvas, its depth and drama bordering on the bizarre, if not impossible.*

What makes everything even more unreal is how privileged I have been and still am. To be sure, I started out with advantages many others didn't have: robust health, a good brain and decent looks, coupled with an upbringing in one of the most stable and prosperous places on earth. Being born into an era of almost unprecedented economic growth and job opportunities, and being showered with mind-boggling and persistent good fortune, also helped.

Time and time again, things worked out far better than I had reason to anticipate. Having seen much of the world, I had modest expectations for a career, yet somehow managed to advance to the senior ranks of the financial industry in a very short period of time. How that happened is still an unsolved mystery to me. Another surprise lay in store after I left Guardian Trust. If someone had told me that, after embracing an absurdly demanding executive position that left little time or energy for my personal life, I'd find my soulmate and have a family, I would have dismissed the forecast as pure lunacy.

And now, having left the business world largely behind me, I find myself deeply contented once again. Having found a good balance between enjoying the outdoors, creative pursuits, interaction with family and friends, engagement with the few remaining clients I have left and the charities I'm involved with, is something I had thought unattainable.

Yes, as I finish these pages, the Covid dynamic complicates and frustrates, tires and divides. But even so, my daily routine manages to bring me unexpected joy.

It's been dusk for nearly a week. The ground is soaked, gurgling when I step on it as I take Hansli for a loop along the nature path. Caroline is spending hours in her pottery shed, tinkering with clay productions that just won't dry. Even when it doesn't rain, the light is blunted by an impenetrable layer of cloud.

In Europe and in the Western part of our continent wildfires rage. Better this, I think, as I look out on the sodden vegetation below me and the restless surface of the lake beyond, the usually vibrant greens and blues reduced to a uniformly gloomy olive-tinged grey. It's what the algae at the bottom of our inlet and the muddy waters around them must look like.

What to do on a day like this? Make a fire, I think. But before doing that I look out at the blurry scene outside my window once more, standing there entranced. The rain is coming down hard now, its sound deafening. I realize that it's been days since I heard any of nature's other sounds—no chirps from squirrels or chipmunks, no slap of a beaver's tail, no loon calls or bird songs. They must all be sleeping.

The world has changed, but I feel at peace. □

In Colorado, with our grandchildren.

Cottage construction: the big barge.

First glimpses of the new cottage.

Signs for the new nature path.

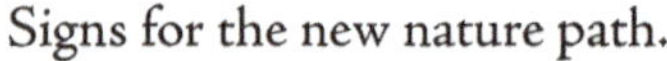

With Stephanie and
Jim in Maine.

With Roman, Flavia
and Mami.

Hansli at the cottage.

Preparing
Thanksgiving dinner
at the cottage.

Canoeing time.

With Melissa, at
the cottage.

The Kasbah at Imlil, with Mt. Toupkal in the background.

Caroline and Abdul.

Goats feasting on
Argan seeds.

Melissa, John and
grandchildren in
Costa Rica.

Rafting down the Balsa
River.

Caroline and Hansli,
spring in Colorado.

Alex, Abby and Cameron.

Melissa and John, with their doodles.

With Cameron,
on the CN
Tower.

Iceberg near
Twillingate.

With Melissa, John, Alex and Abby in Newfoundland.

The garden in Snowmass Village.

Notes and Acknowledgements

A THOUGHT: WITH my memoir at its end, how will I fill the two or three hours I devoted to it each day, for the better part of the past five years? Will I finish 'The Sweet Spot', the novel that's largely written and has been awaiting completion for the past fifteen years? Or is the newspaper column I sometimes fantasize about going to become a reality? If so, it will help revolutionize the charitable universe, getting donors to give more effectively and holding charitable institutions more accountable. Perhaps I'll devote my freed-up hours to painting or mask-making again. Or I'll start working on the many pieces of wood I've collected over the years, some spectacularly disfigured by insects, woodpeckers or rot. I'll sculpt and carve them until they take the shape that I envisioned when I found them along the nature path at the cottage.

Contemplating these options is intriguing. Painting, mask-making or woodworking are challenging, but they also demand an attitude of acceptance which can be extremely liberating. Once the paint dries on the canvas or the chisel has done its work, the creation is final, whether I like it or not. In other words, the outcome is irreversible.

Writing is distinctly different. Typically, once I conclude that I'm done with a project, I learn that it's not done with me. Whether it's a short-story, an essay on geopolitics or a novel I'm working on, some lines, pages or entire chapters call out to be tweaked or rewritten, sometimes repeatedly. Yet I love writing. What makes it all worth it are the moments when creation flows through me and entire passages effortlessly descend onto paper or screen, without me even having contemplated them. To make even minute changes is unthinkable then.

So, for now I'll open myself to possibility, as I've always done. Chances are I'll wake up one morning, five days from now or in a few months' time, and I'll know exactly what to do next.

IN THE MEANTIME, I'm still spending too much time on getting this three-volume retrospective to print. Pandemic-related delays and other unexpected events have hindered progress on both the design and production fronts. I finished my writing in late 2021 and now it's early 2023.

A year and a half is a significant period of time, especially in the context of all that's happened. As I had feared, government overreach intensified further, especially in Canada where a deranged Prime Minister introduced the Emergencies Act, temporarily suspending key parts of the Charter of Rights and Freedoms. Elsewhere too, popular unrest grew as the Covid craze and government mandates severely damaged the economy and financial markets, divided society and fast-tracked surveillance and the digitization of everything. Then Russia invaded the Ukraine, which unleashed a dynamic that could well lead to World War III. Given these grave developments, was it not logical to add a chapter or two to my opus?

In the end I decided not to, applying the same standard I have used throughout this work. I've already written extensively about these issues, particularly in the final volume. While deeply disturbing, the latest developments haven't changed the course of my life, so there is no need to elaborate further.

MOST AUTHORS END their works with a long list of acknowledgements. I'm not sure how appropriate that would be. After all, there was no agent, editor or publisher involved. Unlike my other works, this one is self-published and not intended for a broad audience. Still, there are those who helped with me with the many logistical tasks that come with writing, revising and bringing a book into print.

Caroline patiently listened to countless hours of my readings, commenting on issues of style and context and sometimes telling me that she remembered an episode we'd experienced together quite differently. All along, my granddaughter Alexandra maintained a spreadsheet keeping track of characters, timelines and locations. And when I felt my retrospective was complete, Carolyn Victoria McKechnie subjected my manuscript to a copy-edit.

My friend Richard Moore took the time to help me with the cover design, at a time when his Vietnam-based firm demanded too much of his energy. The result is no less magnificent than his previous designs, which grace the covers of my earlier works, the social study 'Tuiavii's Way' and my first novel 'A Dangerous Remedy'.

Another old friend, fellow writer Larry Gaudet, read the completed opus and sent me commentaries that dramatically expanded my understanding of how different readers can relate to a writer's offering. His insights were invaluable.

And finally, Toronto-based Laura Brady came to my aid, devoting herself to layout, design and digitization tasks, and getting my three volumes print-ready.

I AM PROFOUNDLY grateful to all who have been part of my life and enriched it in countless ways—the Swiss family I was born into and the Canadian one my wife Caroline and I made for ourselves; the friends who accompanied me through my childhood and in my adult years; the colleagues and bosses with whom I shared my professional life and the people who accompanied me on my philanthropic journey; the hundreds of others who influenced my thinking, from philosophers, teachers and academics to backpackers, monks, artists, poets, novelists, politicians, criminals and those who fit no particular definition.

They're all part of this work. They've all helped me define myself.